Timed out

MANCHESTER 1824

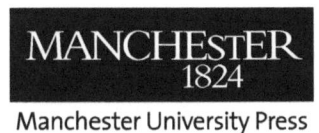

Manchester University Press

rethinking
art's histories

SERIES EDITORS
Amelia G. Jones, Marsha Meskimmon

Rethinking Art's Histories aims to open out art history from its most basic structures by foregrounding work that challenges the conventional periodisation and geographical subfields of traditional art history, and addressing a wide range of visual cultural forms from the early modern period to the present.

These books will acknowledge the impact of recent scholarship on our understanding of the complex temporalities and cartographies that have emerged through centuries of world-wide trade, political colonisation and the diasporic movement of people and ideas across national and continental borders.

Timed out

Art and the transnational Caribbean

Leon Wainwright

Manchester University Press

Published by Manchester University Press
Altrincham Street, Manchester M1 7JA, UK
www.manchesteruniversitypress.co.uk

British Library Cataloguing-in-Publication Data is available

ISBN 978 0 7190 8484 3 hardback
ISBN 978 0 7190 8594 9 paperback

First published 2011

Typeset in Minion with Myriad display
by Koinonia, Manchester

Contents

List of illustrations

Museum, New York. Purchased with funds contributed by Dakis Joannou and by the International Director's Council and Executive Committee Members, 2001.

Every effort has been made to contact the copyright owners for the images used in this book. If you have any queries, please contact the publisher.

Acknowledgements

In 1999, whilst a doctoral student at the School of Oriental and African Studies (SOAS, University of London), I had a letter of invitation from the literary scholar, Sandra Courtman, asking if I would contribute to an annual meeting of the Society for Caribbean Studies (SCS). For showing that my work could find a ready audience among Caribbeanists, I want to thank Sandra, as well as Gad Heuman, Amanda Sives, David Howard, Peter Clegg, Ruth Minott Egglestone, Diana Paton, Mimi Sheller, David Lambert, Jean Stubbs, Mary Turner, Kate Quinn and many others of the SCS who have since made up that audience.

The SCS became for me a much needed space in which I could benefit from an Area Studies expertise and share art historical research in an atmosphere of freedom from disciplinary conformity. It was a fitting prelude to the sort of generous and open exchange of ideas and knowledge that characterises the milieu of art practice, criticism, curating and historiography in the Caribbean and its diaspora. The artist Sonia Boyce had kindly introduced me to the independent researcher of Caribbean art and literature, Anne Walmsley, who had put Sandra on to me. Anne was gently influencing the society behind the scenes by insisting that a panel on visual arts ought to feature prominently at its international conference. As I would come to learn, these aims extended much further, in her unstinting efforts to show that a deeper understanding of the Caribbean and its diaspora may be reached with attention to the visual arts. Over the following decade and with Anne's direction and friendship, I would seek out ways to explore her sense of art's significance for the Caribbean, and in turn the value of the Caribbean for art history as a discipline.

If this book takes its point of departure from such UK beginnings, it has been shaped more deeply from time spent in the Caribbean itself. With support from The Leverhulme Trust (an Early Career Fellowship) and the University of Sussex, I went to live in Trinidad and Guyana in 2004–2005, and have made return visits to the region almost every year since. Even so, I should count my exposure to the Caribbean as rather limited were it not for the extraordinary amount of time given to me by people there. As a British subject visiting a part of the world under British rule a little before my lifetime,

I had anticipated some resistance to my presence in the Caribbean. But the consideration and patience that I have been shown there has helped to make any less than satisfactory encounters easier to understand and, above all, more historically readable. I have benefited from the wide personal knowledge and experience of many of those I have met and for this I would like to thank a great number of individuals whose names I can only begin to list here. In Trinidad: Patricia Mohammed, Rex Dixon, Christopher Cozier, Nicholas Laughlin, Marlon Griffith, Leroi Clarke, Eddie Bowen, Kim Johnson, Rachel Rochford, Radica Mahase, Raymond Ramcharitar, Adele Todd, Georgia Popplewell, Peter and Bonnie Doig, Anu Lakhan, Charlotte Elias, Kathryn Chan, Ashraph Ramsaran, Marsha Pearce, Peter Hanoomansingh, Wendy Nanan, Burton Sankeralli, Mario Lewis, Makemba Kunle, Jaime Lee Loy, Sean Leonard, Susie Dayal, Adrian Camps-Campins, John Stollmeyer, Tessa Alexander, Bobby Lee, Stuart and Mary Hahn, Andy Jacob, Gerry Besson, Martin Mouttet, Lesley-Ann Noel, Mary Adam, Geoffrey MacLean, Carlisle Harris, Irenée Shaw, Che Lovelace, Babu Ketema, Shastri and Shirley Maharaj, Ken Crichlow, Pat Bishop and the late Richard Bolai. I am grateful also to those who attended my education seminars at Caribbean Contemporary Art (CCA). In Guyana: Elfrieda Bissember, Rupert Roopnaraine, Vanda Radzik, Jynell Osborne, Oswald Hussein, Jocelyn Dow, Ruel Johnson, Bernadette Persaud, Joanne Wright-Haley, Nelly Singh, Ian McDonald, and Ameena Gafoor, and the staff of the National Archives, and at the Library of the University of Guyana. In the UK, Barbados and Jamaica: Frank Bowling, Rachel Scott, Maridowa Williams, Charlie Gore, Fiona Saffron-Wilkes, Reyahn King and the staff of the Walker Art Gallery (National Museums Liverpool), Rasheed Araeen and all my colleagues at the journal *Third Text;* Therese Hadchity, Stanley Greaves, Alison Chapman, Alissandra Cummings, Allison Thompson, Jane Bryce, Philip Nanton; Annie Paul and Veerle Poupeye.

In 2008 I delivered a series of open seminars at the University of California, Berkeley, through which the theorisation of my material properly began. For this progress I have to thank all those who attended to make the series a success, including Darcy Grigsby, T. J. Clark, Michele Rabkin and Laura Paulini, most of all Whitney Davis, who has kept that conversation alive and given me every encouragement to pursue a widely reaching programme of enquiry in art history. I am grateful to that Berkeley Fellowship and for the support of the Yale Center for British Art, New Haven, where this book was substantively drafted during my stay in 2009 as a visiting scholar. This was thanks to Gillian Forrester, Lisa Ford, Amy Meyers, Marcia Pointon, Petrina Dacres, Andrea Korda, Tamara Sears, Hazel Carby, Anna Kesson, and the students of the Department of African American Studies. I found courage through Amelia Jones and the editors at Manchester University Press who have warmly encouraged this book to publication. Without Paul Wood of the Open

University, I would still be doubtful about presenting this volume; he brought a rare and expert eye and the final burst of energy and good humour that it needed. I acknowledge my former colleagues and students at Manchester Metropolitan University, and partial funding assistance from the Manchester Institute for Research in Art and Design (MIRIAD). The visual culture scholar Simon Faulkner has listened with unfailing patience whenever I have formed even the faintest idea.

Final work on this book was conducted as part of the project 'Creativity and Innovation in a World of Movement' (CIM), which is financially supported by the HERA Joint Research Programme and co-funded by AHRC, AKA, DASTI, ETF, FNR, FWF, HAZU, IRCHSS, MHEST, NWO, RANNIS, RCN, VR and The European Community FP7 2007–2013, under the Socio-economic Sciences and Humanities programme. The 2011 Publications Grant, awarded by the Historians of British Art (affiliated to the College of Art Association in the United States) helped toward the cost of images. My partner Anna Lora-Wainwright is the open secret of my successful authorship of this book, even as she has worked to write a book of her own at the University of Oxford. Family, at home and abroad, have held my duffel coat while cheering me onto the pitch. All these people have understood why I have cared enough to bring this book about. They have given me the time it needed when I needed them most and I remain ever in their debt.

Introduction:
a transnational art history

These basic building blocks of the new global universe we inhabit confront a blank and uncomprehending provincial 'Englishness' as if fitfully glimpsed from outer space. Beyond sea, sun, sand, reggae and ganja, the fantastic intricacies of the 'transculturation' of European, African and Indian elements over centuries, which have produced the variety and vibrancy of Caribbean 'creole' cultures, is another Great Unknown.[1]

From the province of my own institutional base in England, the aspect of the Caribbean's 'Great Unknown' that demands the most urgent attention is its history of art. The Caribbean is a region that art history has hardly noticed, even as it embarks on its current rethinking along more global lines. If our aim is to understand the modalities of connection that make up an expanded field of art history, and to mistrust the discipline's older limits, then the Caribbean has a large part to play. The truth, however, is that the Caribbean has never really been absent from the history of art. There have always been relations of proximity between the centres of power and knowledge of the metropolitan 'global North' and the Caribbean, essential for understanding the historical developments of ideas and practices of art associated with modernity. There is a concrete and irrefutable record of interaction between the Caribbean and the wider Atlantic, which is configured in the field of art and the experiences of artists.

Even during the process of decolonisation, in the twentieth-century moment of heavy outward migration, a 'counterflow' from the Caribbean extended the region's influence in a process sometimes described as 'colonisation in reverse'. Artists of the Caribbean began to move between national settings and provided novel ways of thinking about the interrelationships between aesthetic value, nation, location and community. Such key experiences were not confined to the first generation of travellers and settlers who moved within and beyond the Caribbean during the collapse of empire; a second generation would also come to play a transformative role in the histories of art. Complex stories of art unfolded as Caribbean artists have positioned themselves in networks of art practice throughout the Atlantic world.

The Caribbean is a vital locus for seeing how creative individuals have negotiated the differences and continuities of art practice across national lines, being active participants in the making of an intricate modernity. In trying to grapple with its significance, this book explores a composite historical picture in which largely familiar – even domesticated – sites of research, such as Britain and North America are revealed to be entwined with the Caribbean. This is in parallel to broader histories of empire that register the entwining of global locations by the circulation of ideas, personnel and populations within European colonies.[2] In addressing the Caribbean, what comes to light is how the very subjects of movement and exchange – individual artists themselves – have coped with historical conditions of art making and reception across a diverse geography. This also brings into view the significance of the Caribbean for the workings of art history as a discipline. The mutual influence of artists through the exchange of ideas and materials is a complex focus for historical study. Yet the altered perception that this offers is also a source of productive analytical challenges. By turning to the Caribbean, what is at stake is not simply the matter of expanding an otherwise unchanged conception of the history of art and, by way of accretion, adding the Caribbean to the topics that have typically come to be of interest. Through a process of realising the Caribbean's profound influence in an Atlantic history of art we may come to wonder why this story was initially erased and, consequently, what vistas of theoretical priority it opens up for the entire enterprise of the historical study of art.

The individuals and artworks examined in this book are not intended to be representative of all those Caribbean artists who crossed the Atlantic, nor the subsequent artists of the Caribbean diaspora. They do, of course, span a fair breadth of their generational, gender, class and national subject positions. In focusing on the path of their movements, attention is especially drawn to Anglophone contexts of the Caribbean. These include former British territories that have received scant art historical treatment: namely Trinidad, of the twin-island republic (Trinidad and Tobago), and Guyana on the mainland of South America, which faces the Caribbean Sea. These are places with less of an archival presence and which have received far less curatorial interest than has the Greater Antilles, where the art histories of Cuba, Puerto Rico, Jamaica and Haiti feature prominently. Survey publications of the wider Caribbean and Latin America have focused first on larger countries, or those with greater visibility in certain art markets. The curiosity about art in 'multicultural' societies has led elsewhere, such as Mexico, Brazil, or South Africa,[3] but the transnational Caribbean may repay similar concerns with the complex significance of art: its role in the making and remaking of place, difference and community, and in imagining the past and future, all of which bear on the goals of this book. A more precise aim is to trace paths through and between Trinidad, Guyana, Britain and North America that would shift these connections away from the margins of inquiry and generate questions about art's histories at large.[4]

The British art critic Guy Brett has suggested a root difficulty for writing about an artist such as Aubrey Williams, born in British Guiana in the 1920s, and present in Britain from the 1950s. It is that art history has remained vague about the possible linkages among various national locations for the making, display and remembrance of art. It is especially uncertain about how to approach such issues in the aftermath of empire. Brett writes: 'Of course, the subtlety of the matter – the complexity of the history that has yet to be written – is that Aubrey Williams's work would have to be considered in three different contexts: that of Guyana, that of the Guyanese and West Indian "diaspora" in Britain, and that of British society.' The several contexts of Williams's life deserve separate consideration, as well as in their interrelationships, 'and all would have to be adjusted in relation to Williams's own desire to be simply a modern, contemporary artist, the equal of any other'.[5] Taking up Brett's call, I am motivated to look further at the issue of how artists such as Aubrey Williams demand a sharper sense of the spatial overlapping or entwining of the Caribbean with the wider Atlantic. This consideration of space may illuminate the experience of the later generations of artists with Caribbean backgrounds who have demanded a stake and an equal place in the canon of modernism and contemporary art.

It becomes obvious, however, that adopting this more complex and transnational approach to historiography also presents certain and perhaps greater temporal challenges. The way in which art history has regarded time and space brings questions of equality to the fore. It is these politics of temporality in particular that I wish to highlight: the ideas about time that have helped to provide the very conditions of artists' struggles and the field of possibilities for overcoming those conditions. My starting point is that there has been a refusal to accept the coevalness or simultaneity of art stories across continents. This has held a primary role in ensuring the almost complete subtraction of the Caribbean from the discipline of art history. C. L. R. James showed that the Caribbean is 'in but not of the West', a description that is indicative of its relationship to dominant historiography. Here I return to that idea and complicate it further by suggesting that it is temporality as much as location, which accentuates the distance between the canonical spaces of modern and contemporary art and artists of the transnational Caribbean.

Anachronism and the transatlantic

The self-reflective debates of anthropology that emerged in the 1980s examined at length how spatial conceptions of 'outsiderness' and the exotic have long been tied to temporal conceptions. Johannes Fabian, for instance, noted that:

… the temporal discourse of anthropology as it was formed decisively under the paradigm of evolutionism rested on a conception of Time that was not only secularized and naturalized but also thoroughly spatialized. Ever since, I shall argue, anthropology's efforts to construct relations with its Other by means of temporal devices implied affirmation of difference as *distance*.[6]

This sparked new interest among anthropologists of art and debates across the humanities. With postcolonial critiques came a more focused interest in the strategic alternatives to the dominant rendering of temporality as distance. The historian Dipesh Chakrabarty has offered a similar gloss on the rationale for the study of much world history, noting an underlying supposition in the discipline which 'makes it possible to identify certain elements in the present as "anachronistic"'.[7] In this line of thought, the reference is quite pointedly to a historicist vision of time and how it influences decisions about who may be considered contemporary and who anachronistic or belated. This happens according to the idea that human development proceeds in stages, with some groups moving on ahead, while others lag behind. It has been shown that such historicism has structured the drive to acquisition and collecting in the ethnographic museum. Among its symptoms are the fear of an expanding, destructive modernity, and a 'salvage paradigm', fixed on halting the disappearance of apparently timeless and discrete cultures by the forward march of history. Within discourses of modern art, the same historicism has framed attention to 'primitivism', with its conflation of spatial and temporal distance, in which the art of others would 'appear to us as present visages of our own pasts'.[8]

This historicism is among the reasons why art history has failed to contemplate the Caribbean. The prevailing attitude to time and space that is present in other, adjacent academic disciplines, has long been seen in the responses of critics and historians to art and artists of the Caribbean and its diaspora. Conventional ideas about temporality have worked to circumscribe the roles and the choices that were presented to artists. With historicism comes the accusation of anachronism that has been an impediment to many Caribbean artists' efforts to claim their place as artists. They have been forced to negotiate the view that their art was 'behind the times', the challenge of being regarded as somehow lagging behind the newest developments in the art of their day. Indeed, anachronism became the defining qualification most attached to artists of the Caribbean and its diaspora in Britain by art critics and art historians during the post-war period. Reviewers subjected their art to accusations of primitivism that presupposed an idea of their works as passé.

Those artists examined here who travelled to Britain in the 1950s and 1960s, were charged with having come 'too late' to be considered seriously, and were seen as 'out of step' with the consensus on what modern art should be. But nowhere was this more marked than in the comparisons between Caribbean artists and widely recognised modernists. The greater the proximity of artists of the Caribbean and its diaspora to the normative centres and celebrated personalities of art, the more vigorously, it seems, was the time–space logic of art history asserted. The challenge these artists faced has in recent decades been described as one of trying to enter 'the citadels of modernism', to use the artist Rasheed Araeen's distinctly spatial metaphor. But no matter how deeply artists of the Caribbean and its diaspora would infiltrate those spaces, it was the politics of time that provided the myth of them as outsiders and mere mimics of European art, only ever in a process of 'catching up' with a heritage that was not theirs. Artists of the Caribbean and its diaspora have struggled to cope with such demands; an experience that they have shared with many of their peers from other parts of the colonial world who have also sought careers as artists in the imperial metropole.[9] Since many of these came to Britain, there is an added complexity to what they found. They were doubly disadvantaged and belated, since British art for much of the twentieth century was itself derogated as backward, relative to the modernist canon centred first on Paris and then increasingly on New York.

All this points to how the Caribbean has been unfavourably subjected to a way of thinking about the history of art as a developmental narrative, a story of 'progress', often parcelled in by national boundaries and expectations of a corresponding ethnic difference, chiefly elaborated through biography. Its artists have been, as it were, placed on the wrong side of history whenever metropolitan centres were dubbed as 'leading', and compared to the ostensibly 'backward' peripheries of the Caribbean 'margin'. Works of self-critique in the discipline, such as Hans Belting's book *The End of the History of Art?*, have shown that the 'progressive' or linear narrative tradition has prevailed since Giorgio Vasari's *Lives of the Artists*, but may now have reached its limits. Other voices have declared such limits to have been overturned by the recent intro-duction of global, pluralistic, spatially aware and 'multicultural' approaches.[10] Even so, these have not guaranteed the end to a tradition of which the Carib-bean has fallen foul. No amount of asserting the conjunctive and integral role of the Caribbean in the formation of modernity, or diversifying art history's geography, has succeeded in dismantling the discipline's normative concep-tions of modernism and contemporaneity.

If art history were to look back differently, it might begin by examining the patterns of public reception for art of the Caribbean and its diaspora. In 1989, Pakistan-born artist and activist Rasheed Araeen, assembled the largest grouping of works by then emerging artists, as well as the older generations of migrants: *The Other Story: Afro-Asian Artists in Post-War Britain*, first exhib-ited at London's Hayward Gallery before touring the UK. Around a third of this work was connected in some way to the Caribbean. What jumps out from the press and media response to the exhibition is not so much that it frequently questioned the exhibition's curatorial rationale, or that it threw up obvious racist dismissals of the work (it did more of the second of these, in fact). It was that any 'positive' review tended to champion the exhibition's historical rather than its contemporary importance, and even its more sympathetic reviewers relegated the exhibition's value to the past. Particular praise was offered to Caribbean, Asian and African artists of the older generations, while the work on display by younger artists was seen as discomforting. It made claims on the present and the future that the parameters of art history found it hard to allow.

In support of *The Other Story*, critic Richard Cork summarised why a lack of awareness among the public of the exhibition's artists would result in so much misunderstanding.[11] The work of young British artists of several diasporas ceased to count under the conditions of reception. More than a decade of what Eddie Chambers called 'arts activism' and 'Black Art' had intended to transform the UK's national, postcolonial 'moment'. Artists such as Sonia Boyce, Keith Piper and Sutapa Biswas demanded not just recognition in the contemporary art scene, but a sea-change to the prevailing notion of the contemporary. They would contest the way in which the complex contemporaneity of their art was obscured and denied. In the arts, in education, in the contested field of cultural heritage, these artists were at the core of rethinking a cultural future for Britain and a place and time for art in the world.

There are countless further ways in which the effort to transform the history of art had to be sustained through confrontations with time. Remaining focused on Britain, exhibitions of the art of the Caribbean and its diaspora have tended to be shown in less mainstream galleries than the Hayward, and so have attracted little or no critical attention. Their appearance in venues which already carry a package of associations with belatedness has contributed most to their overall circumscription. The impressive, purpose-built art gallery of the Commonwealth Institute in London, opened in 1962, hosted the majority of both group and individual exhibitions of work by Caribbean artists. Yet, the ambition of artists from the Commonwealth was for acceptance less on the basis of their deep imperial legacy, than as proponents of the art of the present. It took until 1986 for 'Europe's first exhibition of contemporary Caribbean art', as it was proudly declared, the staging of *Caribbean Art Now*. This was the Commonwealth Institute's only Caribbean show to be widely and seriously reviewed, despite its venue. In the same gallery, *Jamaican Intuitives* (1986) and, at the Hayward Gallery and touring, *The Other Story* and *New World Imagery: Jamaican Art* (1996), were well conceived, closely researched and well presented Caribbean-related shows, all in major galleries. Their titles – with a firm emphasis on the 'new' and the 'now' – betray an inherent struggle over time, a temporal competition being waged in battling the ignorance of critics and the wider hegemony of historical value.

Other exhibitions met with less comprehension, especially those at the Commonwealth Institute Art Gallery: from Aubrey Williams's major series of paintings, *Shostakovich* (1981) and *The Olmec Maya and Now* (1985), to *Trinidad and Tobago Through the Eye of the Artist: From Cazabon to the New Millennium, 1813–2000* (1997–98). Smaller London galleries such as the 198 Gallery (Steve Ouditt, 2000; Petrona Morrison, 2004; Mario Lewis, 2005) and The October Gallery (which has shown works by Aubrey Williams seven times since 1984: Trinidad and Tobago painting, 1992; Jamaican artists, 1994) have tended to be overlooked in the art press owing to the connotations of 'non-Western' art as the poor and primitive relation to mainstream modernism. Limited funding has meant that venues have reached only local Caribbean diaspora audiences, such as Islington Arts Factory, London, with its *Caribbean Connections* series (1995, 1996, 2003 and 2004). Significantly, belated recognition of Frank Bowling came in 2005 with his election to the Royal Academy. Since its 2001 launch, the Tate Gallery on Bankside (Tate Modern) and Tate Britain have made better progress in according a place for black British artists than for artists of the Caribbean. If, as Stuart Hall has suggested, Caribbean artists have been 'quietly written out of the record; not British enough for the Tate [Britain], not international enough for Bankside',[12] then the Institute of International Visual Arts, London, has staged exhibitions and events (*Aubrey Williams*, 1998; *Steve Ouditt: Creole Processing Zone*, 2000), frequently extensively documented, that are intended to break that dichotomy.

Assessing the terms of curatorial selection in Britain and their consequences for art audiences, British responses to art of the Caribbean continue to employ typologies that have historically worked against artists' own declared interests. This is not simply the result of the obvious axis of former colonial connection between Britain and countries of the Anglophone Caribbean. It is common to art history in the main: in its use of spatio-temporal devices, which establish a pattern of classification that is generative of historical knowledge of the art of the Caribbean region as a whole.

The uses of temporality cannot be overstated in their persistent bearing on the reception of art of the Caribbean and its diaspora. In 1985, the reviewer Liz Waugh indicated 'two streams' of Jamaican art,[13] distinguishing between trained and untrained artists, 'cosmopolitans and intuitives'. This rehearsed a controversial hierarchy of value, energetically promoted in Jamaica since 1979, which represents the pervasive influence of a modernist teleology within the national cultures of the post-Independence Caribbean. A review in the *New Statesman* of *The Elders* (The South London Gallery, 1999), which placed Stanley Greaves (b. British Guiana, 1934, based in Barbados since 1987) with Brother Everald Brown (b. Jamaica, 1917, d. 2002), sought to overcome such a preoccupation about these artists' contrasting access to education, styling both men 'metaphysical artists'. This tag was especially devastating since it effectively distanced Greaves and Brown not only from the secular space of modern art, but also from secularised time. Their art was dubbed 'metaphysical' within a framework of progressive modernity in which the Caribbean occupies a time out of time, and is reified as sacred. Since such a description is broadly in line with the primitivism of the early twentieth-century avant-garde, these artists seemed like a throwback to a moment that is widely regarded as over and done with, rendering the art of the Caribbean redundant, being nothing more than food for a lost (European) appetite. More than ten years later in the United States, and art of the Caribbean was still being kept out of dominant definitions of the contemporary. Holland Cotter, a notable reviewer of the Brooklyn Museum's *Infinite Island: Contemporary Caribbean Art* (2007), wrote disparagingly that: 'Multiculturalist terms like identity, hybridity and diversity may sound like words from a dead language in Chelsea, but they are the lingua franca of the Brooklyn show.' He paused to contemplate that perhaps New York is 'just one of many art centers doing their local thing'. He gave some concession to the idea of a more devolved and decentred geography for contemporary art. Yet, ultimately, Cotter took the view that striving to be 'post-identity' should be the eventual and inescapable aim of all Caribbean artists wishing to compete with New York's lead.[14]

Without playing down these inequalities of reception, it is possible to point to another, more intriguing and indeed brighter side of this Atlantic story. I show how being received as both 'out of date' and 'behind the times' – both phrases that individually evoke time and space – has a formative role for artists of the transnational Caribbean. They have resisted the prevailing terms of their reception and sought a different place within the politics of time. Being able to see this politics more clearly demands that we develop approaches other than postures of protest and historical revisionism. Simply to lament the charges of anachronism made to artists of the Caribbean would not illuminate the deeper operations of the dominant historical imagination. Other programmes of critique have undermined the imperial measure which placed the Caribbean 'behind' and 'outside' the time and space of the modern and the metropolitan, such as Stuart Hall's exposing of 'the temporal enigma' in the relation between colonial and postcolonial subject formation.[15] Hall has revisited this theme after a distinctly spatial turn, dubbing the Caribbean 'a quintessentially modern zone',[16] which has prompted Hazel Carby to ask: 'What could we gain by focusing on the geo-politics of encounters, the where in addition to the when, of subject formation?'[17]

These and other voices have exposed as imperial fictions the largely national narratives of modernist universal inclusion; they have deplored their impact on subjects who were disregarded as modern, or left 'outside of the temporality, and of the place of the [British] nation'.[18] But this path has not led to a transformative view of the specific challenges for artists and artworks of the Caribbean and its diaspora and how to involve them in a more ambitious rethinking of art's histories. We have yet to observe how artists have set out to do more than undermine a spatially exclusive definition of modernism and contemporaneity. They have aimed to undo the label of anachronism which is doubtless an obstacle, often by actively engaging with the concept. This has required a variety of approaches, with artists disclosing the diverse benefits of being able to understand and manipulate the concept of time as a creative resource.

In grasping this more fully, I prefer to speak of anachronism as simply a by-word for belatedness, rather than to dwell on the sense of the term as being about a clash or misfit of one conception of time against, or within, another. I appreciate that anachronism may be essentially a scene of conflict where a given temporality aims to dominate by describing alternative times as misplaced and 'out of time'. Even so, this second notion of anachronism – as a temporal misfit – is precisely the one that artists of the Caribbean and its diaspora have encountered in the general assumption of their art story as occupying an 'other' time: as a separate history of art that stands outside the normative one. Only in the most generous analysis might this separate story have a correspondingly progressive status of its own, with its own chronology of creative patterns and drives. In general, the mismatching of one sort of progressive tale with another is always supposed to be less self-aware and less dynamic. It is certainly never valued as authentically cosmopolitan, when compared to the main and hegemonic story of modernism. For this reason, I am also generally unsure what purpose is served by identifying multiple or 'other modernities', or by relocating cosmopolitanism among 'vernacular' registers of creativity. Such claims seem only to smooth the way for unfavourable cultural comparisons on the basis that separate temporalities are hardly of parallel or equivalent historical value.

To remain on this point, I do share the aim for a more diverse sense of the shapes of modernism as well as the end to an absolutist chronology of art. Still, the historiographic purpose of pluralising modernism – with the aim of granting a place to the Caribbean context – has not delivered that outcome. Despite efforts to dismantle hegemonic historical narratives, those associations of inferiority and distance, which artists of the Caribbean and its diaspora have experienced to the point of alienation, remain intact. These are individuals who have regarded their practices as contributing to the larger history of critical art making of the twentieth century and into the present, but which the fragmenting of the historical record has not achieved. This book makes this vividly clear, while showing that the engagement with the politics of time for artists of the transnational Caribbean has brought about often surprising results. This subverts the conventionally reductive view of this art and insists that we embrace time as the generative element of a more redemptive historical awareness.

In his magisterial study *Real spaces*, David Summers has made plain the need to address art that lies outside the boundaries with which dominant art history is familiar. He suggests that the developmentalism I have described in art history is ethnocentric and that the prevailing principles of theory for the discipline are those that necessarily fit into a history of Western modernism, for instance in the central attention to what he terms 'representationalism'.[19] Consequently, Summers extends his analysis to traditions of art making that have no historical connection to the assumptions of Western representationalism. My aim in this book is distinct from his in that I seek to bring into view precisely those aspects of Western modernism which are actively displaced by such ethnocentrism but ought never to be approached as disconnected from modernism. Of course, this requires that we refuse to see modernism and ethnicity – or ethnic particularity – as contiguous and mutually indistinct, or indeed as necessarily mutually defining. This frees us from accepting that if there are multiple ethnicities then there must also be a corresponding range of multiple modernisms. I make this point in order to suggest that modernism may be a more complex domain than the question of ethnicity allows, and that Summers' acknowledgement of the ethnocentrism of modernism is instructive for reasons that he has not fully explored. I would emphasise that there is an implicit and overlooked temporal dimension in the *ethnos* of ethnocentrism; that the roots and uses of this term have to do with a classificatory *order* of difference and of developmental assumptions, largely and extensively elaborated in the historical record through the idea of culture.

The spatiality in the 'centrism' of ethnocentrism is a little more plainly indicated by the term itself, connoting the distinction of centre and periphery – one that surfaces frequently in the reception of Caribbean artists and their works. These temporal and spatial features of ethnocentrism should underline our suspicion about ethnicity as having a theoretical usefulness for understanding art in the Caribbean context. I am concerned to challenge the assumption that knowledge of the Caribbean will truly benefit from art history arriving at a consensus about modernism that is drawn along the territories and boundaries of the 'outside' versus the 'familiar'. There is an established field of debate on time and space which Summers and others have left aside in proposing a global relevance for art history on the basis of a supposedly corresponding relation between modernism and ethnicity.[20] The overall purpose of this book, therefore, sits apart from the general shape of these reconsiderations in art history. Its starting point in the historical representation of the art of the Caribbean opens on to a wider aim to scrutinise the dominant mode and scope of art history. This is with the specific end of seeing what the Caribbean offers to the discipline's future, and how art history may contribute to what Stuart Hall had called (as in my opening epithet) the 'basic building blocks of the new global universe'.

Timed out

Art of the Caribbean extends beyond its national borders, and finds points of articulation in the migration of peoples and the movement of visual ideas and forms. But along those migratory routes it encounters the limits of the pervasive shapes of time. Questions of contemporaneity and coevalness attend the periodisation and identification of the Caribbean and its art within debates about modernity. The mid-twentieth century to the present has been the most vigorous period of Caribbean migratory traffic to Britain, and has seen the historical emergence of Caribbean-descended artists of second and third generations. The record of art display and remembrance highlights the intersections of time and belonging, time and generation, memory, alterity and space. Observing this at work more directly is the key to knowing what new relations have come into being between global movement and visual experience, and to what extent ideas of the Caribbean seem forever enfolded by time.

For this reason, I am less interested in the project of defining Caribbean philosophies or social practices of time, such as those that enliven some of the literary and intellectual traditions of the region and its diaspora.[21] Equally, there is nothing in the art historical outlines of this book that would claim a distinctive 'Caribbean time', as in the ethnography of temporality.[22] The aim instead is to consider the limits of current and canonical thinking on the matter of time in art history as a disciplinary practice, and in its adjacent contexts of curating, display and criticism. This means drawing attention to political processes by which the art and artists of the transnational Caribbean have found themselves excluded from the time of modernism and contemporaneity. This does not always correspond to a simple model, in which ideas about art emerge at the colonial or former colonial periphery of empire, and are then received at the (post)imperial metropole. In that sense, this book seeks to participate in the formulation of a new, integrative model of the cultural politics of decolonisation in which the matters of influence and transmission are problematised. It tries to link the question of time as a local concern (colonial and metropolitan) with the more general processes of imperial power and decline, setting out to show how the notion of time as a cultural category has diverse permutations. This should cause us to rethink the interconnections of colonial and postcolonial experience, and the common geography and global imaginings directed to the historical study of art.

Consequently, this book seeks to unfold the politics of time from art history. It shows that the Caribbean may illuminate how time has functioned in the structuring of art historical knowledge, and how current concerns for change in the discipline may draw instructively from Caribbean-based study. This is the sort of change that allows us to think about what is impeding the development of new global applications for historical study, even in a climate of growing demand for a global or 'world art history'.[23] What I have to say will identify the convergence between self-critical thinking here and in other disciplines, namely anthropology, postcolonial and cultural studies, and in the avant-garde dimensions of twentieth-century art and theory. I am especially interested in how their shared effort to expose and dispense with parochialisms of aesthetic discourse might benefit from a turn to the political dimensions of time and space. Even in the growing light cast on art in its global locations, it might be argued that a persistent blind spot remains – a 'drop out' of vision – that has to be recuperated if we are to succeed in promoting the virtues of the comparative study of art in diverse locations. There are those who seek to illuminate the outer- or transnational dimensions of creativity and historical change as if this would somehow guarantee a transformation in the production of knowledge. Yet it may take more than these initiatives alone to make another world possible in the field of historical representation.

Caribbean works of art and their artists are among the defining elements of transnational connectedness and globalising processes have always been integral to the Caribbean in its Atlantic context. This was articulated most forcefully during the anti-colonial moment – when international political 'equivalences' were creatively realised – and through the mobilities of Caribbean people over those and subsequent decades. However, this transnational experience is far from utopian. Art of the Caribbean and its diaspora occupies an ambivalent place both within and outside the centripetal power of the current capitals of the art world. The celebration of the Caribbean as a seminal example for the new global geography of border-crossing, intermixing and mobility needs to be handled more carefully. The idea of transnationalism may be assimilated as a label, a means for marking out artists as fashionably exotic, for ethnicising them and setting them apart from the usual run of attention. It is worth being wary of the idea that any sort of focus on the Caribbean will bring about an entirely novel way of looking at the art historically overlooked; the challenges run deeper than that for the formation of another and alternative perspective. Certain outlines of this context need to be traced before we may claim to have discovered a way beyond the current circumscriptions and the familiar structures of art historical knowledge.

I would lay the problem chiefly at the matter of time. Time bedevils the aim of assembling such a differently spatial composition for art historiography, and it is the key to coming to terms more fully with questions of power in relation to art of the Caribbean. We need first to understand how space is intersected by time in the orthodox distinctions between the 'mainstream' and the 'margins', along the scale of inclusion, marginality and exclusion, and in the optimistic declarations that such differences dissolve with global, transnational movement and new spatial arrangements and networks. Spatiality as a theme of art discourse is anchored, trapped even, inside an abiding and influential temporal scheme. The spaces that appear to be opened up by transnational approaches to study have still to contend with how time governs and constrains the generation of any such expanded or novel geography. Prevailing models of temporality in particular (with 'the North' cast in a leadership role, as in the common histories of modern art, or the notion of where and when contemporary art may be found) have made it more difficult for a more globally distributed geography of art to evolve.

The present challenge is to reflect on the continuing attachment, in art history and curating, to reputedly 'leading' metropolitan centres, and 'belated' peripheries. This means confronting and undoing not only the orthodox attachment to spatio-temporal narratives of cultural value, but the entire cross-matching of 'over there' and 'back then', which suffuses even the 'global turn' in art history. I argue that we can see how firmly this persists even when the Caribbean's heterogeneity and transnationalism become fashionable key words for the institutions and audiences of contemporary art. By addressing the politics of time, what emerges is a clearer image of how notions of temporal backwardness may be used to cut in different directions, assisting Caribbean agency in struggling with the precariousness of the opportunities that the turn to the global presents. Consequently, artists of the Caribbean and its diaspora should be seen as engaged on several historical fronts. These are not all about battling to undermine the legacy of former imperial centres and how they temporally displace their former colonial peripheries. In some cases, there are ongoing and powerful displacements that result from an idea of 'the contemporary' which has no obvious centres or peripheries. Whatever the setting may be, my aim is to make transparent the complex ways in which such experiences are tied to a normative spatio-temporality in historical representation that will require a continual effort to expose and disrupt.

Much of this book consists of biographical studies of artists who have lived and worked in various circum-Atlantic locations. This is a means to understand how individual creative subjects transmit visual knowledge across colonial and postcolonial territories and national borders and through new networks of connection that refuse to resemble the postcolonial critiques of space and time. Art historical representations of art of the Caribbean hold in common an embedded notion of temporality that operates on a distinctly teleological measure. Chapter 1, 'Painting in the aftermath of painting' configures one such intersection between an artist of the Caribbean and orthodox art historical classification. In the 1950s and 1960s, Guyana-born (then British Guiana) artist Aubrey Williams (b. 1926) experienced critics' attempts to categorise his paintings in terms of 'connections' to either a 'Caribbean' or 'European' heritage. Critics in Britain wrote about the 'primitive urgency', evidenced in the 'tropical forests and primeval ritual dances' that they saw in his canvases, a description of him as primitive and therefore not modern. This was perhaps a familiar response to artists of the Caribbean, Asia and Africa, who converged on Britain intending to establish themselves there during the period of decolonisation. What makes Williams's reception especially significant is the sense of disappointment among critics that his time in Britain had made his primitivism seem less 'urgent' than when he first arrived. They wrote that 'England had tamed him', and that his tropicality had receded in time – that, perhaps like food, his art would pass from the raw, to the cooked. Critics arraigned against him a politics of artistic development that was seen as inevitable and teleological so that, whatever Williams's 'progress', he was reminded that he had to play catch up against the historical clock.

This chapter shows how ideas about time, and connected ones to do with space, are also implicit in the contemporary, more revisionist interest in Williams. Indeed, there are some unexpected continuities with the longer history of his reception as an artist. The redeeming basis for rethinking the terms of Williams's reception and his posthumous inscription in art history and curating may be found in his art itself. Williams and his art have remained a locus of criticism through their associations with outdatedness and anachronism. These terms may be recuperated, however, as part of a general framework for analysing the historical positioning of an artist who continued to be occupied with painting, even as the medium became increasingly outmoded. As such, Williams's art represents a key contribution to the politics of anticolonialism in its dealings with the status of painting, and also causes us to examine other contexts of painting differently, namely Britain. It prompts an appreciation that anachronism has a less than essential character, and that it offers a useful margin for ambiguity – since the accusation of being late and out of date can still be turned on its head.

Chapter 2, 'Varieties of belatedness', relates how a slightly younger artist, Frank Bowling (b. 1936, Bartica, British Guiana), was dogged by the same expectations as Williams. Yet he was also forced to negotiate with certain associations of belatedness and provincialism that arose from the larger process of canonisation, which took place around British art during the moment of decolonisation. This chapter shows Bowling as a participant in Pop art, and one of the peer group of artists that included David Hockney, R. B. Kitaj, Derek Boshier, and others who studied at the Royal College of Art in London during the early 1960s. Bowling failed to be considered as one of the 'Young Contemporaries' of Pop. Despite some initial success in the London art scene, he quickly became an outsider to Britain and its art story. This status was constituted differently from the fashionable belatedness and the regional provincialism commanded by those who have come to stand as the celebrities of British Pop. Bowling could not be feted for hailing from England's regions, its working classes, or for being gay or Jewish, and his own background of displacement was at odds with Pop.

In this chapter I suggest that British art, and British post-war figuration in painting, actually prided itself on being anachronistic in the face of American popular culture and abstraction-focused modernism. British art in this period was suffused by provincialism and backwardness, qualities that were essential for recuperating Britain as an alternative space of modern art. Hockney, Kitaj, and so on (and Peter Blake during the preceding decade) were 'genuine outsiders' of the British establishment and yet as a group this personified the overall outsiderness that British art endured vis-à-vis developments in American art and popular culture more broadly. They were fashionably late and valued for their distance from American-based modernism. This held implications for the way Bowling was understood. The Pop artists had usurped the familiar vocabulary of displacement, leaving Bowling – the displaced postcolonial subject – with nowhere to go. As I argue, temporality is at the heart of this system of value and remembrance. The Pop artists were desirable outsiders thought to transcend the weight of history, while Bowling was trapped by it. With his distinctive Bradford accent and working-class identification, Hockney was a suitable subject for the aspirational, class-crossing permissiveness of London's Swinging Sixties. Famously pictured by photographer David Bailey wearing a gold lamé jacket, Hockney would be immortalised. He graduated from the Royal College of Art with a gold medal. Bowling crossed the line in second place, represented a less fashionable alterity, and had to settle for the silver.

To understand the greater complexity of Bowling's experience is to recall the wider conditions in which the canon of British Pop was produced, and the subsequent patterns that the phenomenon entailed. Bowling's presence in Britain – as much as Williams's – was part of the larger trend of Caribbean migration and British geo-political decline, figured in the transformation of territories of the British Empire into new nations. Such change, and its impact on Britain, framed the way that the Pop story was told and allotted Bowling his marginal place beyond its boundaries. This chapter shows how the social and political changes associated with decolonisation granted an overall layer of meaning to British Pop. They shaped its reception and self-understanding and made clear why Pop became a moment in Atlantic art history whose temporal and spatial logic was shaped by the Caribbean.

Chapter 3, 'Mutual temporal ground' examines a particular moment when art history as a discipline was first seriously regarded as a crucial part of the institutional apparatus of Caribbean nationalism, and how this has since changed in debates over art, difference and canonisation. In the immediate period of Independence in the English-speaking Caribbean, concerns about cultural representation, diversity and inclusion took centre stage. Meanwhile, similar discourses of nation building and nationhood also came to be of interest to artists of the Caribbean diaspora in Britain. One of my principal concerns is to demonstrate how those debates taking place during the late 1960s and 1970s in Guyana are instructive for understanding what happened later in Britain during the 1980s, and indeed up to the present.

Adopting a transatlantic perspective on these histories offers a clearer sense of how attempts to assemble inclusive canons of art history are mounted and, in turn, critiqued. It also demonstrates why there is a need to challenge the assumption of Caribbean anachronism. The Caribbean has seen continuing attempts to settle the matter of how to assemble a consensual cultural canon. These have ranged on a variety of scales, from the national to the regional, and more recently to the transnational. The vigour and deep historical roots of this tradition of debate has bequeathed a distinctly art historical shape, and much may be learnt outside the Caribbean from this locus of concerns about art and representation.

In the 1980s and 1990s, black British artists – in art galleries, in the critical reception of art, art patronage, and art history – were, again, kept out of 'the contemporary'. Throughout this period there was always the spectre of 'ethnic art' as a label that figured particularly prominently in terms of funding patterns. This obvious refashioning of 'primitivism' would be rejected in favour of a vocabulary of 'cultural diversity' and 'cultural difference'. There is a similarity with Guyanese initiatives in theories of art, cultural canons and racial and ethnic difference, which may be examined in the writings of Denis Williams. This comparison establishes what interconnections there may be in the politics of curating and art scholarship across the transnational Caribbean when racial and ethnic difference infuse contexts of art historiography, display and patronage. This chapter compares the theorisations of artistic community and difference that emerged in immediate post-Independence Guyana, with the moment of British 'Black Art', and deals critically with perspectives on art and multiculturalism that have emerged in their aftermath. This produces a sharper sense of the shared or mutual ground of challenges faced in the Caribbean region and its diaspora in Britain over several decades.

Chapter 4, 'Emotional chronology', addresses the battle to be included in the contemporary art scene in Trinidad when, as for Shastri Maharaj, one identifies as Indo-Caribbean. This artist's story – beset by episodes of failure – throws up some revealing historical difficulties. After training abroad, it was obvious for Maharaj that signifiers of Hindu religion and generic motifs of South Asian dress and customs were anachronistic, at least once measured against the values of 1970s conceptualism. The purposeful, self-conscious use of these elements in his painted works of the early 1980s in Trinidad thereby became a tactic of anachronistic reversal.

This was in response to the challenges of building a national art scene in Trinidad and the demands for recognisable traces of ethnic difference that prevailing models of cultural community at that moment engendered. In terms of his efforts to participate in the local art community, such ethnicising of Maharaj and his work has brought about an unsatisfactory position for him, while his attempt to recuperate anachronistic forms in his paintings has led to only relative success. As this chapter demonstrates, the artist is troubled by the difficulties of working within the confines of Trinidad's particular landscape of ethnic differences. In order to evaluate this context more fully, I submit the idea that we need to look at the emotional dimensions of this artist's experience. It is imperative therefore to seek out ways in which emotions may be highlighted as meaningful elements of his experience and career as an artist, in contrast with the more familiar critical approaches to historicising conditions of marginalisation. If the tendency to read ethnic difference from the signifying surface of works of art must be resisted, then an 'emotional chronology' of Maharaj serves to show how he has suffered such readings. This chapter thereby discloses what further historical, even aesthetic, experience is being covered over by concerns about difference and the way beyond this analytical impasse.

The strong feelings that have been generated around the Indo-Caribbean presence is an issue concerning the relation of ethnic difference and art, and yet it also occupies a distinct analytical space of its own. How such feelings can change is shown to be contingently related to the national context of Trinidad. Here I identify what may be described as a temporal space of the emotions: a way of thinking about how artists may apprehend their situated experience, and how they have tried to think and feel beyond their historical circumscriptions. Carefully examining the subjective dimension of Maharaj's experience shows how an artist may be 'timed out' of a contemporary art space. This chapter clarifies why there is a struggle to offer alternatives to the ways in which ethnic difference is mapped onto national space and time in Trinidad. It raises the matter of the hegemonic position there of blackness and creolisation as a 'leading' national identity, and the artistic and emotional dimensions of this Caribbean story.

With this history in view – of discontent among Caribbean individuals of the Indian diaspora toward the hegemony of blackness – the concluding chapter, 'New provincialisms' shows how the transnational Caribbean has itself come to be positioned by a normative understanding of the African diaspora as featured in art historical representations. There have been recent attempts to see art as a crucial linkage for diasporic, postcolonial and transnational networks that operate 'without locus'. However, it is evident that older patterns of centre and periphery that such theorisations have sought to displace have been carried over into the present, and what I have called 'new provincialisms' have emerged. This chapter examines the relation between attention to Caribbean culture and contemporary trends in diaspora research, in the Caribbean, in Britain and in the United States. Art historical interest in Caribbean culture has been generally subsumed into the study of the black or African diaspora, often choosing to emphasise 'black internationalism'. However, in the yearnings for affiliation and solidarity that determine such accounts, it might be argued that current articulations of the notion of transnationalism have often rested on distinctively national priorities, largely those that centre on the United States. Although transnationalism in art history has been engaged as a concept that would link the United States to the Caribbean and black Britain, these latter regions are, nonetheless, rendered peripheral to expressly black American identities and philosophical goals. A fuller explanation is, therefore, needed of the temporal dimension of this peripheral positioning; an account that is capable of illuminating the intersections of time and space in the representation of transnationalism and art practice.

As we attempt to bring to light the growing global influence of the US's 'domestic script' on race, it is also possible to recognise attempts by artists and curators to turn this orientation around. The display and historiography of art in the Caribbean and Britain shares a familial proximity with the United States but, even so, this hegemonic arrangement also elicits some dynamic tensions, and the project of reconceptualising a creative (visual) community has taken some novel shapes. This concluding chapter shows how curating and its concomitant practices of documentation hold out a promise of dismantling and disavowing the hegemonic uses to which race and the diaspora concept have been put as founding categories of art historiography. These competing areas of activity are examined from the different directions of the Caribbean and its diaspora. This opens on to a debate about 'contemporaneity', and the extent to which declarations of inclusivity and 'horizontalisation' in the field of contemporary art may be tested by Caribbean art histories.

A general turn toward visual evidence in the discipline of history, simultaneous with a widening interest in art and transnationalism, presents renewed opportunities for understanding diverse global visualities. There is much awareness of the multiple reasons to avoid the search for a global art history that sits in a mythically detached cultural zone – a world 'outside' – which neatly and sequentially follows in second or third place after a notional First World. However, a similar wariness ought also to extend to hegemonic forms of temporality: those schemes of historiography that provide a generally unquestioned logic for art history through the tacit work of assembling categories of sequential, hierarchical order. Promoting an expanded geographical scope for art display and art history does not thereby guarantee a sea-change in the terms and values of the prevailing historical order. It is too easy to extol the benefits of surveying beyond the conventionally seen physical outlines of art history, without reflecting on the motivations and tools of this search. Investigation of what lies beneath the traditional attachments and limits of the art historical and curatorial imagination is needed more urgently.

Notes

1 S. Hall, 'Whose heritage? Un-settling "The Heritage", re-imagining the post-nation', *Third Text*, 49 (Winter 1999–2000), 3–13, p. 12.
2 C. Hall, 'Histories, empires and the post-colonial moment', in I. Chambers and L. Curti (eds), *The post-colonial question: Common skies, divided horizons* (London: Routledge, 1996); a later development of this idea appears in C. Hall, *Civilising subjects: Metropole and colony in the English imagination, 1830–1867* (Cambridge: Polity, 2002). It also parallels the direction taken in historical geography and among human geographers, such as D. Lambert and A. Lester (eds), *Colonial lives across the British Empire: Imperial careering in the long nineteenth century* (Cambridge: Cambridge University Press, 2006), and Doreen Massey, who has written of patterns of involvement in which: 'Arriving in a new place means joining up with, somehow linking into, the collection of interwoven stories of which that place is made.' D. Massey, *For space* (London: Sage, 2005), p. 119.
3 See, for instance: E. Gabara, *Errant modernism: The ethos of photography in Mexico and Brazil* (London and Durham NC: Duke University Press, 2008); J. Mraz, *Looking for Mexico: Modern visual culture and national identity* (London and Durham NC: Duke University Press, 2009); A. Coombes, *History after apartheid: Visual culture and public memory in a democratic South Africa* (London and Durham NC: Duke University Press, 2003).
4 In disciplines such as anthropology, the Caribbean is an exemplary site for inquiry and its status is far from marginal. Among the vast literature on Trinidad alone, see: M. Herskovits and F. Herskovits, *Trinidad village* (New York: Octagon Books, 1976 [1947]); D. Crowley, 'Plural and differential acculturation in Trinidad', *American Anthropologist*, 59:5 (1957), 817–24; K. A. Yelvington (ed.), *Trinidad Ethnicity* (London: Macmillan Caribbean, 1993). An extended bibliography appears in: A. Khan, *Callaloo nation: Metaphors of race and religious identity among South Asians in Trinidad* (London and Durham NC: Duke University Press, 2004). While much of the present book makes it clear that the discipline of art history has not paid such equally central attention to the Caribbean, I argue that there is no reason why this situation should continue.
5 G. Brett, 'A tragic excitement', in A. Dempsey, G. Tawadros and M. Williams (eds), *Aubrey Williams* (London: Institute of International Visual Arts and Whitechapel Gallery, 1998), pp. 22–35, p. 24.
6 J. Fabian, *Time and the other: How anthropology makes its object* (New York: Columbia University Press, 1983), p. 16.
7 D. Chakrabarty, *Provincialising Europe: Postcolonial thought and historical difference* (Princeton: Princeton University Press, 2000), p. 12.
8 D. Miller, 'Primitive art and the necessity of primitivism to art', in Susan Hiller (ed.), *The myth of primitivism* (London and New York: Routledge, 1991), pp. 50–71, p. 56. See also: J. Friedman, 'Civilisational cycles and the history of primitivism', *Social Analysis*, 14 (1983), 31–52; H. Foster, 'The "Primitive" unconscious of Modern Art', *October*, 34 (1985), 45–70; F. Myers, '"Primitivism", anthropology, and the category of "Primitive art"', in C. Tilley, W. Keane, S. Kuechler, M. Rowlands and P. Spyer (eds), *Handbook of material culture* (London: Sage Publications, 2006), pp. 267–84.

9 See for instance: C. Moody, 'Ronald Moody: A man true to his vision', *Third Text*, 8/9 (1989), 5–24; C. Moody, 'A way of life', *Caribbean Beat* (Nov./Dec. 2000), 54–9; Olu Oguibe, *Uzo Egonu: An African artist in the West* (London: Kala Press, 1994). For a curatorial view of Chandra see: Horizon Gallery, *Avinash Chandra* (London: Horizon Gallery, 1987); R. Araeen, *The essential black art* (London: Kala Press, 1988); M. Shemza, 'Anwar Jalal Shemza: Search for cultural identity', *Third Text*, 8/9 (1989), 65–78.

10 I use the term 'multicultural' here in the sense that the philosopher of art David Carrier does in his account of new departures away from 'monoculturalism'. D. Carrier, *A world art history and its objects* (Pennsylvania: Pennsylvania State University Press, 2008), pp. 27–44.

11 R. Cork, 'Buried treasures: an art world that makes you feel an outsider', *The Listener* (December 1989), p. 8.

12 M. Jaggi, 'Prophet at the margins: interview with Stuart Hall', *The Guardian* (8 July 2000).

13 L. Waugh, 'Two streams of Jamaican Art', *Circa*, 23 (1985), 24–7.

14 To quote him in full: 'A few decades back, when the art world was smaller and easier to police, and "international" meant Manhattan and Western Europe, New York more or less dictated what kind of art would be looked at, what ideas would circulate, what would be cool. But this is no longer so. The arena has expanded. Although economically powerful, New York is increasingly just one of many art centers doing their local thing. Most work that turns up in Manhattan galleries has little connection with, or pertinence to, what artists are doing and thinking about in Africa or India or even in the Bronx. And what's happening in those places apparently holds little interest for Manhattan.' H. Cotter, 'Caribbean visions of tropical paradise and protest', *The New York Times* (31 August 2007).

15 S. Hall, 'Negotiating Caribbean identities', *New Left Review*, 209 (1995), 3–14.

16 S. Hall, 'The Caribbean: A quintessentially modern zone', in G. Tawadros (ed.), *Contemporary art and ideas in an era of globalisation* (London: Institute of International Visual Arts, 2004), pp. 296–9; and S. Hall, 'Thinking the diaspora: Home-thoughts from abroad', *Small Axe*, 6 (1999), 1–18.

17 H. Carby, 'Becoming modern racialized subjects', *Cultural Studies*, 23:4 (2009), 624–65, p. 628.

18 Carby, 'Becoming modern racialized subjects', p. 653.

19 See especially pp. 15–41, D. Summers, *Real spaces: World art history and the rise of Western modernism* (London and New York: Phaidon, 2003).

20 For instance when modernism is treated as 'homogenous, empty time', to use Benjamin's phrase. W. Benjamin, *Illuminations*, trans. H. Zohn (London: Jonathan Cape, 1970), see especially 'Theses on the philosophy of history', part xiii; B. Anderson, *Imagined communities: Reflections on the origins and spread of nationalism* (London: Verso, 1983), especially chapter 2. H. Bhabha, *The location of culture* (Routledge, 1994); on 'spacing' and 'temporalising' within the limits of the text see: J. Derrida 'Differance', in *Speech and phenomena and other essays on Husserl's theory of signs*, trans. David B. Allison (Evanston, Ill.: Northwestern University Press, 1973), pp. 129–60; M. Foucault, 'Of other spaces', trans. Jay Miskowiec, *Diacritics*, 16 (1986), 22–7, which introduces a notion of 'heterotopias' or 'counter-

sites … in which the real sites, all the other real sites that can be found within the culture, are simultaneously represented, contested and inverted', p. 24. For a direct look at the 'chronopolitics' of empire and decolonisation that revisits Benjamin through a critique of Anderson, see J. Kelly, 'Time and the global: Against the homogeneous, empty communities in contemporary social theory', *Development and Change*, 29:4 (1998), 839–71.

21 Caribbean proposals for a metaphysics of time, and their relation to modernism have been vividly defined in the region's print culture. M. L. Emery, *Modernism, the visual, and Caribbean literature* (Cambridge: Cambridge University Press, 2009).

22 K. K. Birth, 'Any time is Trinidad time: Social meanings and temporal conscious-ness: A review', *Journal of the Royal Anthropological Institute*, 9:1 (2003), 819–20.

23 I set out the British background to this interest in: L. Wainwright, 'On being unique: World art and its British institutions', *Visual Culture in Britain*, 10:1 (2009), 87–101. Recent notable volumes in English include: K. Zijlmans and W. van Damme (eds), *World art studies: Exploring concepts and approaches* (Amsterdam: Valiz, 2008); J. Elkins (ed.), *Is art history global?* (London and New York: Routledge, 2007); and J. Onians (ed.), *Compression vs. expression: Containing and explaining the world's art* (New Haven: Yale University Press, 2006). See also C. Harris, 'The Buddha goes global: Some thoughts toward a transnational art history', *Art History*, 29:4 (2006), 698–720.

1   Painting in the aftermath of painting

The Guyana-born (then British Guiana) artist Aubrey Williams (b. 1926, d. 1990) has been approached in a range of ways in scholarship and exhibition display. The range reflects the artist's ability to be situated in several places in the twentieth-century history of art. First, Williams has attracted attention for his role in the cultural debates entailed by anti-colonialism, especially in the context of the Caribbean Artists Movement (CAM).[1] Since he was largely based in Britain after 1952, there is also the study of his participation in the national story of British art,[2] but an overlaying concern is to bring about a change in the artist's largely neglected status in mainstream art history. This has coincided with a generally concerted effort to shift or to rescue him from the lesser known provinces and margins of the modernist canon. The intention is to relocate Williams in the common or normative accounts of art in the twentieth century and to treat him as a foremost presence within British art. A more radical aim is to regard his art as a locus of its own; a centre-point around which the post-war history of painting can be rearranged, such as the ambition to establish him at the forefront of transatlantic post-war abstractionism.[3]

Although, as yet, there is no full biography of Williams, some detailed scholarship has allowed the circulation of his art to be mapped onto a global network of significant places – Guyana, the United States, Britain, Jamaica, France.[4] He moved through these diverse locations and lived a life that entwined otherwise apparently unrelated histories of art. Waiting to emerge more fully is a sense of how these places may be found to relate in the course of Williams's experience. To situate Williams at the overlapping of these contexts would amount to a larger task of historical analysis that has not yet been attempted, despite the breadth of current interest in his career. He is exemplary of the manner in which modern subjectivity and creativity developed during decolonisation by virtue of the multiple movements that criss-crossed the Atlantic in the period of its heaviest migratory traffic.[5] A more specific challenge remains to investigate how Williams's art and career brought together the complexities of nationalist resistance in colonies of the British Empire and the enfolding of British post-war modernism.[6]

While such a challenge might be answered in an extended critical study, or indeed, an exhibition of the art of Aubrey Williams, there is still the question of what can be learned from his example for an art history of the Caribbean and the politics of time. This book shows how ideas about time, and connected ones to do with space, are implicit in contemporary interest in him, as much as in the longer history of his reception as an artist. Consequently, there is much to explore in the way that he was represented over several decades during his career, and subsequently. It is significant that emphasising Williams's rightful 'place' within normative art historical narratives is an aim which, by definition, relies on both temporal and spatial metaphors. Such metaphors become even more instrumental when there is a motivation to see his career as prismatic of the development of Caribbean transnationalism. It is a concept that again enfolds considerations about time and space, aiming to understand a geography that transcends any single national story.

There is a widespread belief that Aubrey Williams's art may provide the basis for a radically different sort of writing and curating about the Caribbean. He is often the touchstone for writing that promises to reverse the historical pattern of marginalisation and exclusion that he and his peers endured. However, particularly troubling for this prospect is the continuity between how Williams was received in his day, and the more revisionist accounts of him. The current attention to Williams has indeed broken away from the omissions of the past and delivered a fresh message. But more orthodox spatio-temporal paradigms persist discernibly in this recent writing; there is a certain convergence in the mode of current interest in the artist and the often limiting associations that attended him throughout his career. I suggest that it is indeed hard to offer radical alternatives to the largely circumscribing, exclusionist treatment of Williams. In this he is, of course, not alone; it is necessary to think more deliberately about ways to accord greater prominence and visibility to art and artists of the Caribbean more broadly.

When he first began to attract the attention of art critics, reviews typically emphasised Williams's origins outside Britain, and tended to stress the exotic character of his work:[7]

> His first paintings … were full of hints of tangled forests and African rituals. England has tamed him, which reduces the strength of his impact, and refined him, which gives him more subtlety and more clarity than he had five years ago. On balance, he has become more acceptable to European eyes but less powerful, though some of the original primitive urgency remains …[8]

This same image of the artist, as embarked on a journey from a wild 'outside' – a hinterland from where he may have physically migrated, but could not disentangle himself – ran as a theme throughout his British reception during the 1950s and 1960s. Such reviewers were absorbed in a language of the primitive and exotic, and an underlying racism. This circumscription of the value of his works was based around a general focus on their exotic 'outsiderness' so that his status on the London art scene was compromised by the perceived incompatibility of his birthplace in the Caribbean with metropolitan success. Such terms of evaluation implied the impossibility of the artist's ambition to practise as an artist, highlighting the supposed failure and inadequacy of his art as a contribution to Western high modernism. By the time the Caribbean Artists Movement was formed in 1966 by artists alongside writers and critics John La Rose, Kamau (then L. Edward) Brathwaite and Andrew Salkey, Williams had started 'to feel terribly isolated, physically and intellectually'.[9] From then onwards, he would spend more and more time working in the Caribbean, and finally in Florida.[10]

Certainly, charges of anachronism had a crippling effect on Williams. They set up a racialised, marginalised reading of works and undermined his significance as an artist. All the more surprising then that not unrelated approaches to the matter of time have persisted in the ongoing attempts to reverse this pattern. Dominant notions of temporality are carried over, even in the service of laudable appeals for Williams and his art to be dignified and seen in a new light. Perhaps the basis for rethinking the terms of Williams's reception, and his posthumous inscription in art history and curating, may be found in his art itself. Williams and his art may be considered through the associations of outdatedness and anachronism – if indeed the two may be thought about together, despite their subtly divergent significance. He made a virtue of the way that painting was losing its status in the context of the decolonising Caribbean, by confronting his audiences there with a modernist practice. In the context of Britain, his presence suggests that we look back with new eyes to the departures from post-war high modernism.

Even so, Williams's simultaneous interest in both figuration and abstraction has to be placed carefully. He was not a conservative artist who persisted with modernist abstraction in the face of post-modernist site-specific art – in this sense he should not be confused with the briefly fashionable and largely reactionary 'New Spirit' painters of the 1980s.[11] The axis on which he moved, between various locations of the circum-Atlantic brought together otherwise disconnected stories of art, so that his art reveals an interaction between the North Atlantic metropole, namely London, and the transformations of colony to nationhood in the Caribbean. Ultimately, he embodied a history of the dynamic entwining of these locations, and his art has to be seen therefore as an indication that, against expectation, anachronism may be reclaimed.

In the aftermath of painting

Williams began his education in Georgetown, Guyana, where he took part in a four-year agricultural apprenticeship scheme, affiliated to University College, London, and was appointed an agricultural field officer in 1944. He studied at the Working Peoples' Art Class, and travelled to Britain to become a painter. After taking part in his first group show in London, in October 1954 at the little-known Archer Gallery in Westbourne Grove, under the direction of Dr Mary Morris,[12] he waited a further five years for a major solo exhibition,[13] which led to invitations to exhibit in Paris, Milan and Chicago.[14] His first serious accolade came in 1963, when he took the only prize at the First Commonwealth Biennale of Abstract Art. Williams's initial success owed much to Denis Bowen, a South African painter and teacher, founder of the New Vision Group in 1951. Bowen and his group were unusual in their inclusive attitude to young artists from outside Britain, and created a range of spaces where they displayed – a central London gallery (the New Vision Centre Gallery), and multi-use spaces around West London.[15]

Williams appropriated to his own ends the association that critics made with his works, as confined to an 'outdated' sort of creative practice. A starting

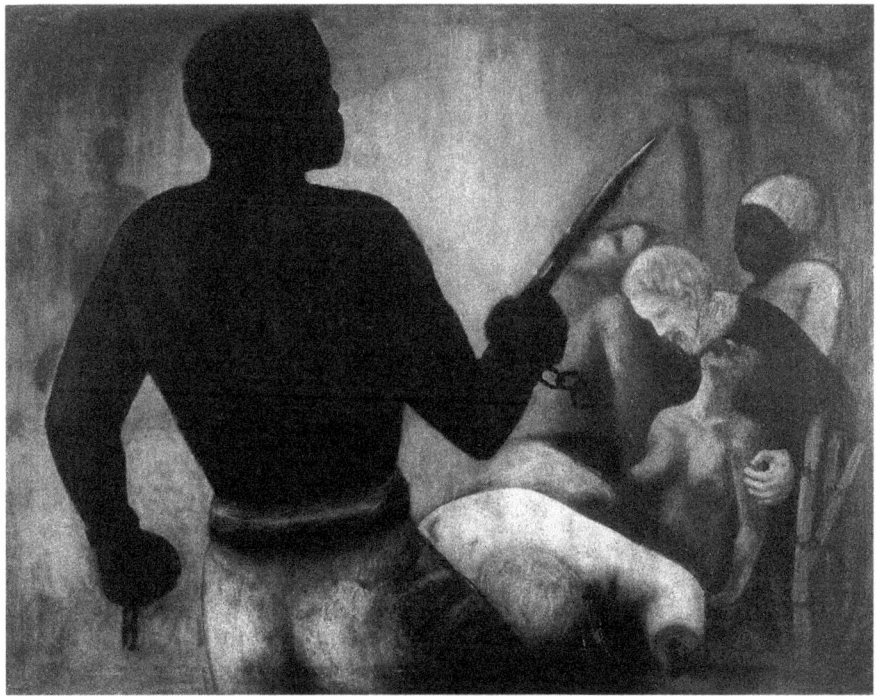

Aubrey Williams, *Revolt* (1960), oil on canvas, 134 × 165 cm.   **1**

point for the way he did so may be found in his painting *Revolt*, of 1960 (figure 1), a work that initiated the sustained apprehension of anachronism that beset his career as a whole. Williams made the painting while attempting to establish himself in the art world of London in the 1950s and 1960s. It is quite unlike his mostly abstract work that went on display at the New Vision Centre, and which had been the basis for the comment by Newton, cited above. *Revolt* has been generally overlooked as an example from his enormous output in painting, and yet it lends itself to thinking more critically about him. The painting offers a way of seeing how Williams's position may have been predetermined by patterns within art reception, but nevertheless that he came to use anachronism to his own ends as an exploitable resource.

An initial reading of *Revolt* offers some immediate, figurative references, while the painting itself has an unusual biography. It was produced in Britain but given by Williams as a gift to the Guyanese people, and is now in the Guyana National Gallery in Georgetown. The painting caused a controversy when the founders and custodians of the Guyana Museum, the Royal Agricultural and Commercial Society (RACS) in Georgetown, refused to exhibit the piece in 1960. There was no public statement of the grounds for this refusal, but the occasion prompted Jan Carew, novelist and art critic, to write:

> … this august and antiquated body was striking a traditional posture of resistance to Guianese freedom. The colonial mentality cannot stand an art and literature which smells of the earth and interprets truthfully the dreams of the people. For 'art and literature are like lightning, and lightning can never be timid'.[16]

Standing as victor over a maimed white body, a stripped white woman, and a helpless white man, *Revolt* is composed around a negative space of silhouette, the outline of an enslaved rebel brandishing a weapon. On a first reading, the piece provokes the same 'tragic excitement' that Guy Brett noted on encountering the artist's predominantly abstract paintings.[17] It captures a historic moment of human tragedy in 1763, when the enslaved leaders Cuffy, Accara and Atta launched a revolt against their Dutch plantation owners in Berbice – now a county of Guyana, then a separate Dutch colony – which ended in failure.[18] Overlaying this eighteenth-century context, is the importance of *Revolt* within the history of Guyana's decolonisation, both before and after its independence from Britain on 26 May 1966. It frames the promise of political freedom in British Guiana as the resolution of a long programme of national struggle, dating back at least to the Berbice revolt. Carew described the painting as a symbol of the new nation rising, 'stretching its limbs, stiff from too much kneeling'. This metaphor links the work to other twentieth-century mass mobilisations embodied in figurative allegory, both in the Caribbean and more globally.[19] Further, the motif of the shackles of enslaved bondage places *Revolt* within a post-1960s trend for commemorating rebellion in the Caribbean. It comes to evoke not so much the deliverance of emancipation, but the winning of freedom.

By this time, however, the period of Caribbean nationalism, the manufactured vision of the enslaved rebel figure as national hero had moved into statuary. The hero was no longer aptly expressed in painting. Indeed, the regional pattern of public monuments in Haiti, Guyana, Barbados and Surinam,[20] suggests that the widespread transfer of the theme of rebellion and emancipation into the medium of monumental sculpture had rendered obsolete the earlier treatment of that theme in paint.[21] Philip Moore's great public work, his *1763 Monument* (1976), popularly known as 'the Cuffy monument', indicates the same historical setting of the Berbice rebellion, cast in bronze.[22] As such, the further importance of *Revolt* stems from the artist's choice of painting for his medium, rather than sculpture. Painting harked back to the older colonial order, rather than in the direction that creativity in the Caribbean had begun to move towards. No longer the sine qua non of the modern, its status was superseded by sculpture, and other time-based, contingent forms of spectacle – dance, theatre, performance, carnival, steel drumming, calypso[23] – while performance also intersected with literature.[24]

The choice of painting underlines how Williams's work was touched by anachronism, in the sense that it depended on a form of address and a context of display that were largely understood and accessed by elite and colonial audiences. Arguably, its associations only 'work' if viewers share the conventions that painting draws upon, whether this be the genre of 'history painting', or more fundamentally, the codes of figuration and portraiture. For *Revolt* to be seen the way Williams intended, it would need to have been shown in the Georgetown Museum, rather than in the manner of the coming Caribbean shift toward a preference for outdoor public space, and either monumentality or performance. Whereas we might expect that the painting was precisely the sort of cultural object that the colonial authorities would gladly promote, his choice of subject would trouble this relation. It did not enjoy the cooperation of the RACS, in their refusal to exhibit the work.

To understand why this happened is to recognise how Williams used *Revolt* to gather together several strands of meaning. First was his self-identification with the enslaved man it pictured, which would be obvious to anyone who was acquainted with the artist. The distinctive profile and build of the figure resembles Williams himself, outlining his then youthful and muscular frame. It was the same profile that Picasso commented on when he met Williams in Paris:

He said that I had a very fine African head and he would like me to pose for him. […] In spite of the fact that I was introduced to him as an artist, he did not think of me as another artist. He thought of me only as something he could use for his own work.[25]

The meeting became a basis for Williams's ongoing and justified complaint that black subjects featured throughout modernism primarily as objects of interest, rather than as artists themselves. *Revolt* allowed him to resist that situation by asserting an authorial position through self-portraiture, and yet this inclusion of himself is underscored by certain other details. The enslaved figure in *Revolt* mirrors the pose that the artist would have struck when standing to paint, with a hand raised to the canvas. In his hand he has placed a blade, a technical procedure of metaphorical substitution, of a weapon for a paintbrush.

The insertion of Williams's own image also conveys the painting's intended reception in Guyana. It is part of the painting's play with the observer's point of view. The enslaved figure in *Revolt* is oriented towards his target of aggression, the Dutch planter, perhaps Governor Hoogenheim himself, and his household. The connotation of a saintly white figure, head bowed in pious martyrdom, is obvious, and yet here that traditional message is subverted. For instead of the viewer's compassion being drawn to the planter, the painting appeals to the righteous rebel – offering a view of the scene as if we ourselves people the ranks of the rebels. By virtue of this choreographic arrangement, the artist forcefully and strategically assumed a viewer complicit with the rebellion. As spectators, we stand behind the rebel, and behind and in support of Williams.

From what is known of Williams's donation of the painting to the colonial authorities, there was, of course, another intended viewer: the government whose minister had asked that the piece be displayed in 1960, but had that wish denied by the RACS. A little of what was discussed is recorded in committee minutes. There is a handwritten amendment, signed by Mr H. R. Persaud, to the draft minutes of a meeting in 1960, called especially to discuss the painting. It makes clear that concern among executive members focused on the consequences for their relationship with a minister: Janet Jagan, co-founder in 1950 with her husband, Cheddi Jagan, of the left-wing People's Progressive Party, both future national leaders of Guyana.[26] The note illustrates the extent to which the RACS was still able to influence the government, even at the level of decisions about the public display of art. Persaud noted that, 'what I said was that if the Society felt that the painting was unsuitable for exhibition, then it ought to have contacted the Minister concerned and asked her to re-consider her decision. The Society's failure to do so had resulted in the slighting of the Minister.'[27] The episode indicates how the balance of power in decolonising Guyana had not yet tipped in favour of a democratic leadership.

The bureaucratic controversy over the painting concerned disclosure of visual knowledge of the historical past, the ostensible topic of *Revolt*. The painting's presence in Guyana prompted the RACS to continue assuming the patrician role it had been assigned at its founding in 1844.[28] Carew's suggestion, therefore, that *Revolt* 'represents a break-through to the hearts of black men'[29] was simplistic, given that the Guyanese elite comprising the RACS in 1960 chose not to identify with Williams's mobilised viewer, electing to place themselves in the position of the Dutch planter.

Revolt entered an environment in Guyana where various ways of seeing were in conflict with one another, resulting in the painting being immediately kept from public attention. Its impact was thus shared between the galvanising of anti-colonial feeling and antagonism among proprietors of British Guiana's leading official cultural institution; between an unequivocal didacticism and local cultural activism. *Revolt* was not to be allowed a showing until 1970, at the Guyana Museum at a *Retrospective Exhibition of Guyanese Artists* organised by an art sub-committee chaired by Williams himself. Noting the circumstances around the event, Anne Walmsley writes that *Revolt* 'was hung prominently in [that] exhibition: an irony not lost on those who knew how the painting had been refused space … nine years earlier'.[30]

Fire and time

These conditions of reception offer a starting point for seeing how Williams approached his practice, and led to considerations about the formal preoccupations of his works as a whole. Again, *Revolt* grants a suitable way into this analysis. While there are inevitable associations with the circumstances around the Berbice rebellion, the painting is also invested with other visual references. The figures in the composition are glimpsed through a red-coloured penumbra in a scene that takes place at night. This surrounding colour forms a light source for the action, covering much of the painted surface – a glowing, colourful background that denotes fire. It is the burning of plantation fields and houses, indicating the destruction of property, the committing to flames of plantation wealth and its mode of production. This is a prototype for how Williams would handle fire in other works, in several of his major groups of paintings, and certain standalone pieces of the late 1960s. The group produced in Britain and Florida, his *Olmec Maya* series,[31] contains shapes that are set against a background of continually burning, colourful flame. In some of the paintings, a mass of flames occupies the central ground of the picture, such as the image dedicated to the plumed serpent, *Queztlcoatl III* (figure 2). The mass is framed by stout blocks of primary colour, and behind it is a ceaselessly swirling surface of flame.

After *Revolt*, seldom did Williams's interest in fire take an illusionistic form. The aim was not to depict fire naturalistically, but to distil its essence and to reassemble its aesthetic qualities. This sort of approach can be seen in

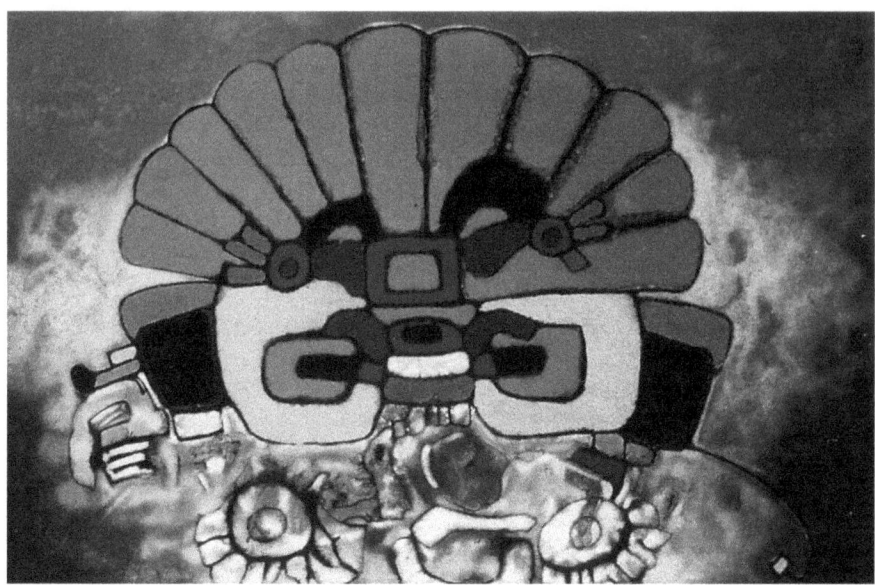

2   Aubrey Williams, *Queztlcoatl III* (1984), oil on canvas, 120 × 178 cm.

some forcefully fiery images, for instance those paintings from *Olmec Maya*, under the title *Hymn to the Sun*. They evoke various Amerindian icons that are illustrated schematically: features of the Central American landscape, transformed by Williams into more ambiguous shapes. The icons are drawn from places that served as the navigation points on pre-European maps, recorded in the cartographic codices that the artist knew from the British Museum.[32] These epic manuscripts illustrate pathways around landmarks and coded indications of the expected time spent in traversing the distances between them. Translating such pictograms into abstract designs on canvas was a huge undertaking. Again, the element of fire is a running thread, drawing them together as a body of works. In many of these, Williams has fitted frames of burning light around notionally Amerindian shapes that change in appearance with each canvas, and the central shapes are lit up as well as obscured in places by flames. They are images of changing objects whose transformations are captured at fleeting instants in time, with some forms shown in the process of being blown apart as if by explosions of light.

Among this series, *Hymn to the Sun IX* (figure 3) epitomises Williams's strategic and ambivalent attitude to modernism. There is a mixed manner in which he approaches the task of painting the sun. As is well known, artists within the modern tradition eschewed the idea of illustration, in the pursuit of autonomous aesthetic effects. Cézanne, for example, spoke of being unable to imitate the sun and having to find an 'equivalent' for it within the decorative scheme of the painting.[33] Williams follows this attitude in part. On the one hand, his works suggest a belief in the modernist idea of the recovery of aesthetic order and depth from inchoate sensation. He chooses not to paint recognisable images of the sun, favouring the alternative: to convey a larger aesthetic totality in which perception is reordered. In parallel, however, some discernible aspects of the composition do remain naturalistic – the burst of rays from behind a cloud and the sharp edges of linear shafts of light. The series thereby constitutes something of a balancing act, both aligned to the abstractionist suggestion of visual essence and yet merged with the faithful observation of nature.

On this basis, Williams proceeds to evoke a specific experience for the viewer. As well as being basic forms of life, for him fire and air are elements with a creative temperament. They have their own personalities, and are transitional, responsive and volatile. The action in his paintings takes place in the moments after the breaking of a boundary – the walls of a biological cell, the surface of a raindrop – in the split second when nothing has yet quite escaped or spilled out. Around these permeable edges are areas of the canvas that seem waiting to be filled. When thought about as the interplay of characters, here is the indifference of space in contrast to the exuberance of flame. As his works develop these positions exchange roles. Apparently static shapes are injected with energy by strokes of paint that melt the edges of a shape under strong light. Williams's *Cosmos* paintings, the series begun in 1985, take up this searching interest in a totally different physical environment among stars and planets, arranged as rings of colour against a dark background, in trails of illuminated dust and pyroclastic debris, arranged as fires in space.

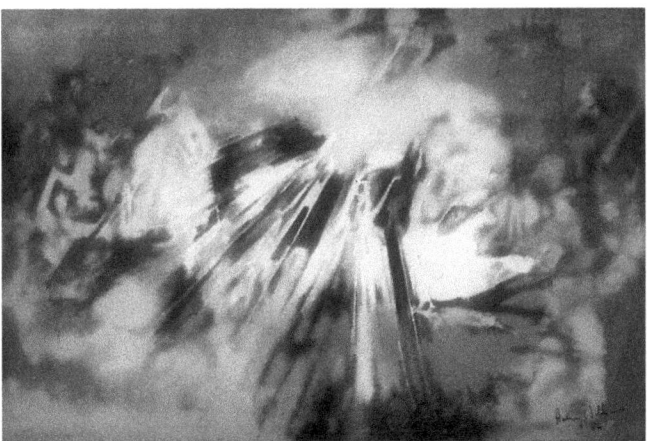

Aubrey Williams, *Hymn to the Sun IX*. From the *Olmec Maya series*, oil on canvas (1984), 119 × 178 cm.

3

From the Amerindian and stellar realms, Williams stole fire to blaze another trail, with the force of fire and light re-emerging in his paintings about music. He was long fascinated by the chamber and orchestral music of Shostakovich and inspired to create a series of thirty paintings between 1969 and 1981 (figure 4). Many of these pieces comprise large, warm blossoms and petals of colour, and tongues or leaves of fire are mixed in with flat and spreading colour fields. In the film about Aubrey Williams, *The Mark of the Hand*, the artist speaks of his early encounter with Shostakovich, on hearing his First Symphony. It suggested to Williams the overlapping of touch, sound and memory which came to enervate his series of paintings as a whole. As he put it, 'I could feel colour.'[34] This conception, which appeals to the tactility of vision and to the cross-matching of the range of our senses, has a long history within modernist abstraction, notably in the theories of Kandinsky. Williams's music series is rooted in this sensorial project, extending the potential of sound to take on shape and texture. It is structured by Williams's ambition to create spatial depth that can be pictured and played with. The painter's response to mystery in his Amerindian works, here gives way to excursions of wonder. Flames blow across the canvases and clear the way for mesmerising vistas, merging the horizons between the vision of Shostakovich, and the listening ear of Williams the artist.

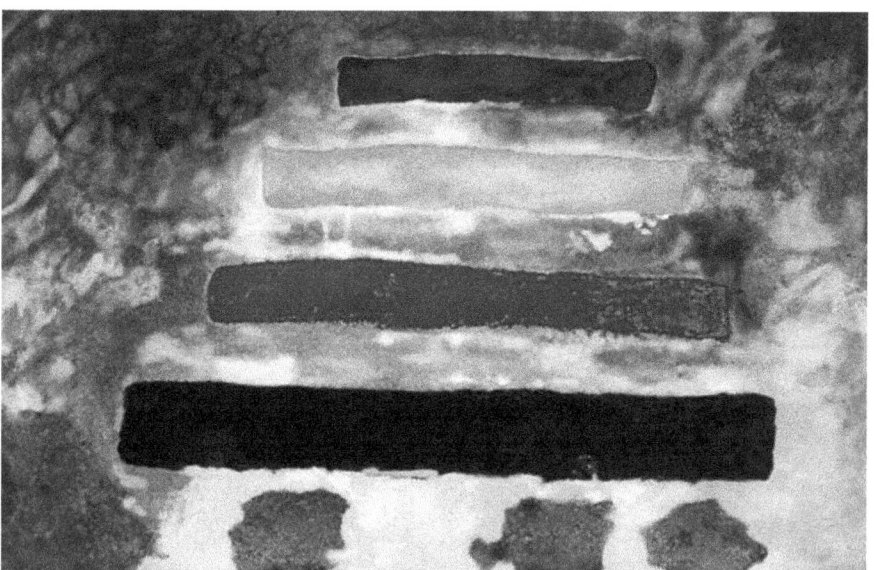

4   Aubrey Williams, *Shostakovich 11th Quartet Opus 122* (1981), oil on canvas, 130 × 203 cm.

The transformation of the painted surface into fire can be traced through the repetition of flame in each of Williams's canvases. In this regard, he carried on with inherently illusionistic, modernist painting despite the claims made for the materialism of the new three-dimensional work. The excitement surrounding this emerging practice focused on the literal movement of the spectator in space as distinct from the fixed viewing point of painting.[35] The response of artists such as Alan Charlton or Frank Stella in defence of painting was intended to undo any of the apparent stability assigned to two-dimensional form.[36] There are traces of this priority with Williams, although presented in a different way – his repeating works on the theme of fire, for instance, which bring another sort of meditation on temporal instability. Paintings such as *Time and Elements* (figure 5) bestow a watchful interest in the duration of flame as a measure of the duration of time. There is no concrete link in Williams's biography to interest in Gaston Bachelard's psychoanalysis of fire,[37] nor to the philosophy of time established by thinkers such as Bergson, but his practice is open to a theoretical inquiry along those lines.

However, Williams was not confined to exploring the consciousness of the temporality of viewing. Broadly, he touched on the same rhetorical significance given to fire in the context of political struggles for equality.[38] More contingently, he extended the critical embrace of fire that was demonstrated

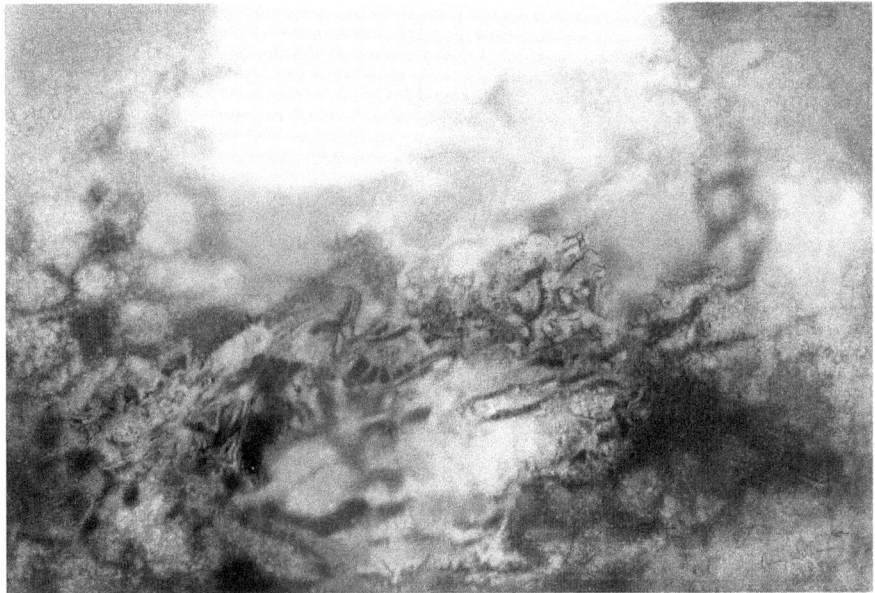

Aubrey Williams, *Time and the Elements* (1985), from the *Olmec Maya series*, oil on canvas, 123 × 181 cm. **5**

by contemporaries such as the Guyanese poet Martin Carter, in his construction of 'a revolutionary alphabet of freedom'.[39] Williams showed how the qualities of fire intersect with the political theorising of historical time. This was vital, given that his reception was so tightly enfolded in the placement of his works along a linear, imperial sense of history. Presenting other ways of looking at painting, much rested on his ability to construct the painted surface as a gradually consuming flame.

Returning to *Revolt*, the painting's purpose during the period of Guyana's decolonisation was thereby augmented by Williams's formal interest in the erasing, excoriating effects of fire. Nowhere was this explored better than through his devices of abstraction. As in the later canvases, large areas of *Revolt* are empty and abstracted. Consequently, the canvas is empty of topographical signifiers; it is neither a domestic interior, nor a landscape marked by ruins, nor a built or urban space. Through the placement of figures on a ground that they do not fully disrupt, the rebellion pictured in *Revolt* is staged in a utopian space, a space without place; not specific to that eighteenth-century moment in Berbice or the twentieth-century moment of a decolonising British Guiana. Unlike the 'history painting' of the nineteenth-century academy, the canvas has an abstract noun for its title, rather than a name, place or date for an event. *Revolt* is, therefore, interchangeable with other gestures from elsewhere and other displays of violent resistance throughout history.

That the subject of Williams's painting is not tied to any particular historical time is a common virtue of his canvases as a whole. It is the basis for the philosophical and critical quality of his art, complemented by a corresponding abstraction of space. Together these interests emphasise Williams's works as a political response to the strictures of being contained within one's own historical moment, which in this sense was the long moment of colonial rule. There was an urgent need to imagine alternatives beyond that present, by envisioning a place within the present of decolonised modernity. Through the medium of painting, Williams broaches Martin Carter's parallel sense of the contingency of time and being, his appreciation of the intersecting nature, the simultaneity or affinity of time and space conveyed, for instance, in his poem 'Our Time': 'The more the men of our time we are/the more our time is. But always/we have been somewhere else.'[40] With Carter, he lodges an appeal to be coeval or contemporary with the time of the modern, to be of the same time. Chakrabarty has reminded us why this yearning should prove to be so crucial. The desire for contemporaneity is a desire to be equal in age to the modern political classes, to be considered mature and ready to participate in democratic rule, rather than consigned to 'the waiting room of history'.

The creation of *Revolt* and Williams's choice to gift the painting to the people of Guyana was driven by the anti-colonial desire for a virtuous state of being which is released and recuperated from the condition of the provincial and belated. Williams was all for expressing a distinctive sense of present-ness, of being in the present, as 'belonging' to the same historical time, not simply as a compatriot to Carter and other Guyanese contemporaries, but at the cutting edge of painting internationally. The 'our time' in Carter's poem is the shared modern time that Williams and his peers aspired to occupy. They had a political desire to reclaim a place in the present – to recover their agency – and to hold a role in the shaping of history, which was denied to colonised subjects. Even so, the use of picturing has a special status in articulating such anti-colonial goals; and its material presence works differently from writing. With *Revolt*, Williams created a physical object which was both present in Georgetown in 1960, yet made absent from public view. The making absent of the work, as the invisible object of controversy, would involuntarily extend the scope of *Revolt* as an artwork. It enhanced its quality as a work of protest, and repositioned its artist as an agent of agitation.

Revolt demanded that the viewer confront and identify with its subjects, preferring that we involve ourselves in a complicit relation to the artist. This was an index of the artist's belief in the need for images to absorb and accom-modate themselves to the viewer. Michael Fried identified a movement toward 'theatricality' in much 1960s art,[41] and although Williams was not in view for Fried, he might have been identified as one of those artists who remained, by contrast, fully engaged with the idea of modernist absorption, despite the rise of theatricality. He found a place at the New Vision Centre Gallery, described at the end of its first year of opening as: 'Fiercely non-figurative … remark-ably international.'[42] Fried saw modernism as being 'at war' with theatre and theatricality,[43] and yet the reception of *Revolt* by the RACS committee was a different scene of conflict. What came to matter there was how Williams's interest in absorption became a sort of criticality, since his conservative audience remained distanced from modernism.

Entwined art stories

Assessment of Williams's practice as a whole has to take into view multiple global contexts and his rather special position as an artist. He remained sensi-tive to Caribbean discourses on the role of the artist there and he was aware of the developments around art in the 1950s and 1960s in Britain. But only with hindsight can we say that he contributed to some of the lasting changes that art went through in the later part of the twentieth century, in moving toward a more global, conceptual approach.

In the first decades that Williams painted, the sense of what made for a relevant, contemporary sort of visual creativity in the Anglophone Caribbean differed from that of the North Atlantic. This separating of the ways has been the object of inquiry in the field of literature, as writers became involved in programmes of independence and nation building, but it has been far less examined in relation to art practice. As noted, the Caribbean would choose not to prioritise painting during the immediate period of decolonisation in the region, since its preference was for art that was monumental and public, a challenge that sculpture was more equipped to meet than painting. A point often overlooked from the Caribbean side is that critiques of painting also took hold elsewhere in the North Atlantic. In the United States this was a critique of the medium-specificity of both sculpture and painting from the point of view of the emerging site-specific based practices. There is no direct link between Williams and this context, or the anti-modernist British art of the 1960s (associated with Barry Flanagan, Richard Long, Mark Boyle, John Latham and so on). We must also consider that, in the North Atlantic, Williams's approach to painting was at odds with the mainstream of modernist abstractionism. This is noted by Kobena Mercer, who has dubbed his link with abstraction as 'discrepant'.[44] His canvases were not purely abstract and for modernist spokespersons such as Fried and Clement Greenberg, Williams's art would have been seen as compromised and provincial in the sense of being backwardly conservative.

Even so, Williams relished the opportunity to hold on to abstraction and figuration together, and looked askance at the leading assumptions of what was modern art, and what was not. Williams had an unusual status in each setting in that he maintained a connection to the Caribbean, lived mostly in Britain, and travelled to the United States, so that his biography entwined spaces that art history has treated as largely disconnected. With the benefit of hindsight, we may see that these diverse settings around the Atlantic were brought together in Williams's experience – that he stood on their mutual temporal ground. There is a certain appeal in the conclusion that Williams raised similar questions in art practice to those that eventually transformed North Atlantic art at its core, that his role was integral in the art historical developments toward new stances and demands on painting. But Williams's story cannot be told in this way if that means claiming from the documentation of his life and from examination of his art that he had an 'integral' relation at the time. It is in retrospect, when the criteria for what is significant have changed, that he comes into focus. He is not just conservative in relation to Morris, Smithson, Andre, Serra and so on, but distinctive for where he came from, and on the basis of the geography of his experience. He was one of several artists who raised the possibility that Greenbergian modernist values could be reworked through a vector to do with place, for instance by extolling the virtues of the 'local' as against the 'universal' and 'international'.

A similarity may be seen with artists in the British setting such as John Hoyland, whose interest along these lines comes to seem more important after considering Williams. This altered picture may be what the critic Guy

Brett has in mind when linking Williams's abstraction to artists such as Peter Lanyon and Alan Davie – for their common connection to music, flight and ancient cultural or environmental heritage[45] – or what the curator Andrew Dempsey detects Williams to have in common with the later non-figurative painters Gillian Ayres and Albert Irvin.[46] This book does not seek to claim Williams as a British artist, but the history of art in Britain comes to look different once we have a deeper understanding of his art.

The Cuban art critic, Gerardo Mosquera has thought in a similar way about Williams's impact on art history of the Americas. Mosquera has included Williams among a list of artists 'for whom the African presence as a conclusive factor in Latin American fine arts can be isolated'. The basis for this is not the survival of myths from Africa, but 'a natural inclination toward the creation of myths … reflecting a reality where magic and myth play a very active role in contemporary problems'.[47] Mosquera's sense is that an 'African presence' resides in the prevalence of myth in Williams's art – his Amerindian works with their human themes and materials foregrounding the significance and ubiquity of myth. The embrace of the material culture of Amerindian experience by way of figuration was an active undoing of the appetite for formal purity, the foil to a modernist 'disinterested' spectator and the ideology of the 'universal'.

Consequently, it seems more pertinent to ask not about the importance of some underlying 'Africanness' or 'Amerindianness', but about the outcomes of a focus on myth – how this aesthetic departure was articulated to Williams's wider search for an approach to painting that would meet with his experience. This can be considered from the perspective of his awareness of those global contexts in which imperialism and capitalism were being undermined during the mid-twentieth century. Williams's art drew lines of equivalence between anti-colonial liberation movements and the new intellectual projects of the political Left. A major challenge to modernist orthodoxy issued from the spaces outside the conventional geographical boundaries of modernism. For the broad programme of alternatives that they posed, he was attracted to the artists Arshile Gorky, Roberto Matta, Rufino Tamayo, Diego Rivera, José Orozco and Wifredo Lam.[48] Following them, he continually resisted attempts to define his paintings as either 'Caribbean' or 'European', thereby frustrating the demand of audiences who assumed easy 'connections' to any single visual heritage.[49] As Williams told fellow CAM members gathered in his studio in 1967, 'I have great respect for world art, especially for European art … [But] the intrinsic trend, the life force of what I'm doing, is not anything to do with the emotional structure of European life.'[50] This was consonant with the debates held among members of CAM on the issue of artistic 'sources', as in Ronald Moody's comment at a meeting in 1968 that 'Each one of us has to … delve within himself and really begin to find out what he is …'[51] Williams's parallel creative focus on Shostakovich's music was especially judicious. Along that avenue he fathomed with the works of an inspirational figure who had remained true to his own vision in Stalinist Russia. Against the background of Williams's anti-colonial biography, he would identify with what it meant to be a creative practitioner in a climate of political ferment and the rethinking of Marxism.

There is a particular way in which this consideration of regional contexts is essential for elucidating Williams. For the most part, he worked on the canvas in order to figure flames, making the painted surface into a metaphorical mass of flame, rather than only depicting or illustrating how fire might appear to the observer. The line between these is subtle, but crucial, in locating his works within a modernist tradition. It was a tradition that the North Atlantic avant-garde was set to displace and render out of date: Robert Morris for instance described painting as having become 'antique', on his move to three-dimensionality.[52] So that when he began the *Olmec Maya* series, or indeed, produced *Revolt*, Williams took up a medium that was already threatened with obsolescence. The claim that he embraced painting for its status within the development of artistic modernism is therefore problematic. The new directions in 1960s art had their critical purchase only when painted elements such as the figure were recognised as anachronistic, and then explored and exploited.

Regardless of how anachronistic figuration had become, it was not seen as such in Guyana by his RACS audience. There, Williams's works were viewed as broadly in line with an outside imposition of progressivism. *Revolt*'s reception restated the conservatism of the colonial bureaucracy, and yet it was nothing compared to the rejection of painting that would become widespread in the Caribbean. Williams was thereby practising in the aftermath of certain modalities of art practice in Britain – abstractionism and figuration – and in the Caribbean setting, the aftermath of painting itself. The criticality of his approach depended on his ability to take account of these differing yet entwined attitudes, and to inhabit their stories.

Revolt was exemplary in its contribution to the politics of an active decolonisation. Williams's self-identification ran beyond the local contexts of Georgetown and Berbice, towards a self-assertion of his place within a genre of 1950s and 1960s neo-figuration in Britain. *Revolt*, therefore, fitted closely within the preoccupations of at least two locales, holding a place among the leading preoccupations of British post-war artists and audiences, while remaining key to the cultural politics of Guyana in its march to independence. That such multiple locations and readings of the painting were possible at all depended largely on the fact of the physical portability of *Revolt* – that it is a painting per se, rather than a large-scale sculpture, as with other treatments of the Berbice rebels and the theme of emancipation. Made in Britain, the painting travelled to Guyana to share a field of effects and diverse reactions. In that politically divided space, where audiences grasped ambivalently at the meaning of decolonisation, the artist's imaginative intervention drew further potency from the fact that the painting was conceived and conveyed from the imperial centre.

Ultimately, this prompts a return to Williams's concern with fire, and the range of ways that fire became crucial in how he negotiated a place and a time for himself. Sculpture has contended with painting in the Caribbean, and yet it is not at root a suitable medium for illusionism: for trying to show that fire is formless. Williams needed a medium that fitted his *incendiary* purpose, that suited his overall motivation of blurring too readily compartmentalised artistic contexts and identities. His aim was to undermine categorisations of visual creativity – such as the division of the 'timeless' and ethnographic Amerindian artefact from modern art; myth from history – and the separation of abstract form from figuration, which came to govern much twentieth-century modernism. *Hymn to the Sun* suggested the virtually religious reverence for its subject matter – painting in devotion to the sun – which modernism had set aside. It is poised between the regard for the sun in Olmec and Maya ritual, and the meditations on the sun that emerged with the new poetry and literature of modernising, decolonising Guyana.[53]

Williams was distinctive for the way he responded to the issues that defined the crisis of modernism in the latter part of the twentieth century. He was an active presence on the British art scene and yet continued to influence the region of his birth, visiting or sending paintings across, and taking part in exhibitions there. He took an active role in both places in debates addressing the nature of the experience of modernity. He was also acutely aware of the political undercurrents that were about to break to the surface in modernism – resulting in an art that became more contingent, plural and global.

The interpretation of modernism that Williams espoused is worth discussing in the context of the claim that temporality has been a governing element in the practice of his painting. He dismissed the distinction that so exercised modernism of a choice between figuration and abstraction, by providing plenty of examples where these approaches to painting could meet on the same canvas. This aspect of his practice upset an older assumption of the need to keep figurative and abstract painting apart. Paintings such as *Revolt* were also redolent of conventions of painting that were emphatically rejected by the avant-garde and discredited by the dominant narrative of high modernism. As such, instead of seeing his mixing up of figurative and abstract elements as representing a belated, provincial lagging behind high modernism, it is more productive to regard it as an anticipation of a fully post-modernist painting. Williams's choices over registers involved shifting between approaches and collapsing conventional distinctions. This placed him ahead of the curve that led beyond modernism, rather than confining him to the label of an artist who came 'too late'.

Anti- and post-colonial uses of anachronism

Williams's temporal placement can be explored further through the language of anti-colonialism and with regard to his insertion in postcolonial debates. It may seem surprising that there is little substantial difference between the language used by Caribbean and British critics of Williams's art, and that what has mattered ultimately is how their contexts rendered different outcomes. The sorts of responses that Williams received in Britain, and those generated in the Caribbean, show the influence in both places of certain attitudes to temporality that were held in common. As Jan Carew put it:

> These paintings of Aubrey Williams ... express in essence a sense of being which differs from that of the European in the same way that the music of the spinnet differs from the rhythm of a drum. ... His art reflects the instinctive sense of rhythm of the Negro fused with the mytho-poetic imagination of Indian-Voodoo and the image of gods and man, the dreams born in cradles of a forest and brought to the city where twentieth-century man paces the pavements of destruction.[54]

Observations on how modern art reception has tended to 'primitivise' artists from Europe's 'elsewhere' have encouraged us to berate Carew for his choice of words.[55] Yet in the immediate era of decolonisation in the West Indies during the 1960s, such stereotypes were embraced and mobilised, with some successful political outcomes. To be able to assert one's identity as a 'Negro' or 'a sense of being which differs from that of the European' (to quote Carew) was to assert an anti-colonial message, as in the Negritude movement throughout the French colonies in Africa and the Caribbean. It provided a means for shaping a cultural category of difference that would force a crucial separation from European, in this case British, cultural hegemony. Carew's goal in supporting Williams was to imaginatively describe his work as a basis for cultural autonomy from British rule.

It is worth comparing Carew's prose with the touching tribute to Aubrey Williams written during a major retrospective of his work in 1998 by the Guyanese artist and academic Denis Williams (no relation to Aubrey):

> the West Indian painter in the metropolis creates problems for himself by adopting paradigms that result from an evolutionary agenda outside his history and impossible for him to share. ... I do not think that Aubrey was temperamentally equipped to challenge any of the assumptions of Abstract Expressionism or to delve into the theoretical niceties of which it was an outcome ... Aubrey thought deeply, of course, but could not cerebrate either in speech or in painting. ... This was a tricky situation for a colonial ... painter.[56]

It is fair to suspect that Denis Williams met with similar criticisms while he worked as a painter in London from 1946, and was writing here from first-hand experience.[57] His comments restate an all too common perception among British audiences of Williams as a West Indian artist. The state of being disadvantaged by 'an evolutionary agenda outside his history and impossible for him to share' is a phrase that captures the sort of cross-matching of space and time, which characterised the charges of belatedness that these artists met with. That they were involved in a 'tricky situation' rather understates the matter.[58]

What was complex about the situation for Caribbean artists is that approaches to painting had their uses depending on the context of their display, which was different in various sites around the Atlantic. The reception of *Revolt* by those who controlled the Georgetown Museum was underlined by parochial and colonial values that mediated an exclusive domain of public display in which they were unable to accept the language of primitivism that surrounded Williams's art in Guyana, championed in print by Carew. Yet the same primitivist language that was invoked in support of Aubrey Williams in the Caribbean would limit his importance when it featured in his British reception. At the very least, this reveals that imperial discourse – in which the intention was to limit the impact of artists such as Williams – depending on where it was exerted, would require different sorts of resistance. Williams would face the uneasy task of pursuing an art practice whose value was unstable and had to consider multiple audiences.

If successful appropriations of primitivism are contingent upon place, the temporal context of anti-colonial articulations is consequently also significant. This is demonstrated by postcolonial scholarship on India where similar strategies are understood to throw up obstacles to freedom.[59] This uncovers, in the present analysis, the temporal contingency of the Caribbean resort to primitivism. Such a resort may even be seen as a consequence, an offshoot, or a reproduction of the colonial order, and as the misrecognition of its subversion. This may be compared to Frantz Fanon's commentary, which unmasks a related outcome in what he knew from French colonies in Africa. He dismissed the relevance to radical political change of certain practices of cultural representation among nationalist artists and writers, suggesting: 'You will never make colonialism blush for shame by spreading out little-known cultural treasures under its eyes.'[60]

These are the broader initiatives that postcolonial thought offers. Art historical study more specifically, however, has hardly broached the matter of how artists practising during decolonisation in the Caribbean – and while on the move between imperial centre and periphery – would objectify their own circumstances. What may lead this work is the effort to understand how the dimension of time dominated in the ways that artists read their own experiences. There was pressure for artists to act as supporters of anti-colonialism, and to relate their works to histories of visual creativity that were temporally disconnected from the present struggles – such as Williams's decision to revisit eighteenth-century Berbice, or pre-Columbian cartography. In his case, these were not the only formative influences; the noted histories of abstractionism and figuration were also of concern. For Fanon, it was obvious which of these elements the architects of decolonising nations would favour. As he warned, 'the man of culture … will let himself be hypnotized by these mummified fragments which because they are static are in fact symbols of negation and outworn contrivances'.[61] Fanon criticised the view that the 'little-known' cultural past was an ample resource to which nation builders could productively double back. Ideas and practices which were rendered out of date, or trapped in a distant historical moment, were thus prime candidates for being released into the present. In that formula, cultural materials that appear anachronistic on account of the colonising process are recuperated precisely because of that quality. They are thought to be able to reverse the outcomes of colonisation and to add depth to the newness of the independent nation, helping to confer its own antiquity.[62] When suitable forms cannot be found, or their coverage of the nation's novelty is thin and unconvincing, what matters then is the search itself. The ultimate priority is simply to question who gets to decide what counts as anachronistic.

The anxiety about being both belated and provincial compels the anti-colonial strategy of self-invention. Rather than anachronism being made irrelevant, it becomes instead the chief site of contestation. Anachronism focuses the reclamation of an outmoded past and the dream of reconnecting with a pre-colonial state of being. With the benefit of historical hindsight, however, the contradictions of this search are clear. Even the process of reclamation remains trapped in a persistently hegemonic, imperialising attitude to temporality. The terrain of imperial time is reaffirmed. Anti-colonial efforts emerge at an intersection of time and space which is mapped and organised into the scheme of a modern centre and belated province. This narrows the range of outcomes for artistic creativity, limiting artists to the task of recovering an imagined past. As it does so, art making moves deeper into the relationship of client to the project of nationalism. That emerging system of value places demands on what art making should deliver; it enlists art in the abstract imagining of national community. What might be called the time of the artwork (the temporary conditions that make it relevant, and its lifespan once these change) is set out on its behalf – while the status of the artist is also tied to this fate. Like the work of art, the artist's temporal context also becomes over-determined.

This predicament is familiar from what we know of the constraints experienced by artists in conditions of modern nationalism. There, the modernist promise of an autonomous future for art practice is deferred by the demands of a continuous present of national construction. This process contributes to the ambivalence demonstrated by artists such as Williams during the histor-ical moment of decolonisation: an interest in the autonomy of form enshrined in high modernism, and yet the competing pressures brought on art practice to relate to the specificity of time and place. Since the nationalist project is ongoing and incomplete, the fulfilment of this autonomy becomes ever more remote. There is an adverse result for anti-colonialism when the modernising, decolonising impulse moves into direct conflict with the yearnings for the artistic freedoms of modernism. A dilemma emerges for the artist, who is required to give up one sort of freedom for another.

This was at work in Williams's own battle in Guyana to display his work, even as the theatricality of sculpture, and theatre itself, threatened to render his canvases obsolete. From this we can see what happens when the intersec-tion of art and nationalism has the added dimension of decolonisation, and with it, an added contradiction. Creativity is subject to circumscriptions that begin to resemble those of centralised imperial control, and to thereby repeat another, more unexpected past: the unthinkable return of foreign rule. This is illustrative of how a newly independent state apparatus may take on aspects of the foregoing colonialist administration, and how the time of colonisation persists in the moment of its intended antithesis. Artists such as Williams may have experienced this situation positively: a vantage point from which to understand the relation between art practice and its historical context. In every sense, his fraught interactions in the Caribbean took place on a distinctly temporal terrain.

It is worthwhile to compare Guyana's anti-colonial positioning of Williams with his British career. Concerns with what is so aptly called Williams's 'place in history' have taken another shape through the curatorial contestation of Britain's national art canon. Here the anti-colonial priority of establishing a relation between art and nationhood is redeployed. Yet it takes an adversarial, more strictly postcolonial mode, concerned with countering the 'invisibility' of exclusion and marginalisation. The exhibition of 1989 by Rasheed Araeen, *The Other Story*, was significant in establishing a historical frame around Williams in relation to Britain. Williams and his peers were displayed in such a way as to turn on their head the usual rendering of artists from Africa, Asia and the Caribbean as secondary, outdated followers or mimics of canonical modernists; of Ivan Peries as following Gauguin, Francis Newton Souza as after Picasso, and so on. The exhibition suggested that these artists – with their sometime anachronistic figurative works – were in fact instructive as precur-sors for the 'figural turn' towards self-portraiture and identification with the human body, typical of much 'Black Art' practice of the 1980s and early 1990s. This curatorial treatment had the same historicist dimension that was typical of the developmentalist tradition of much art history. It emphasised an unfolding history of art that could be traced out through comparisons of visual motifs over several decades, setting in motion the sort of iconographic analysis that has subsequently been addressed to a story of art in 'Black Britain'.[63]

The exhibition plumbed several decades of works by 'Afro-Asian' practitioners, to emerge with an 'untold story' of the underlying tendencies that result in the art of the present. Its distinctly developmental model of art history was assisted by the idea of a longer running movement that spanned the post-war period. One intention for the exhibition was to address an audience that knew little or nothing of what preceded them: the generation of artists from diverse, largely diasporic backgrounds, who emerged in the 1980s. Through the exhibition they would be able to see more clearly the legacy of earlier generations. It was therefore essential to Araeen's thesis that a larger shape of historical time could be sketched out, in which it was made clear that these younger artists had practised despite certain knowledge of the past being conspicuously unavailable to them. In that sense, the fact that this was a story being told for the first time did not detract from the credibility of an already existing story. There was indeed a paucity of documentation and curatorial representation supplying the 'other' narrative. There was little knowledge of the Caribbean Artists Movement (CAM) among artists of the 1980s (Anne Walmsley's group biography was not to appear until 1992) and the mounting of *The Other Story* was the first substantial historical exhibition surveying that and previous decades.

However, if Araeen rationalised his exhibition on a historicist basis, it was that very historicism which came to make Williams appear in some way 'out of date'. This also happened when Williams met with the self-declared 'Black Art' postmodernists of the 1980s: made public in the heated exchange with the artist Sonia Boyce at a seminar organised by Creation for Liberation in Brixton in 1987, when Williams addressed younger, British-born artists of a range of ethnicities.[64] The root of their conflict was that Williams's outlooks seemed untenable to younger artists of African, Asian and Caribbean descent. Even among critical, postcolonial artists and curators, he was again handed the label of anachronism.

What has yet to be explained is why an artist charged with being out of date could have such an abiding presence throughout the Black Art decade of the 1980s, when he prompted a debate about the complex issue of generation and time with regard to creativity in Britain. A similar emphasis on generational questions was shared with many of the CAM group, as Stuart Hall expressed it at one of their meetings in 1968: 'The task of any intellectual and any writer in relation to ... [the next generations of West Indians in Britain] is pre-eminently to help them see, clarify, speak, understand and name the process that they're going through.'[65] Certainly, what Williams shared with the subsequent generation of British artists of Caribbean descent was the need to establish an authorial position through self-portraiture, even if their approach to realism[66] was less oblique than in Williams's mix of abstraction and naturalism. By putting their own bodies in the frame in a variety of new encodings, these later artists aimed to identify their simultaneously British and politically black presence as a framework for their art practice.[67]

Such generational questions are still proving to be central in research on diaspora culture in Britain.[68] Williams's participation in the art debates of the 1980s may demonstrate what Stuart Hall has described as a 'condensation of dissimilar currents' or 'two moments condensed into one', as he interacted with younger artists.[69] A more complex view of time is suggested by the political philosopher Giorgio Agamben, writing on what may be recuperable from a belated or anachronistic status. It suggests another way of seeing how Williams was positioned by the self-declared divergences and discontinuities of 1980s 'Black Art'. Agamben reminds us of the potentially positive qualities of what he terms 'dyschrony', by which he means a sense of adhering to one's time by standing at a distance from it. As he writes:

> But you have to understand that this appointment is not a chronological one, but rather something that transforms chronology. Anachronism allows us to grasp our time in the form of a 'too early', which is also a 'too late', of an already that is also a not yet. And at the same time, to recognise in the darkness of the present, the light which without ever reaching us, is perennially, permanently travelling towards us.[70]

The most remarkable feature relating to the representation of Williams is how the basic terms for historicising his works have persisted even into the postcolonial treatment of him – a lasting impulse to address his art through stagist concerns with time and space. We should pause to ask why this is so, and in what ways Williams provides the basis for a larger study of how Caribbean art and artists are implicated in dominant models for thinking about visual creativity. His efforts as a painter were pitted against prevailing ideas about temporality, in which the former imperial metropole is firmly cast in a leadership role. Yet even when the aim is to undermine such common teleologies of modern art, these are found difficult to break from. Less critical approaches to time are generic in the commentary on artists of the Caribbean and its diaspora, and they have made temporality seem an unlikely focus for analysis. Williams's presence in art history is epitomised by the persistent application of spatio-temporal schemes in which 'over there' and 'back then' are cross-matched or coordinated, or else, it is wrapped up in the contradictions that arise from their subversion. Time haunts even those concerted attempts to address art of the Caribbean according to a newer geography.

Any future departure for understanding Williams will have to contend with the persistent problem of temporality. The present challenge goes beyond trying to release art history from any attachment to the formula of 'leading' metropolitan centres versus 'belated' peripheries. It is about seeing what role temporality holds in the global mapping of art history, and to know where this awareness may be of use for the Caribbean. On the whole, Williams has been disadvantaged by time, but so has a more transnational art history. He was once put on the wrong side of modernism because of his Caribbean birth, but he has the added disadvantage of the particular approach to time taken by postcolonial historiography. The centrally critical question in understanding Williams and other artists who are similarly positioned is how to refuse to serve the interests of prevailing trends in historical remembrance and visual reception. Their lives and works may be the source of alternative resources for critical study. Painting was becoming anachronistic by the highpoint of Caribbean migration, and Williams encountered the problems this entailed, while also seeing clearly the possibilities that lay beyond. If this can be achieved in art practice, then there should be hope still for art historical method. The example of Williams will help to work through a complex Atlantic space whose outlines are drawn by the question of time.

Notes

1 A. Walmsley, *The Caribbean artists movement: 1966–1972* (London: New Beacon Books, 1992); A. Walmsley (ed.), *Guyana dreaming: The art of Aubrey Williams* (Aarhus: Dangeroo Press, 1990); W. Harris, 'Aubrey Williams', *Third Text*, 10:34 (1996), 79–82; S. Harvie, 'The search for a Guyanese identity: The evolution of the fine arts in Guyana with special reference to the work of Aubrey Williams' (unpublished MA thesis, Centre for Caribbean Studies, University of Warwick, 1993).

2 R. Araeen (ed.), *The other story: Afro-Asian artists in post-war Britain* (London: The Hayward Gallery, 1989); R. Araeen, 'When the naughty children of Empire come home to roost', *Third Text*, 20 (2006), 233–9.

3 K. Mercer, 'Black Atlantic abstraction: Aubrey Williams and Frank Bowling', in K. Mercer (ed.), *Discrepant abstraction* (London and Cambridge MA: Institute of International Visual Arts and MIT Press, 2006), pp. 184–5.

4 Walmsley, *Guyana dreaming*; A. Dempsey, G. Tawadros and M. Williams (eds), *Aubrey Williams* (London: Institute of International Visual Arts and Whitechapel Gallery, 1998).

5 Indeed, this was the premise for the exhibition that I co-curated with Reyahn King at the Walker Art Gallery, Liverpool. See: L. Wainwright, 'Aubrey Williams: Atlantic fire', in Reyahn King and The October Gallery (eds), *Aubrey Williams: Atlantic fire* (National Museums Liverpool and The October Gallery, 2010), pp. 46–55.

6 The beginnings of this are sketched out in L. Wainwright, 'Francis Newton Souza and Aubrey Williams: Entwined art histories at the end of Empire', in S. Faulkner and A. Ramamurthy (eds), *Visual culture and decolonisation in Britain* (Aldershot: Ashgate, 2006), pp. 101–26; L. Wainwright, 'Aubrey Williams's art of transnationalism: Entwining histories at the end of Empire', *The Arts Journal*, 2:2 (2006), 116–39; and L. Wainwright, 'Aubrey Williams: A painter in the aftermath of painting', *Wasafiri*, 24:3 (2009), 65–79.

7 In this regard, Walmsley brings into view Eric Newton's response that: 'His tortured, interwoven forms, on dark, sinister backgrounds, leave one in no doubt about their connection with tropical forests and primeval ritual dances'. E. Newton, 'Round the London galleries', *The Listener* (28 August 1958), p. 310. This passage is quoted, but incorrectly cited in Walmsley, *The Caribbean artists movement*, p. 17.

8 Newton (1963), quoted in Araeen (ed.), *The other story*, p. 32.

9 R. Araeen, 'Conversation with Aubrey Williams', *Third Text*, 2:1 (1987), 25–52, p. 27; For a thorough documentation of the history of CAM, see Walmsley, *The Caribbean artists movement*.

10 See Walmsley, 'Chronology', in Dempsey, Tawadros and Williams (eds), *Aubrey Williams*, pp. 65–101.

11 See for instance: N. Serota, C. M. Joachimides and N. Rosenthal, *A new spirit in painting* (London: Royal Academy of Arts, 1981).

12 Williams's recollection in 1972 of this event as compared to documentation from 1954 is commented upon in Walmsley, 'Chronology', p. 71 and in D. Bowen, 'Obituary of Aubrey Williams', *Art Monthly* (1990), p. 35. Bowen also mentions a small solo exhibition of Williams's work held at the same gallery in 1956; see Walmsley, *Guyana dreaming*, p. 101.

13 New Vision Centre, *Aubrey Williams: Exhibition of paintings and gouaches* (London: New Vision Centre, 1959).

14 Walmsley, *The Caribbean artists movement*, p. 17.

15 Walmsley has noted: 'The group was open to any artist interested primarily in non-figurative work and to all nationalities, and provided such artists with opportunities to show their work'. Walmsley, *The Caribbean artists movement*, p. 16. Walmsley goes on to quote Margaret Garlake's history of New Vision: 'The practice of giving unknown, young, foreign artists one-man shows was almost unique in London at that time and was only possible because the gallery was a non-profit-making organisation. Few commercial galleries were interested in non-figurative art'. M Garlake, *New vision 56–66* (Jarrow, Tyne and Wear: Bede Gallery, 1984), p. 4.

16 J. Carew, 'Revolt', *Tropica* (December 1960), p. 4. Carew's brief commentary on this episode carried terms that he used in his later writings to describe similar, culturally formative 'fulcrums of change'. 'Archimedes once said, "find me the fulcrum and I will move the world", and what we need to search for, and to discover as we rewrite the history of the Caribbean peoples, are new social, political, economic, historical and cultural fulcrums of change. For by discovering these, we can more easily bring the past back to life so that it can remain impregnated with the smell of the earth and the primordial dreams of the people'. J. Carew, 'Fulcrums of change', *Race and Class*, 26 (1984), 1–13, p. 1.

17 G. Brett, 'A tragic excitement', in Dempsey, Tawadros and Williams (eds), *Aubrey Williams*, pp. 22–35, reprinted as 'A tragic excitement: the work of Aubrey Williams', *Third Text*, 48 (1999), 29–44. The term 'tragic excitement' was first used by Williams himself in interview in 1987: 'It's excitement. Excitement is not pleasure. It's a tragic excitement'. Quoted in Araeen, 'Conversation with Aubrey Williams', p. 40. Reprinted in Walmsley, *Guyana dreaming*, p. 48.

18 Carew, 'Revolt', p. 4.

19 Paintings of this kind had first appeared in large numbers during the early to mid-nineteenth century, when the motif of broken chains vied for predominance over that of unfastened manacles, a suggestion of competing notions about the path to emancipation as claimed or won by the enslaved, rather than granted by European piety. French salon painting, such as the 1848 sketch by Nicholas-François Gosse *L'esclavage affranchi* (today known as *Liberté, Egalité, Fraternité*) and the large painting of 1849 in Versailles by François Biard, *Proclamation de la liberté des noirs aux colonies*, indicate this dynamic. Both are reproduced in H. Honour (ed.), *The image of the black in Western art, Vol IV* (Boston and London: Harvard University Press, 1989), pp. 171–2. Long disfavoured was the scheme in which an enslaved figure was shown kneeling in supplication, as popularised by abolitionists and those who wore the Wedgwood medallion. I refer also to the ceramic 'slave medallion' made by Josiah Wedgwood for the Society for the Abolition of the Slave Trade in 1787; the political significance of its motif and the nature of its circulation and use are described critically in M. Guyatt, 'The Wedgwood slave medallion: values in eighteenth-century design', *Journal of Design History*, 13:2 (2000), 93–105.

20 R. Price, 'Monuments and silent screamings: a view from Martinique', in G. Oostindie (ed.), *Facing up to the past: Perspectives on the commemoration of slavery from Africa, the Americas and Europe* (Kingston: Ian Randle and Prince Claus Fund Library, 2001), p. 58.

21 That sculpture has remained its predominant medium can be seen in: Karl Broodhagen's *The Emancipation Statue*, commonly known as 'Bussa' in Barbados; Albert Mangonès's *Le Marron Inconnu de Saint-Domingue* in Haiti; and Laura Facey Cooper's *Emancipation Song* in Jamaica. For a discussion of public sculpture in the region see: L. Brown, 'Monuments to freedom, monuments to nation: The politics of emancipation and remembrance in the Eastern Caribbean', *Slavery and Abolition*, 23:3 (2002), 93–116; also, D. Lambert, '"Part of the blood and the dream": Surrogation, memory and the national hero in the postcolonial Caribbean', *Patterns of Prejudice*, 41:3/4 (2007), 345–71.

22 Aubrey Williams initiated and coordinated this work, as Eve Williams has described it, '... the first home-grown, large-scale public monument in Guyana'. As she continues: 'The artist Philip Moore was repatriated to Guyana from the United States to undertake this work. His fifteen-foot bronze statue, weighing two and a quarter tonnes, was cast for Guyana at Britain's famous Morris Singer foundry in Basingstoke where the work was overseen by Williams in his role as Director of Art for the History and Arts Council of Guyana. The original maquette Moore had sculpted in wood was also cast in bronze and later formed a central exhibit in Guyana's exhibition at the Jamaica Institute during Carifesta 1976.' E. Williams, *The art of Denis Williams*, forthcoming monograph, Chapter VI.

23 G. Rohlehr, 'The Calypsonian as artist: Freedom and responsibility', *Small Axe*, 9:5:1 (2001), 1–26.

24 For some examples in Guyana, see: A. Creighton, 'The metaphor of the theater in "The four banks of the river of space"', *Callaloo*, 18:1 (1995), 71–82; H. Maes-Jelinek, '"Carnival" and creativity in Wilson Harris's fiction', in M. Gilkes (ed.), *The literate imagination: Essays on the novels of Wilson Harris* (London: Macmillan Caribbean, 1989), pp. 45–62.

25 R. Araeen, 'A conversation with Aubrey Williams'. The meeting with Picasso has prompted further discussion: S. Gikandi, 'Picasso, Africa, and the schemata of difference', *Modernism/Modernity*, 10:3 (2003), 455–80; L. Rosenberg, 'Caribbean models for modernism in the work of Claude McKay and Jean Rhys', *Modernism/Modernity*, 11:2 (2004), 219–38.

26 Cheddi became President of Guyana in 1992, and Janet Jagan, in 1997–99.

27 Any regret for the refusal to show the painting was confined to this matter of protocol: 'having lent the hall [a display space for *Revolt*] we had no control over what was exhibited, and that informing Mr. Burrowes [E. R. Burrowes, artist, educator and founder of the Working People's Art Group] of the rejection of the picture was not the right course of action: we ought to have asked the Minister to review her decision to have the painting exhibited'. See National Archive of Guyana, *Royal Agricultural and Commercial Society*, 'Culture' file 8, 'Meeting to discuss painting by Aubrey Williams entitled "Revolt"', 13 November 1960.

28 These are set out in the 'Royal Agricultural and Commercial Society Ordinance', *The Laws of British Guiana*, chapter 202, among which are: 'To promote, as far as possible, the improvement and encouragement of the agriculture of the Colony, and of every branch of industry, whereby the resources of the Colony are likely to be developed and increased, to promote science, art, music and literature and to collect and disseminate useful information on those subjects.' This would, in part, entail the establishment and maintenance of 'suitable public rooms in the City of Georgetown for the use of members, such as an exchange room, a reading room, a museum and model room, and a library'.

29 The full quote reads: 'Williams's painting is instinct with a freshness and a barbaric power. It is as though he captures colours, images, forms which lay gestating through dark and lost centuries, waiting for the right moment of birth. *Revolt* brings to life the sense of struggle, the pristine strength of a people searching for a true image of themselves. This painting represents a break-through to the hearts of black men, scanning new horizons, impatient with bondage, wanting nothing less than full independence and freedom.' Carew, 'Revolt', p. 4.

30 Walmsley, 'Chronology', p. 82.

31 Williams's three great series of the late 1970s and 1980s were all painted in Florida.

32 G. Brotherstone, *Painted books from Mexico: Codices in UK collections and the world they represent* (London: British Museum Press, 1995).

33 '"I wished to copy nature," said Cézanne. "I could not. But I was satisfied when I had discovered that the sun, for instance, could not be reproduced, but that it must be represented by something else … by colour."' Quoted in: M. Denis, 'Cézanne', originally published in French, translated by Roger Fry in *Burlington Magazine*, XVI London, Jan–Feb. 1910, 207–19 and 275–80, anthologised in C. Harrison and P. Wood, *Art in theory 1900–2000: An anthology of changing ideas* (Oxford: Blackwell, 2003), pp. 39–46, quotation from p. 44.

34 I. Bakari, *The mark of the hand* (The Arts Council of England and Kuumba Productions, 1986, 51 mins). This concurs with Wilson Harris's recollection of seeing Williams's paintings: 'I remember the first time I met Aubrey Williams was in 1970. The first time I saw his painting, what I felt then was a music coming out of his canvases. A music; I looked at the paintings and I heard a silent music. And

this is what I mean when I say "created a sound that was red", … a comparison … between the sound and the paint – the paint that gave out a sound that you hear. The eye and the ear; the linkage of eye and ear.' H. Maes-Jelinek and B. Ledent (eds), *Theatre of the arts: Wilson Harris and the Caribbean* (Amsterdam: Rodopi, 2002), p. 242. In Harris's fiction these associations are elaborated further: 'They [*sic*] seemed survival blood had stained its feathers in rare fire. The fire was so unnerving, so matchless, it created a sound that was *red,* a scarlet sound' (emphasis in the original). W. Harris, *The dark jester* (London: Faber & Faber, 2001), p. 21.

35 This distinction in examined in depth by Potts, who explains: 'If, with painting, instability is created by the ostensiveness of the spatial fields and shapes its flat surfaces evoke, with sculpture we are made more aware of the instabilities inherent in our perceptual encounter with the work itself as object or environmental configuration.' A. Potts, *The sculptural imagination: Figurative, modernist, minimalist* (New Haven: Yale University Press, 2000), p. 8.

36 A. Charlton, *Alan Charlton* (London: Institute of Contemporary Arts, 1991); W. Rubin, *Frank Stella* (New York: Museum of Modern Art, 1970).

37 G. Bachelard, *The psycho-analysis of fire*, trans. A. C. M. Ross (London: Routledge & Kegan Paul, 1964).

38 J. Baldwin, *The fire next time* (London: Michael Joseph, 1963). Jan Carew has recalled, of the late 1960s, how cities of the United States such as Chicago, Newark and Baltimore were damaged by fire. Remembering too Baldwin's prophetic prose, he reflects upon the role of fire in cultural rejuvenation and Caribbean histories of rebellion. 'The anatomy of America's inner cities was laid bare in the wake of those cleansing fires. The culture of the streets then burst out of a humus of decay like exquisite wild flowers flourishing in a dung heap.' J. Carew, 'Culture and rebellion', *Race and Class*, 35:1 (1993), 1–8, p. 1. By contrast, M. Hanchard has drawn Baldwin's writings into a discussion of time and modernity. He is less interested in his use of fire than Baldwin's relation to examples in the history of the African diaspora that reveal 'the ethico-political relationship between temporality and notions of human progress'. M. Hanchard, 'Afro-modernity: Temporality, politics, and the African diaspora', *Public Culture*, 11:1 (1999), 245–68, p. 257.

39 G. Robinson, '"If freedom writes no happier alphabet": Martin Carter and poetic silence', *Small Axe*, 8:1 (2004), 43–62. See also Carter's collection of poems first published in 1951, *The hill of fire glows red*, reprinted in M. Carter, *Selected poems* (Georgetown, Guyana: Red Thread Women's Press, 1997).

40 M. Carter, 'Our time', *Poems of affinity* (Georgetown, Guyana: Release Publishers, 1980), pp. 14–15; G. Robinson (ed.), *Martin Carter: University of hunger. Collected poems and selected prose* (Tarset: Bloodaxe, 2000), pp. 40–3; G. Rohlehr, '"Assassins of the voice": Martin Carter's poems of affinity 1978–1980', in S. Brown (ed.), *All are involved: The art of Martin Carter* (Leeds: Peepal Tree, 2000), pp. 183–99, pp. 184–5.

41 M. Fried, 'Art and objecthood' (1967), reprinted in G. Battcock (ed.), *Minimal art: A critical anthology* (New York: Dutton, 1968), pp. 139–42; M. Fried, *Absorption and theatricality: Painting and beholder in the age of Diderot* (Berkeley: University of California Press, 1980).

42 Quoted in M. Garlake, *New art, new world: British art in post-war society* (New Haven: Yale University Press, 1998), p. 28.

43 Fried, 'Art and objecthood'.

44 Mercer, 'Black Atlantic abstraction', pp. 184–5.

45 Brett, 'A tragic excitement', p. 28.

46 A. Dempsey, 'Curator's Foreword', in Dempsey, Tawadros and Williams (eds), *Aubrey Williams*, p. 12.

47 G. Mosquera, 'Africa in the art of Latin America', *Art Journal*, 5:1:4 (1992), 30–8, p. 34. See also: G. Mosquera, 'Introduction', *New art from Cuba* (New York: SUNY College, 1985), pp. 1–3.

48 Dempsey, Tawadros and Williams (eds), *Aubrey Williams*, passim.

49 Walmsley, *Guyana dreaming*, p. 61.

50 Quoted from A. Walmsley's notes drawing on the unpublished transcript of a recorded conversation between Aubrey Williams, Wilson Harris, John La Rose, Edward Brathwaite and Andrew Salkey, 'Aubrey Williams in his studio: 23 June, 1967', p. 61.

51 Quoted in Walmsley, *The Caribbean artists movement*, p. 181.

52 As he writes: 'The trouble with painting is not its inescapable illusionism *per se*. But this inherent illusionism brings with it a non-actual elusiveness or indeterminate allusiveness. The mode has become antique. Specifically, what is antique about it is the divisiveness of experience which marks on a flat surface elicit. There are obvious cultural and historical reasons why this happens. For a long while the duality of thing and allusion sustained itself under the force of profuse organizational innovations within the work itself. But it has worn thin and its premises cease to convince.' R. Morris, 'Notes on Sculpture, Part 3: Notes and Nonsequiturs', *Artforum*, 5:2 (1966), 20–3, p. 20. This move to three-dimensional work would also come to be outmoded by 1970s conceptualism, focused on a related anxiety over anachronism, as in Victor Burgin's memorable declaration of painting as 'the anachronistic daubing of woven fabrics with coloured mud' and sculpture, 'the chipping apart of rocks and the sticking together of pipes'. V. Burgin, 'Socialist formalism', *Studio International*, 191:980 (1976), 148–54; see also: J. L. Walker, *Left shift: Radical art in 1970s Britain* (London: I. B. Tauris, 2002), p. 114.

53 See, for example: W. Harris, 'The sun (Fourteen poems in a cycle)', *Kyk-over-al*, 20 (1955), 175–82; W. Harris, 'Sun poem XV', *Kyk-over-al*, 23 (1958), 7, also in G. Lamming and M. Carter (eds), *Guyana independence issue* (Georgetown, Guyana: New World, 1966), p. 54. What Harris calls 'the originality of the sun', a concept expressing the source of creativity, is introduced in his 1990 lecture 'Creative and re-creative balance between diverse cultures', reprinted in A. Riach and M. Williams (eds), *The radical imagination: Lectures and talks by Wilson Harris* (Liège: Liège University Press, 1992), pp. 103–15. See also, the influential anthology of writing: A. Walmsley, *The sun's eye: West Indian writing for young readers* (Port of Spain and Kingston: Longman Caribbean, 1968).

54 Carew, quoted in Araeen (ed.), *The other story*, p. 32. See also Wilson Harris's observation of 1967 that aesthetics in the West Indies has focused on the 'human' through rhythm. See K. K. Birth, *Bacchanalian sentiments: Musical experiences and political counterpoints in Trinidad* (London and Durham NC: Duke University Press, 2008), p. 213.

55 As have Araeen and Tawadros, who both cite Carew in this regard; see Araeen

(ed.), *The other story*, p. 32; G. Tawadros, 'Running with the hare and hunting with the hounds' in M. J. Beauchamp-Byrd and M. F. Sirmans (eds), *Transforming the crown: African, Asian and Caribbean artists in Britain, 1966–1996* (Chicago: Chicago University Press, 1998), pp. 58–62, p. 59.

56 D. Williams, 'Aubrey Williams in Guyana', in Dempsey, Tawadros and Williams (eds), *Aubrey Williams*, pp. 36–45, p. 44.

57 In Chapter 3 I outline Denis Williams's career in greater detail.

58 See, for instance, my account of Denis Williams as an art historian and critical phenomenologist concerned with pre-colonial models of multicultural society: L. Wainwright, 'Speaking to contemporary art history: Denis Williams and Guyana', in C. Williams and E. Williams (eds), *Denis Williams: A life in works: New and collected essays* (Amsterdam and New York: Rodopi Press, 2009), pp. 65–76.

59 Ashis Nandy, for example, observes of the South Asian context: 'The imposed burden to be perfectly non-Western only constricts his, the everyday Indian's, cultural self, just as the older burden of being perfectly Western once narrowed – and still sometimes narrows – his choices in the matter of his and his society's future. The new responsibility forces him to stress only those parts of his culture which are recessive in the West and to underplay both those which his culture shares with the West and those which remain undefined by the West. It in fact binds him even more irrevocably to the West'. A. Nandy, *The intimate enemy: Loss and recovery of self under colonialism* (Oxford: Oxford University Press, 1983), p. 73.

60 F. Fanon, *The wretched of the earth*, trans. C. Farrington (Harmondsworth: Penguin, 1965), p. 178.

61 F. Fanon, quoted in K. K. Birth, *Bacchanalian sentiments: Musical experiences and political counterpoints in Trinidad* (Duke University Press, 2008), p. 213.

62 If this is another way of saying that in Caribbean anti-colonial nationalism, time plays a central role, this is not necessarily a 'Caribbean' conception of time at all. 'Outside' models of the nation state were accommodated into discourses of Independence, notable in the 'foundational' forms of culture, and 'culturalism'. Today, the remains of these discourses may be read in the angst that settles on the forms emerging in former cultural symbolisations of nationhood such as carnival, which are a consequence of the late capitalist development of carnival as a branch of the cultural industries. Anachronism is at odds with the 'pretty mas' in Trinidad, and the 'all-inclusive' party culture surrounding carnival, even as nations such as St Vincent and the Grenadines, Barbados and other stakeholders in the Caribbean tourist economy promote their own indigenised carnival celebrations. In Trinidad the 'middle-class cosmopolitanism' (G. Aching, *Masking and power: Carnival and popular culture in the Caribbean*, Minneapolis: University of Minnesota Press, 2002) entailed in carnival is seen as an affront to the ostensibly more authentic values of 'ol' mas' and the 'continuous' traditions of the 'blue devils' of Paramin. The cultural nationalism of Independence and the developmental agenda around carnival may be at odds, yet they each share a similar stagist approach to temporality, in which present-day manifestations of carnival seem to threaten the past with obsolescence.

63 K. Mercer, 'Iconography after identity', in *Shades of black: Assembling black arts in 1980s Britain* (London and Durham NC: Duke University Press, 2005).

64 See Walmsley, *The Caribbean artists movement,* pp. 320 and 340. This was recalled during a discussion I had with Sonia Boyce during the study day focused on Aubrey Williams, Tate Britain (21 September 2007). It was recorded for the Tate archive and subsequently made available online.

65 Quoted in Walmsley, *The Caribbean artists movement,* p. 164.

66 The broader cultural politics of such realist techniques are outlined in M. Sealy (ed.), *Vanley Burke: A retrospective* (London: Lawrence & Wishart Ltd, 1993).

67 An inspiration for such approaches, and a deeper study of the political and aesthetic desire for visibility, was the self-authored monograph by R. Araeen, *Making myself visible* (London: Kala Press, 1984).

68 In the field of performance studies, for instance, see: M. Macmillan, 'From generation to generation: Notes on black performance in Britain', *Performance Research,* 9:3 (2004), 54–68.

69 S. Hall, 'Black diaspora artists in Britain: Three "moments" in post-war history', *History Workshop Journal,* 61 (2006), 1–24.

70 G. Agamben, *Che cos'è il contemporaneo?* (Rome: Nottetempo, 2008), p. 17, my translation.

2　Varieties of belatedness

The genuine precursor usually appears upon the scene of a provincial civilization, where people have long been the recipients rather than the originators of
new behaviour. (George Kubler, *The Shape of Time*, 1962)[1]

Frank Bowling was born in 1935 [sic] in British Guiana, where the multi-
racial situation has not yielded any predominant culture, or anything else very
much except a luridly black and white impasse between the exploiters and the
exploited. (Snowdon et al., *Private View*, 1965)[2]

New York remains the metropolitan center for the visual arts, to which artists
living in the rest of America, in Holland, Germany, Brazil, England, France,
Japan, Australia, etc. stand in a provincial relationship. (Terry Smith, 'The
provincialism problem', 1974)[3]

Chapter 1 showed that understanding of the artist Aubrey Williams is suffused
with a tendency to evaluate artists of the Caribbean as if they belong behind
or outside the history of artistic modernism. Williams is not untypical of
artists of the Caribbean. The prevailing terms for evaluation have historically conflicted with Caribbean experience and failed to meet the interests of
artists seeking to practice within a common space of modernist creativity. The
charge of belatedness in particular frustrates the ambition to join in a shared
space – and time – of art production. Involving himself in this politics of
time, Williams was concerned to recuperate something positive from anachronism itself and in an effort to turn his situation around, chose painting as his
medium. He found ways to press its knowingly 'backward' associations into
the service of a broad field of questions about historical understanding, place
and temporality. The object of a critical art practice in rising to this challenge
was the purposeful troubling of the values surrounding such imputations of
belatedness.

Consequently, my treatment of art of the Caribbean has extended beyond
the usual preoccupation with inclusion and exclusion, which has attended
much discussion of the negative reception that Williams endured. Indeed,

addressing the matter of time in relation to the art of the Caribbean causes us to think more carefully about the shape of art historical narratives of the mid-twentieth century – such as in the canonical mapping of 'our time', against 'the time of others'. A politics of time is complicated by the migration and the movement of artists and works of art between Caribbean territories and Britain; spatial conditions that hold implications for how the manipulation of painting as an anachronistic form may operate at the level of reception.

This chapter examines a similar situation in which time and space have again operated contingently in the reception and reputation of an artist of the Caribbean: Frank Bowling, who was born in British Guiana and migrated to Britain in 1950. Bowling began his career in the much celebrated moment of Pop art of the early 1960s. Like Williams, he met with some initial success before encountering marginalisation. But the setting of British Pop differs from the context experienced by Williams. Here, by contrast, the avant-garde embrace of the virtues of temporal backwardness and outsiderness took centre stage and held dominant. Williams's experience illuminated a politics of time that has a particular role in the canonisation of Pop, in which Pop is announced as a recuperation of temporal and spatial 'alterity'. Its canonisation is itself affected by the notion of a recuperated 'outsiderness'. These conditions throw up particular challenges for the ways of engaging the issue of historicising Bowling.

Against this background, the stakes were raised for Bowling in his ambition to practise as an artist. Much as in the current scholarly drive to dignify Williams's legacy, revisionist historical study of Bowling has tried to reverse his fortunes by providing an alternative narrative in which Bowling is added to the cast of characters comprising British Pop.[4] There is, however, something inherently limiting about the way this has been done. The problem of thinking art historically about both Bowling and Pop is more intractable than revisionism can combat. To understand the greater complexity of Bowling's experience is instead to recall the wider conditions in which this canon was produced, and the subsequent patterns that it entailed. Bowling's presence in Britain – as much as Williams's – was part of the larger trend of Caribbean migration and British geo-political decline, figured in the transformation of territories of the British Empire into new nations. Such change, and its impact on Britain, also framed the way that the Pop story was told. The social and political changes associated with decolonisation granted an overall layer of meaning to British Pop, orienting its reception and self-understanding. Pop was a moment in Atlantic art history whose temporal and spatial logic was in part shaped by the Caribbean.

The belatedness of Pop

The story of British Pop art, as it is commonly told, begins with the first use of the term 'Pop' among members of the Independent Group (IG) in London during the early 1950s, to indicate a general sense of popular culture at large. The group's young artists, critics and architects would lay the way for developments in British art in the later 1950s and early 1960s when Pop became a synonym for the leading edge of contemporary art. It signified a style of art that drew on popular imagery from advertising, comics and other printed sources. Much activity took place around a certain group of British artists trained mostly at the Royal College of Art (RCA). The week in, week out interactions among the RCA crowd that shaped Pop involved, at least, Barrie Bates (later Billy Apple), Derek Boshier, Frank Bowling, Patrick Caulfield, David Hockney, Allen Jones, R. B. Kitaj, Peter Phillips and Norman Toynton. These students experimented with the challenge of superimposing styles and devices from older artists, such as Francis Bacon, and with sources and elements from far outside the tradition of British art, often spliced and resized to evoke a dry comedy based on jarring incongruities of place, time and association. Notions of identity and context were plainly regarded as a focus for imaginative manipulation as Pop became synonymous with visual jokes. There were the toothpaste paintings of Boshier and the portable giant tube – with removable cap – carried casually by Claes Oldenburg among bemused London shoppers. Such works had their genesis in an appreciation of how objects and images are not only open and available to recontextualisation, but also demand it.

Students of Pop at the RCA were quick to seize opportunities. They showed what new intersections could be made with painting as a cardinal category of high art by mobilising quotidian objects. Significantly, this would extend to showing how alterity itself, as a general category of being, could give rise to new 'transpositions' (following Baudrillard),[5] and to contest and revolt. The immediate, local result of their provocations was to embarrass the art school by questioning it from within. This quickened a growing generational split between students at the RCA and the British establishment. At the institutional level it brought repercussions in the form of expulsions. As Frank Bowling recounted:

> Six of them went on the same day. They were these heavy duty men who had done their national service, had all been in the army one way or another, like David Hockney, who had worked in a hospital for two years. … I think that the staff had to stamp their authority. If you could imagine a school with Kitaj, Hockney, Peter Philips, Boshier and myself, I think the staff was intimidated.[6]

Pop began as a local transformation in which students channelled their impatience toward the previous generation of RCA staff and students. The critic and juror Lawrence Alloway, who collaborated in showcasing the Pop artists, attributed the RCA's importance to 'spontaneous activity among the students, and not as a result of staff influence'.[7] Alex Seago has aptly called their actions 'burning the box of beautiful things', an attempt to destroy the 'the culture of a supine, reactionary Establishment'[8] and the eccentricity of English painting espoused by tutors at the RCA. As an outpouring of dissent, British Pop was assembled on the opportunity to disavow and disrupt all that was most rarefied and exclusionary about the art school.

It still seems surprising that the stance and the art of the students of Pop were so quickly and warmly feted in the neon lights of the London art world. But the support for Pop issued from the new and increasing interest in the arts in general during the 1960s, and a celebration of Britishness that composed Pop as a crucial chapter in the national art story. The continuing popularity of the RCA artists during Pop has much to do with the dramatic unravelling and remaking of Britishness, and of British art, as the Empire faced decolonisation. Pop can be read primarily through Britain's evolving nationalism at the end of the Empire, as Britishness was reshaped by the anti-colonial movement and a changing attitude within the imperial metropole toward its colonies. The cult of national character displayed in the Lion and the Unicorn Pavilion of the Festival of Britain may have been appreciated by many RCA students of the early 1950s.[9] But British art and design of the immediate post-war enshrined a worldview in which Nkrumah's Independent Ghana and a sovereign West Indies seemed unimaginable. By the late 1950s, the approach to art practice that the RCA had to offer its students was deemed no longer affirming or tenable.

The social and political changes wrought by decolonisation and the Caribbean dimension of that process have not been much explored in relation to British Pop art. They were tied closely to the dawning realisation that Britain was lagging behind the transformations by commerce of everyday life in the United States. In art, specifically, Britain had arguably always been 'behind' other art centres, namely Paris, and the pace was now being set by New York. This positioning gave rise to the mood of belatedness which touched the artists and critics of Pop in a mixed and paradoxical way. The young Pop artists would respond obliquely to decolonisation and its engendered confusion about British 'greatness' by embracing the sophistication and energy of American culture, its painting, music and graphic design. In turn, they incurred the wrath of critics who, in Andreas Huyssen's words, 'denounced Pop art as non-art, supermarket-art, Kitsch-art and as a coca-colonization of Western Europe'.[10] Significantly, each of these positions was marked by ideas about time. Britain's growing sense of the anachronism of its pretension to remain a global power can be read off from the commentary on Pop and the 'spontaneous activity' of the young Pop artists. Art making in Britain was deemed to be somehow out of time, or behind in time, and the attempted reversals and what were often elaborations on the theme of this status became the story of Pop.[11]

Consequently, in order to reach a fuller understanding of Pop it is essential to see more clearly how such preoccupations with belatedness and provincialism were formative of the period. The epithet at the start of this chapter, taken from George Kubler's study of 1962, summarises a line of thinking among artists and art historians who are unable to accept the assumption that there is a single 'development' in which all art may be placed. In the United States throughout the 1960s several artists drew direct inspiration from Kubler, such as Robert Morris, Ad Reinhardt, and most notably Robert Smithson – as first suggested by his 1964 working notes for his neon sculpture *Eliminator* and subsequent writings.[12] Kubler's thought signalled the recognition of 'many histories of art made up of open numbers of more or less local interactions', as David Summers has described his contribution.[13]

There is nothing like a traceable line of influence between Kubler and British Pop, as there is in the American avant-garde (indeed, the desire to trace one out would demonstrate the sort of weak historicism that Kubler abjured). But much commentary on art of this period in Britain took up a similar attitude. The idea that temporal and spatial provincialism was fully capable of recuperation appealed to artists and their commentators in London during the 1960s. While seeking stances of opposition and alternatives in the academy, the fact of Britain's art scene being overshadowed and provincialised by North America became implicit in the worries expressed about Britishness during Pop. The canonised artists of the RCA exploited that stream of thought in which 'the scene of a provincial civilization' might be a fitting location for 'originators of new behaviour'. As such, the tropes of anachronism and provincialism became the basis for an ameliorating position for Britain within the history of art. In rather Kublerian language, the phenomenon of Pop exploited the intersections of spatial and temporal distance in order to render accounts of its 'originality', and to identify its 'originators'.

I am preoccupied with showing why the Caribbean should hold such a major role in defining how we now think about a key chapter of canonical art history such as Pop. This opens on to more widely reaching art historical questions, not least about how separable the Caribbean is from the more familiar territory of the discipline. That Britain's art scene was becoming belated and provincial subject to developments in North America was implicit in post-war anxieties over nationhood and Britishness and the collapsing Empire. It energised the stances of generational difference and revolt that were famously taken up, such as among the artists of the RCA, soon to be put into the national spotlight. By the late 1950s, art making in Britain was deemed to be somehow behind in time, or out of time, even out of place. The attempted reversals, along with active recuperations of this status, have animated the Pop story.

British Pop as a whole would be oriented toward finding a solution to the problem of provincialism and backwardness. What it failed to examine, however, and this is no less true of subsequent commentary, was the background of reasons that had contributed to a sense of British insecurity and belatedness in the first place. For this reason, it is the contribution to Pop made by the British Guiana-born artist, Frank Bowling that may provide a way of reconsidering how such an important movement in art history, apparently without a Caribbean dimension, may be so deeply inflected by it. Chapter 1 showed how Aubrey Williams held on to painting. In Bowling's interactions with Pop, the continuing attachment to painting and the desire to be remembered became another site of Caribbean struggle.

Outsiderness as Pop

For British art of the 1950s a sense of provincialism and its temporal connotation of belatedness presided over the relation of Britain to America, punctuated here and there by reminders of Britain's shrinking Empire. That political map lay heavy on how the role of individual artworks and the biographies of certain artists were to be understood within a national art history. Implicit across the longer period of post-war British art is a vocabulary of 'the leading' and 'the led' – an idea of Britain's sometime leadership superseded by that of America – which was current in the decades well before and after Pop.[14]

When recalling the art of Pop, these two national locations comprise a lively economy of aesthetic and social relations, distinguished by its emphasis on temporal as much as geographical distance. The influential commentaries on Pop retain a vivid sense of Britain's international connections by looking mainly to the United States,[15] with areas of perceived equivalence with the United States, as well as crucial discontinuities.[16] That shared concern with the national is significant of how reflections on Pop in Britain even at its outset were dominated by an emphasis on place and locality, and found an ultimate expression in the conception of time. The combined efforts of artists, critics and what Thomas Crow has called 'the faceless workings of markets and institutions'[17] sought to configure London in particular as a leading cultural metropole. Pop emerged from the production of 'urbanity' that was post-war London, in view of any shared ground with art from the wider Atlantic, and in the hope of claiming this country's vanguard position on the global map of high modernism. If this goal was not achieved in art practice, it might be said that only in the area of Pop music can Britain be said to have had a leading global influence, such as with the Beatles. To borrow Lawrence Alloway's phrase in describing Paolozzi, the challenge for Britain was to defend its seeming inviolability against being 'bombarded by mass media imagery', the international visual culture considered to have emerged from an American epicentre, while still maintaining its historical 'lead'.[18]

A clearer understanding of this moment in the history of art might be based on important considerations of nationalism, class and age or generation. In introducing a Caribbean dimension to this analysis, I am less interested in adding to these the significance of race and ethnicity, than bringing to bear concerns about the geography of Pop and a related focus on time. During the early 1950s, from within the United Kingdom's state of economic austerity, the graphic art and advertising that arose from the consumerism of the United States were viewed with envy and desire, handled like cult objects heralding a seductive future. New York was clearly 'ahead', when measured by the IG's sudden self-awareness of London as a locus for dated design, of art 'in arrears'.[19] As the novelist Len Deighton, who originally trained as a graphic designer, eloquently put it:

> Sometimes during the 1950s a film reviewer said the hero was two jumps ahead of the police, but three behind the audience. Some of us who were art students during that period knew the feeling well. New York was exploding with graphic ideas – wonderful typography and unsurpassed illustrations by such artists as David Stone Martin and Bob Peak – while British advertising and magazines were controlled by people preoccupied by Victoriana.[20]

If American Pop was seen to have the advantage of sitting 'ahead' and 'at home' in a land of commerce (even if its art world operated within Cold War strictures), there were still mixed feelings about its influence on Britain.[21] Among the IG there was always a paradox in the left-wing embrace of American popular culture: the group's delight in the material trappings of capitalism as a way of critiquing the elitism of high art. Certainly, the admiration for American popular culture was mixed with disdain for its globalising spread, which settled on a sense of Britain as suffering decline.[22] Like the IG, the British Pop artists battled for originality in the rush to escape the embarrassment of anachronism, a battle that they deemed American Pop to have won, on the 'long front' of a conflict between old and new.[23] The battle at home was largely with the elders of the London art world, as Christopher Finch recalls:

> When I enrolled at Chelsea School of Art in September 1957, London was a city still hung over from the effects of World War II. ... [I]t was acknowledged as provincial even by the artists who lived and worked there – many of them liked it that way.[24]

Although vivid concerns with temporality shaped the art and the record of this period, art history's attention to the study of time has been rather selective.[25] Still to emerge is the sort of critical writing on Pop which would ask how art and artists at the RCA were implicated in the intersection of belatedness and provincialism. A composite spatio-temporal paradigm underscores the conception of Britain's demise, facing the challenge of North American political dominance and creative 'leadership'. It is a paradigm that closely informs the remembrance of Pop, giving rise to the notion of the quintessential British Pop artist as 'outsider'.

The art and biography of Peter Blake, forerunner to the RCA students of Pop, offered one of the first opportunities for audiences to see that a virtue could be made of a sort of Britishness which purposefully traded on its belatedness and outsiderness. His popularity seems to rest on the sort of description that the curator Natalie Rudd gave of him:

> Many critics have considered his work too whimsical, too jokey; too far removed from the serious issues of the day to warrant prolonged consideration. But the very qualities that render his art so out of touch are exactly those that make it so intriguing. Blake is a genuine outsider.[26]

Rudd also writes about 'roots' for Blake and his 'affection for his native soil' and location.[27] When 'the serious issues of the day' have precisely to do with the American advertising and everyday style that became so crucial in Britain from the 1950s, as they were for the generation of Pop, the seriousness of Blake's contribution becomes more obvious. On this account, Blake's often remarked species of Englishness becomes an index of originality and radicalism, delivered through, and not despite, the inclusion among his works of American pop-culture referents.

Peter Blake's 'genuine outsider' status was also guaranteed by the connotations of social class that played around his career, nearly as much as with David Hockney's. Known for his frivolous statements, for his contrariness toward the art world, his distinctive northern accent, dyed blond hair and heavy spectacles, Hockney was amusing for those of the 'swinging' elite who sought a fashionable association with the package of anti-Establishment symbols that he formed.[28] Hockney wrote about the basis of such appeal that: 'If you're a working class person from outside London you're an outsider, just like a foreigner.'[29] At the centre of an artistic career that was launched during Pop is the matter of entitlement – to visual pleasure and desire, to free movement and to spaces of leisure and erotic encounter. Hockney explored these in favour of others like him who have endured the position of the 'outsider'.

The related response of R. B. Kitaj gained nuance from his status as an American-born artist who was domiciled in Britain for over thirty years. Kitaj was fascinated with the expatriate, the dispossessed and the exile, and a search for identity within his own secular Jewishness. As Aulich and Lynch have suggested, Kitaj created in his canvases 'a portrait gallery of individuals who are *marginal*, yet whose existence is *essential* to the mainstream, as if they were part of a repressed cultural subconscious' (original emphasis).[30] Often issued together, such themes of alterity and newness have attended the popularity of Kitaj in Britain. This is in spite of those modernist critics who saw figuration as not properly modern, and the favouring of abstraction.[31] The claims for the artist's distinctiveness and his 'exilic internationalism' are therefore significant of the ways in which Britain was grappling with being chronologically outpaced or made anachronistic by the values attached to art elsewhere. The keen reception of the figure in Pop art stood at the centre of how this country negotiated its provincialism, and how it grappled with the profound preoccupation with belatedness and the outsider that surrounded Pop.

When an artist of Pop is Caribbean

The abiding question about the Caribbean connection in the story of Pop is why claims about belatedness and alterity have been used to valorise some of the artists of Pop and not others. It still needs to be explained why the period's ostensibly radical social inclusions went so far, and no further. In beginning to trace out some kind of answer, it is worth focusing on one of the RCA students who has typically remained absent in the record of Pop.

Frank Bowling entered the RCA in 1959, where he soon gained recognition by winning a life-drawing prize in his first-year examination. 'That's what I was doing all the time, I guess. And it was very amusing, because Kitaj, who wasn't very good at drawing, had to borrow some of Hockney's drawings to pass. It was really quite funny.'[32] As a student, Bowling's early pieces contributed to Pop's rejection of the legacy of English painting on which the RCA curriculum was founded. He did so by much less gentle departures than his contemporaries who employed collage – photographs and anatomical images as a pictorial trigger and aide-memoire for their painted figures. Bowling augmented that practice by drawing readily on first-hand knowledge and by peopling his canvases with confidently repeating themes. For example, a series of 'Birthday' paintings[33] stemmed from his own experience in Notting Hill before he was a student when he had helped a young Jamaican woman in childbirth. He had also assisted in the delivery of his own son, and along with many others was disturbed at the prospect of fathering a child when the side effects of the thalidomide drug were becoming public. His 1961 painting, *The Martyrdom of Patrice Lumumba* (figure 6),[34] responded to news of the assassination of the first elected Prime Minister of the Democratic Republic of the Congo in January that year. This work indicated the global range of Bowling's attention and linked his practice to a wider scope of historical contexts and geography of political and psychic struggle that illuminated his transnational background and connections to decolonisation.

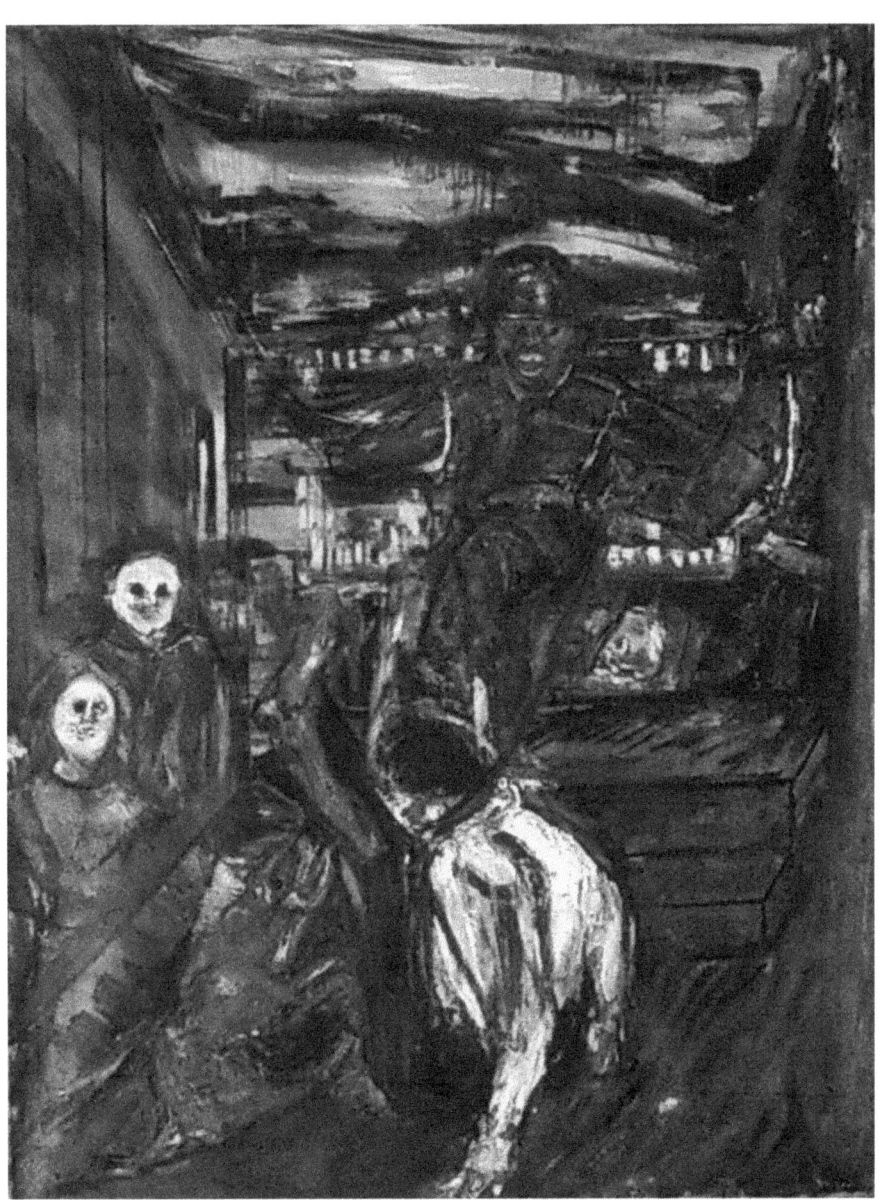

Frank Bowling, *The Martyrdom of Patrice Lumumba* (1961), oil on canvas (lost),   **6**
304.8 × 228.6 cm.

In September 1960, owing to the RCA's constitutional ban on marriages between students and staff (Bowling's partner was the college registrar), he was forced to leave, continuing his studies for a term at the Slade School of Art, before being invited back after his then wife transferred to Chelsea

College. However, on returning to the RCA in 1961, Bowling found that he was not included in the *Young Contemporaries* show. This was a major vehicle for elevating its artists at a crucial point of their emergence, and has remained a common touchstone of the Pop canon. Time at the Slade had brought him into contact with a wider range of artists, and in response, he joined an alternative, rival assemblage, the Young Commonwealth Artists Group. Bowling recalled the conditions under which it formed:

> It was made up of guys from places like Australia, New Zealand, the Caribbean, Jamaica, Canada, Singapore, India, South Africa, Pakistan, Sri Lanka, and a couple of very good sculptors from the southern part of Rhodesia. A lot of guys from the Indian subcontinent were at the Slade, there were oodles of them there, but none at the Royal College – people like Shemza. The reason this came about, it was obviously a student gathering, is that it was felt that the people from the Commonwealth were being edged out by the English provincial lot: people from Yorkshire, and Manchester, really heavy duty guys from up North, and the Welsh.[35]

From the division Bowling describes between the Young Contemporaries and the Young Commonwealth Artists it is obvious that the forms of mobilised provincialism, so central to the Pop artists, clashed with the provincial identities of those artists from a wider global geography. What they had jointly failed to see was a shared condition of provincialism – what might have become the very foundation for a common art space in which questions of power and the purpose of art making could be raised.[36]

We might say that Bowling sought to identify as both 'Commonwealth' and 'Contemporary' and despite their constitutive tensions, initially found success. An independent attitude emerged in the way Bowling would organise himself for public display. Derek Boshier and Bowling, in their joint show *Images in Revolt* (1962),[37] would gain the lead on their RCA peers, being the first to exhibit away from the support lent by the larger group show format. Such work drew the attention of critics including Lawrence Alloway and David Sylvester. Andrew Forge recognised the artist as exceptional, overrunning with praise pregnant with classical references to Bowling's triumphal affront to the 'Baconianism' indulged by the artists (and critics) of his generation.[38] In the same year, without meeting the critic, he had impressed Norbert Lynton with his first show, especially the two versions of a work entitled *Painting 1962*, and a triptych entitled *A Mirror, Three Windows,* and *A Door,*[39] bought by the Calouste Gulbenkian Foundation. A reproduction of two parts of that painting was carried by *Art International* alongside Lynton's review.[40]

Bowling went on to graduate from the RCA, winning a silver medal for painting, while David Hockney famously took the gold. This secondary position created for Bowling by such a system of reward and visibility has become a focus for the revisionist accounts of him in relation to Pop.[41] In his later works he would return to the theme of his time at the RCA. He signalled to the widely celebrated artists of Pop in two paintings in particular, *Who's Afraid of Barney Newman?* (1968, figure 7), presented to Tate Britain in 2006, and a work made much later, in 1986, *Spread out Ron Kitaj*. The first is directed to Barnett Newman whose work dominated, perhaps even intimidated Bowling and other students at the RCA in their attitude to painted colour, 'hero-figure for the younger generation of British artists', as Alan Bowness recorded.[42] The canvas is a sort of pun in response to Newman's painting, *Who's Afraid of Red, Yellow and Blue*, which Bowling considered to be a swipe at the sober modernist paintings of Piet Mondrian. The second is dedicated to the inspirational quality of Kitaj which Bowling felt as his peer, as he indicated in his letter to the Tate, written in the same year that it was painted:

> We were all painting from newspaper cuttings, photographs, films, etc, but I wasn't allowed to be a Pop artist because of their preoccupation with what was Pop. Mine was to do with political things in the Third World ... I did not paint Marilyn Monroe because she did not interest me. Kitaj did not paint Marilyn Monroe either; he painted 'The Murder of Rosa Luxemburg'. Kitaj was closest to me in political preoccupation.[43]

A sense of Bowling's relationship to the canonised artists of Pop gains definition from mapping the interpersonal divisions and alliances that emerged among artists, and what was plainly on view in the contours of their social geography on the London 'scene'. There is ample evidence of the contestations and lines of competition within the Pop group in their everyday encounters in the institutional setting of the RCA. Certain departments within the RCA by the end of the 1950s were known for being choosy and territorial about their affinities. Prior to the building of the 1960s' block, even if students were part of departments that were housed elsewhere than in the main building, the junior common room and pubs nearby provided a setting for interaction. Friendships between the painting school and the sculpture school were rare, as compared with graphic design and illustration, housed in the painting school. There were strong ties between Alisdair Grant (sometime editor with John Hedgecoe of the RCA's *ARK* magazine, which ran from 1950 to 1972), Richard Guyatt (who allegedly first used the term 'graphic design' in Britain)[44] and Edward Ardizzone. Students in fashion, housed on Gloucester Road, not far from the Commonwealth Institute, formed more fruitful relations with these painters than with those at the nearby sculpture school, with some lasting friendships, and with some of them marrying.

Similar divisions could be mapped onto London more widely, with two very different locations emerging for the interactions of artists. There were

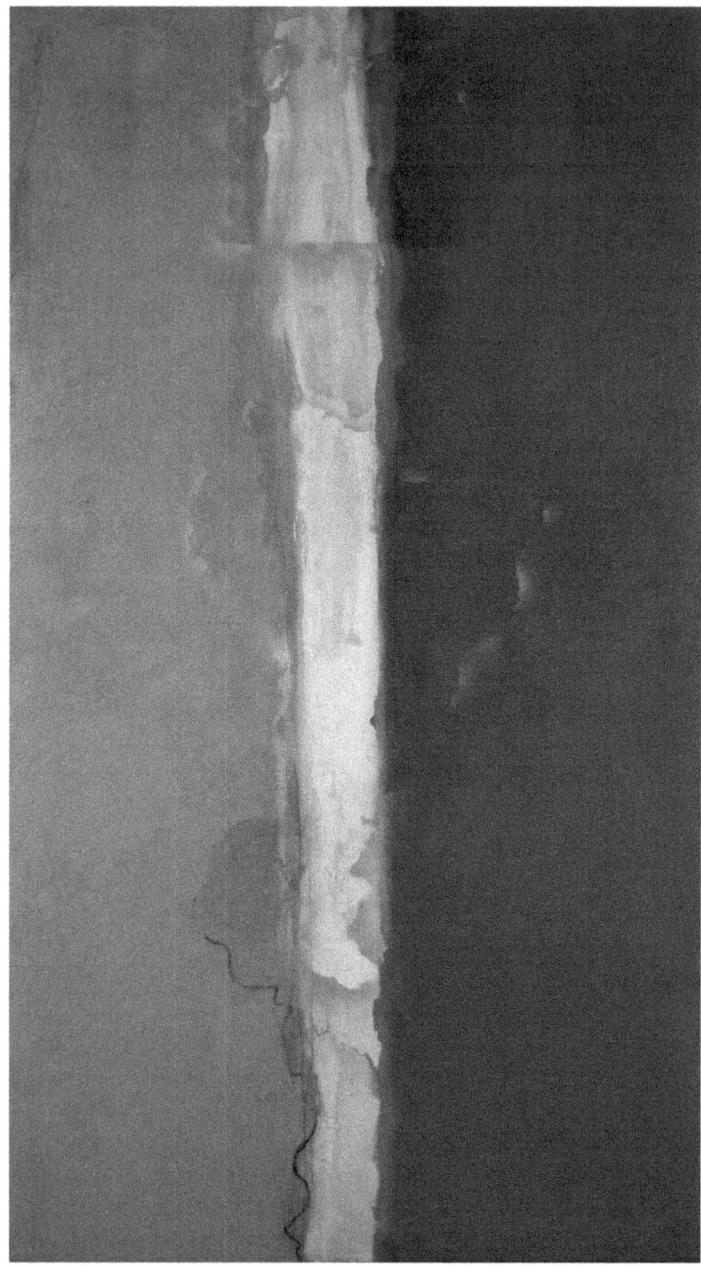

7   Frank Bowling *Who's afraid of Barney Newman* (1968), acrylic on
           canvas, 236.4 × 129.5 cm.

those students who would join successful artists like Liz Frink, Francis Bacon and Lucian Freud for daily informal meetings and drinks at venues in Chelsea, Fulham Road and King's Road. Meanwhile a separate grouping at Ladbroke Grove and at Portobello Road became a more intense site of artists vying for position.[45] Of the liveliest contexts for drinking and contact – Soho, Portobello Road and Chelsea – Bowling enjoyed keeping up with them all, moving around seamlessly despite the territorialism of the RCA's departments and disciplines.

Such circumstances contributed to which of those students would be included in the success story of Pop. They belie those accounts which seek only to amplify the sense of a productive and shared attitude to image making at Pop's formation. They also indicate how the historiography of Pop is founded on the biography of a group whose local and mundane interactions were never closely examined. If they were more seriously addressed then there would need to be greater transparency about the values which govern those accounts of Pop written within the analytic of belatedness and provincialism. The preservation of these values has lasted through to the present with consequences for how Bowling has been remembered. In the catalogue for a major retrospective of the work of Peter Blake at Tate Britain in 2003, we are told that: 'Roots are important to Blake. Although locations are seldom specified, his work exudes an overall feeling of Englishness, reflecting the artist's affection for his native soil.'[46]

Roots are also important to the hegemonic art historical record; indeed they have proved vital to the story of Pop, ultimately disenfranchising Frank Bowling, despite his evidently integral participation. The emphasis on the Britishness of the celebrated Pop artists involved their canonisation as virtuously provincial 'outsiders' yet simultaneously intimate 'natives'. Such artists could be openly identified as displaced and distinct by social class, region, religion, or sexuality, and by residing in Britain rather than the United States. The recently asked questions about gender and Pop also follow this pattern, showing how displacement affected the RCA trained artist, Pauline Boty. Boty, who appeared alongside Blake, Boshier and Philips in Ken Russell's film *Pop Goes the Easel*,[47] battled with the 'institutionalized sexism' of the RCA, when 'the ethos and structure of the college was deeply gendered'.[48] Boty's part-Iranian ancestry recedes from view in the late celebration of her unique persona within Pop as 'the only blonde in the world'.[49]

British Pop prided itself on its belatedness and provincialism in the face of American popular culture and abstraction-focused modernism. Most favoured is the sort of art that played with recuperations of this status. This has ironically had the effect of concealing a comparable marginalisation – with its politics of displacement – that is associated with artists of the Caribbean as postcolonial creative subjects.[50] The celebration of Pop is consequently underscored by an energetic insistence on the centrality of the trope of the 'outsider', and on Pop as a story of spatio-temporal alterity made good. Yet it has involved the rejection of further 'outsider' identities, Bowling's not least among them. Pop valorised various forms of alterity and was yet reluctant to countenance the alterity of ethnicity. But the greater reluctance was about coming to terms with the correlation between Britain's changing imperial status and the way in which art in Britain was narrated. Bowling's description (quoted above) of the creation of the Young Commonwealth Artists Group bears upon this difference: 'The reason this came about, it was obviously a student gathering, is that it was felt that the people from the Commonwealth were being edged out by the English provincial lot.' The problem for Bowling is not that he was never associated with the status of the provincial – with his birthplace in the West Indies and his African descent – it is that he could not boast his own provincialism in the same nativist terms as the artists of Pop.

Indeed, the separate grouping of artists, as either Young Contemporaries or Young Commonwealth, was an outcome of the struggles that followed from the decolonising process. Artists from the Empire overseas shared London with those who were participating for the first time in elite art spaces, each seeking the advantages of change at the former metropole, not least, its appetite for a domestic brand of difference. How artists such as Bowling encountered the limits of the Pop art canon is easily visible through the lens of British imperial decline, and the concomitant realisation in the 1960s that British art lagged behind an American 'lead'. Each was entwined with what Bowling represented: a no longer 'contained at a distance' colonial subject but a child of Empire, home to roost. Through Bowling's presence, we can understand the historical basis for the nature of the Pop story as a whole. His being in Britain was contingent with why Pop became a narrative about how its artists were regarded as an embodiment of belatedness and provincialism.

The outcome for Bowling is that the canonical proliferation in the varieties of belatedness leaves the unacknowledged Caribbean participant of contemporary art with nowhere to go. This says something about the available strategies for countering the omissions of the twentieth century art canon. It causes us to think again about the value of appealing to a politics of marginal subjectivity, as presented in much postcolonial theory. The story of Pop shows that we would do well to consider how easily such a politics can be pressed into the service of other, far less marginal, agendas. British art and artists have been rendered in a similar light to the way Caribbean alterity has been posited. To make this clear will inevitably change the way that British Pop is understood. But the details of this story have more pressing implications for how to critically approach the task of historicising art of the Caribbean more broadly.

It may be instructive to look at how the writer Kobena Mercer has raised an argument about marginalisation in an attempt to tackle the relation of Bowling to Aubrey Williams, writing that:

the universal relevance of the themes of loss, separation and survival that feature in their work can be understood to flow from the specificity of diaspora subjectivities that have been historically shaped by collective experiences of trauma and catastrophe. While such complex issues went unrecognised in the discourse of cultural nationalism, they also fell below the radar of the normative formalism that regarded issues of identity and context as irrelevant to the disinterested univeralism of 'pure' abstraction. By employing the alternative vocabulary of diaspora, we may loosen the double-bind created by these seemingly disparate varieties of essentialism…[51]

For Mercer, a closer understanding of Bowling's legacy in paint rests on the significance of his 'diaspora subjectivity'. Yet in an effort to bring out this connection in his works, as in Williams's – to describe how this 'diaspora' element appears in their art practice – Mercer uses terms of description that might apply just as aptly to the artists of Pop. In that sense he misrecognises as diasporic various aspects of the more canonical art history (and sets out an interpretation of Bowling using the same postcolonial vocabulary that is appropriated in the canonisation of Pop). For instance, taking into account the contextually scurrilous irreverence of Pop, it is obvious that, like Bowling, none of his RCA contemporaries aimed for 'pure' abstraction or even 'normative formalism'. That pursuit remained in the domain of earlier modernists and was thoroughly ousted by the contextual values of the Pop artists.[52] On the lips of its detractors or its supporters, Pop was widely established in its day as having avoided 'disinterested universalism'. Indeed, it was the disregard for purity that caused the critic Clement Greenberg to argue that he failed to see Pop as 'original' in any sense, dismissively dubbing it 'neo-dada'. Its mix and match aesthetic was even deemed excessive, adding up to nothing more than a movement of mere 'novelty'.[53] More significant still, for the critic Lucy Lippard, Pop was already an entertainingly historically hybrid form.[54]

If Mercer has mistaken the hybridity and syncretism associated with Pop for an 'alternative vocabulary of diaspora', then by now it should be clear why this is so easy to do. Pop was about exploring the shifting status of anachronistic forms such as painting, in the face of newer media, and produced a characteristically hybrid product. The Pop generation stood at the interstices of fine art and the rapid perceptual shifts happening beyond the artist's studio in the visual field, in film, advertising, music, fashion and photography. This aspect of Mercer's misreading is less grave than the one of distancing Bowling from Pop, and Pop from decolonisation. The British art system was absorbed with the positionality of belatedness and provincialism, which was impossible to detach from the larger devolving imperial frame. Separating Bowling from the deeper complexities in which he is embedded – in search of the 'diaspora subject' of Pop – is not 'alternative' at all, and certainly not one that suits Bowling's demand for joint participation in British art. If there is a tale of 'trauma and catastrophe' for the artist it is his excommunication from the mainstream body of art historical narration. The complex aesthetic commanded by Bowling should hardly be taken as a premise for isolating him from his Pop contemporaries, but as the grounds for their contingency.

Finally, Bowling has issued a very forceful objection to being singled out from among the artists of Pop on the basis of a concern for ethnicity. Mercer suggests that the artist demonstrates a form of 'Black Atlantic abstraction', yet this fits uneasily with the artist's own characterisation of his practice. As Bowling makes clear: 'I have a real sort of instinctive anger about this constant harping on Black.'[55] This is the message that he has carried throughout his career, encapsulated in a series of elegant writings in the art press of the late 1960s and 1970s. An especially unequivocal statement of 1971 examined the demand for a form of racially conscious 'black art'. It queried the need for black nationalism to have any significant influence on modern art making. Marking his own approach to modernism, he concluded: 'Should works of painting and sculpture continue to be a black issue and not an art issue, it is my considered opinion that these works will suffer.'[56]

Bowling's mirror

In 1966, Bowling produced a monumental painting entitled *Mirror* (figure 8), which is instructive for examining Pop as a half-told tale, and for assessing Bowling's own meditation on its history. The main subject of the painting is a spiralling staircase modelled on one at the RCA, and which serves as the pivot or vortex of an art-creating machine, implicating Bowling's London contemporaries. Different styles are used for the figures in the painting, mostly tied to the artists that they portray. Such styles also become spaces, and spaces styles. At the same time, *Mirror* neatly frames the moment of Pop in the rigid sense of being a summation of the turbulent decade that Bowling had spent among a coterie of hallowed English painters, only to emerge apparently empty-handed, passing without due recognition. The result is a sort of large-scale painted resumé of those artists who stood out for Bowling, which elaborates a skein of formal relations among them.

Mirror was first shown at the Royal Academy Summer Exhibition and declared 'Painting of the Year'. This was on the occasion that Bowling was first asked to become a member of the Royal Academy, before the honour was withheld.[57] That the painting attracted such interest epitomises how systematically, by 1966, British modern art and artists of the 1950s and 1960s had become institutionalised, and how their sometime radicalism had become defused and outdated. Partly, the painting was devised, rather impishly, to confront British audiences about their taste for Bacon (the 'Baconianism' decried by Andrew

Forge, above). It did so by showing Bowling to be in youthful command of illusion and pictorial space, as he put it, 'more flattened out' and 'integrated' than Bacon knew how. At odds with Forge's view, one of the main alibis among critics for underplaying Bowling's contribution to British painting has been to mark him down as derivative of Bacon.[58] But *Mirror* speaks back to their clumsy handling of that relation and succeeds in switching and reversing its hierarchy. As he explains:

> I think that the fact is that most of those people who were writing about the art weren't looking at art. They couldn't see the difference between what I was doing, and what Bacon was doing. What they saw was this superficial, one-dimensional aspect which was that I was dragging paint. I was using paint

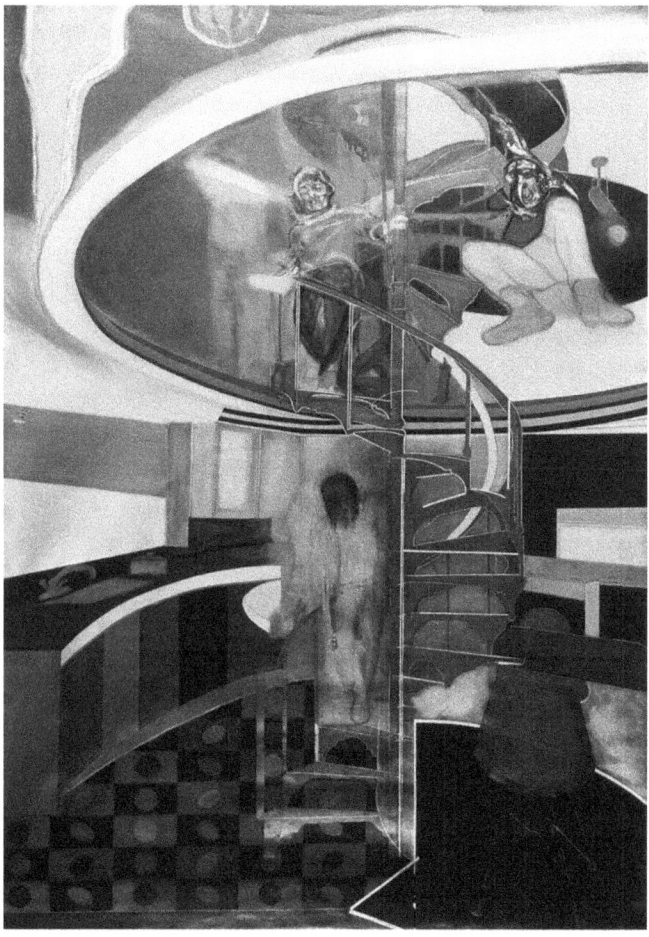

Frank Bowling, *Mirror* (1966), acrylic and oil on canvas, 304.8 × 213.4 cm.   **8**

you could say in a similar way to Bacon's, dragging the paint, using the material to express in my case, you know, hurt, agony, this kind of thing. I suppose that you could say that Francis was doing the same thing as me. But the main difference between us, and I asked Francis about this at the time, is that he didn't understand space. He had to make all these artificial devices to hold space on his canvases together. Whereas I was leaning very heavily on old master art to get the space in my work. And the space as a result in my work was more flattened out than his interior design, perspectival devices. I wasn't into that. The background of my pictures was stained. I didn't fill the space up the way Bacon did with one colour and then impose an image on it and then try to hold the image together in space. My work was flatter and more integrated as a result, as space, I felt.[59]

As if on the surface of a playing board, the snakes and ladders scheme of *Mirror* – in which artists jostle in an ambitious game of fleeting ascendancy – involves the prize-winning artists of the day. The composition orders their personalities into a hierarchy with the benefit of loose caricature. A stocky Bacon in mustard roll-neck glances towards the viewer, head tilted as he descends the stairs. We can see the transformations of Duchamp's 1912 nudes clothed in the same painterly 'accidents' that Bacon used – an interest in Duchamp that links Bowling to several other Pop artists who caught on to his devices.[60] As another artist hurries to be at the top of the staircase, he has lost his footing altogether. Boldly outlined as in the figural works of Kitaj, he is buoyant and unanchored, bobbing undignified near the ceiling, frozen in a jockeying pose.

Bowling employs *Mirror* to confront his audience with their appetite for British painting. He responds to Richard Hamilton's frequent pastiche of modern design, commenting on high art's relationship to new icons of the popular: the fitted kitchen sink, repeating wallpaper, formica and styrofoam of *Mirror* furnish the technicolour interior of a large, elliptical space. A collage of English painters is framed at its upper edge by a pink crescent like those of Patrick Heron, matched to a space suggesting the landscapes of David Hockney. At the lower left are geometrical patterns that gently repeat Victor Vasarely's Op Art. They repeat the configuration of his portfolio *Planetary Folklore* of 1954, which Bowling might first have seen at London's Hanover Gallery in 1965, which was a key venue for Bacon. At the foot of the stairs is Bowling himself, pivotally placed and swathed in light. Taking a step, he is also gesturing to leave. It is a stained and unfinished portrait and a conclusive mark of self-erasure.

Given his choice of a title for *Mirror*, and that between 1962 and 1966 critics had cooled on Bowling while his abilities with paint rapidly matured, the piece invited a further irony. A notable case of Bowling's exclusion from the story of Pop was the large survey show, the 1964 Gulbenkian Foundation

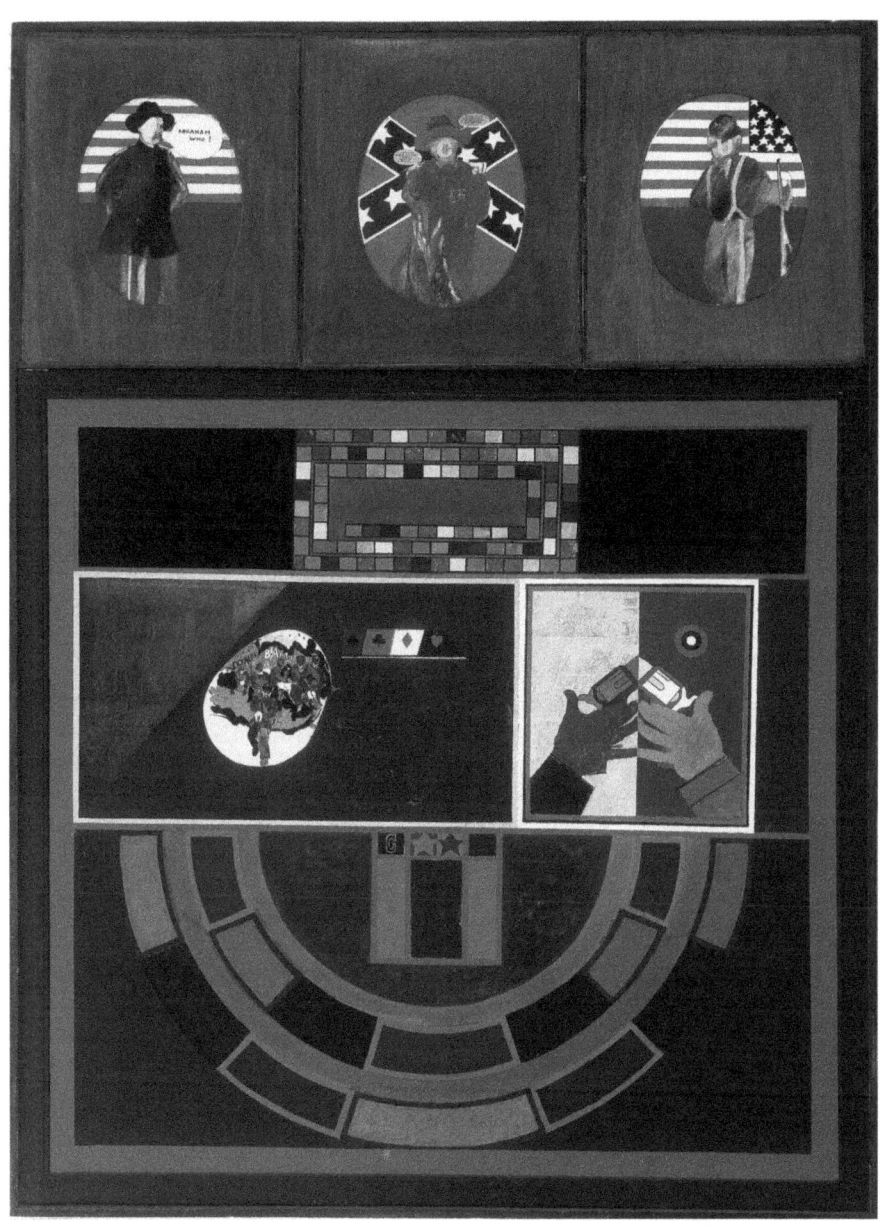

Peter Phillips, *War/Game* (1961), oil and wood on canvas, 213.36 × 152.4 cm.   **9**

exhibition at the Tate Gallery, *54–64: Painting and Sculpture of a Decade*, which he had presumed he would contribute to, given the Foundation's previous commission and purchase of his work.[61] The excuse for his omission was that his inclusion would look too much like nepotism since his then wife was involved in the selection. *Mirror* offers Bowling's own review of the years 1954–64, refashioning many of the personalities caught in the scope of that exhibition. It brings home the theme of conflict, the 'game format' that had vaguely occupied Peter Phillips in his work of 1961, *War/Game* (figure 9) with its elements of pinball machines, gambling tables and heraldic devices. It is a conflict coded in the heraldry of noted British painters, and hung within bright, manufactured surroundings.

In late 1966, Frank Bowling left Britain for the United States. On moving to New York (until early 1967), the artist lived in the Chelsea Hotel, comfortable and excited to share a milieu with Jasper Johns, who also lived in the hotel, and Warhol, Rothko and many others. Until he was able to afford a large loft space on Broadway and Spring Street, the hotel was a space of induction and what Bowling has termed a 'ready-made learning process'. Another temporal distinction (already existing, 'ready-made') Bowling's subsequent record of achievements in the United States contrasts with Britain's shortcomings, for him. By 1966, when the symposium 'Destruction in Art' was staged at London's Africa Centre, arguably Britain's first truly international post-war event,[62] Bowling had left the country. When considered together, the slow timing of that symposium and the success following from Bowling's Atlantic migration are another historical measure of the belatedness and provincialism of British art. The ultimate subversion of that status by an artist of the Caribbean was simply to relocate; from 1966 onwards, Aubrey Williams too would spend more and more time away from Britain, working in the Caribbean, and finally in Florida.[63]

In Bowling's new home in America, he would engage with a wider circle of interlocutors and tackle head on the question of the status of painting. His migration marked the firm start of the abstract work for which he is now far better known, in a turn away from the 'new figuration' of Britain and Pop. In New York, he painted *Mother's House* (1967, figure 10) and *Bartica Born II* (1969),[64] which declared lines of connection with the newly independent state of Guyana, and of his childhood memories there. These were executed in a manner that combined cheap printing techniques with painting, indexing directly to a mainstay of Pop, yet extending to open identification with his birthplace among the gingerbread jalousies and whitewashed wooden lanes of Bartica, a small river depot on the Essequibo. Familial associations with Bartica are elaborated by the repeating transfer of an image of the Bowling family home onto canvas, a detail first used in his *Cover Girl* of 1962 (figure 11) and a work on paper, *Beware of the Dog* (1966, figure 12). A more hidden reference hinges on associations with Bartica as a figure of political history. The town carries a locus of references as the nearest settlement to the seventeenth-century Dutch fortress Kyk-over-al (literally, 'see over all' or 'lookout'), now a ruin on a tiny uninhabited island at the confluence of the Essequibo, Mazaruni and Cuyuni rivers.

Through this metaphor of an empowered, non-Anglophone vision, Kyk-over-al has long connoted a mode of visual knowledge able to shift between linguistic registers and traverse contested terrain. The name was cannily assumed in 1945 for a leading journal of critical writing that would carry works by Martin Carter, poet and spokesperson for the independence movement, during his 1953 imprisonment by the British administration.[65] His *Poems of Resistance from British Guiana*, printed a year later in London, included 'The University of Hunger', which encapsulates the deep learning through deprivation suffered by colonial subjects: 'is the university of hunger the wide waste'.[66] Bartica changed hands several times as a European possession and is a micro-organism of imperial incursions and trade-offs whose twentieth-century fallout was being increasingly felt at the time Bowling was

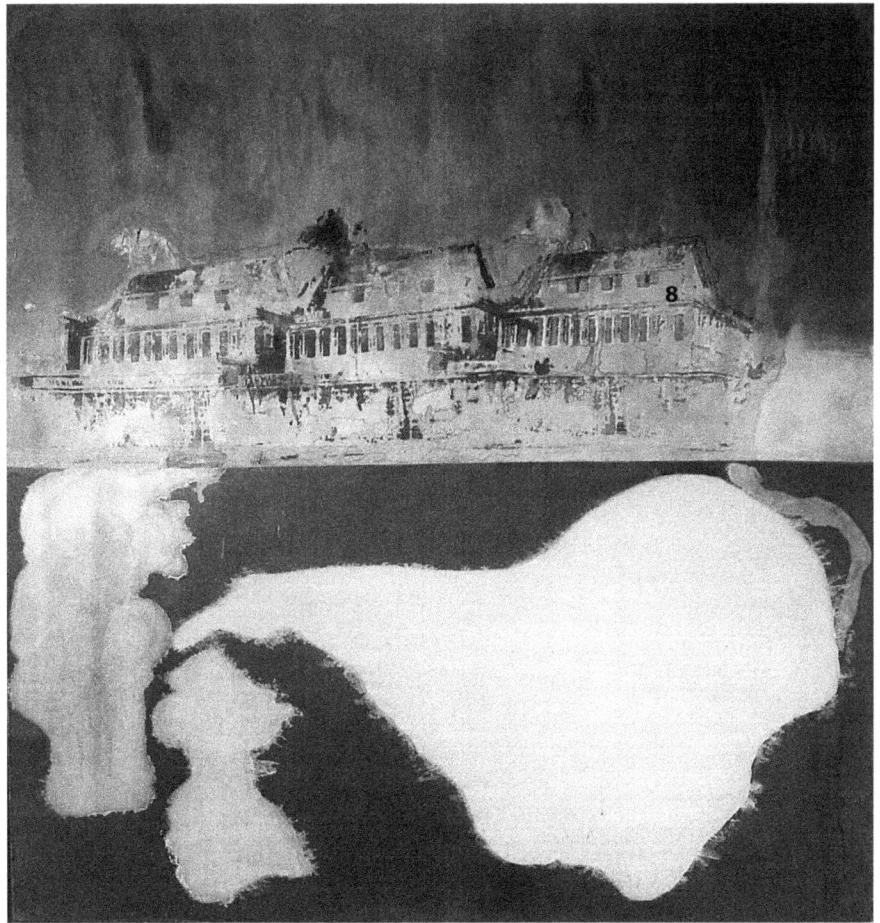

Frank Bowling, *Mother's House* (1967), acrylic on canvas, 157.5 × 167.6 cm.   **10**

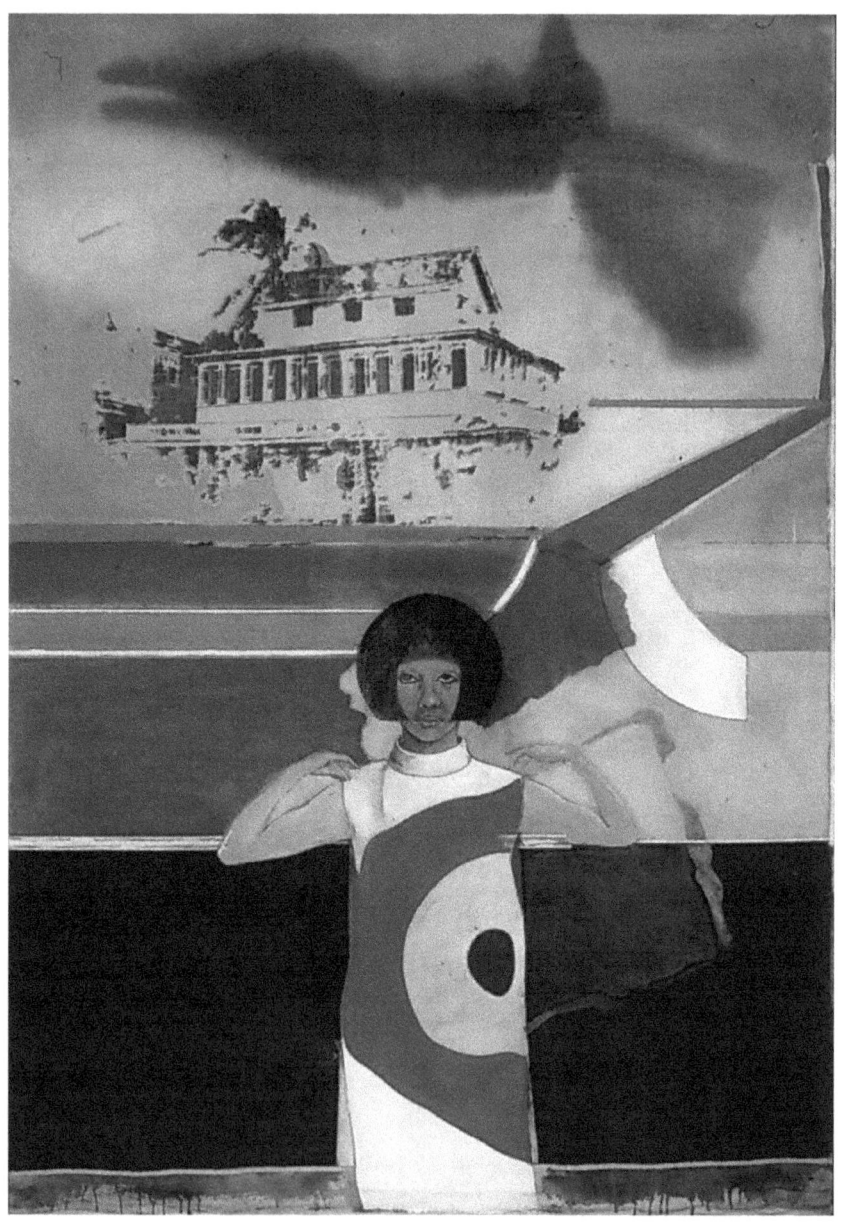

11   Frank Bowling, *Cover Girl* (1964), acrylic and oil on canvas, 144.8 × 101.6 cm.

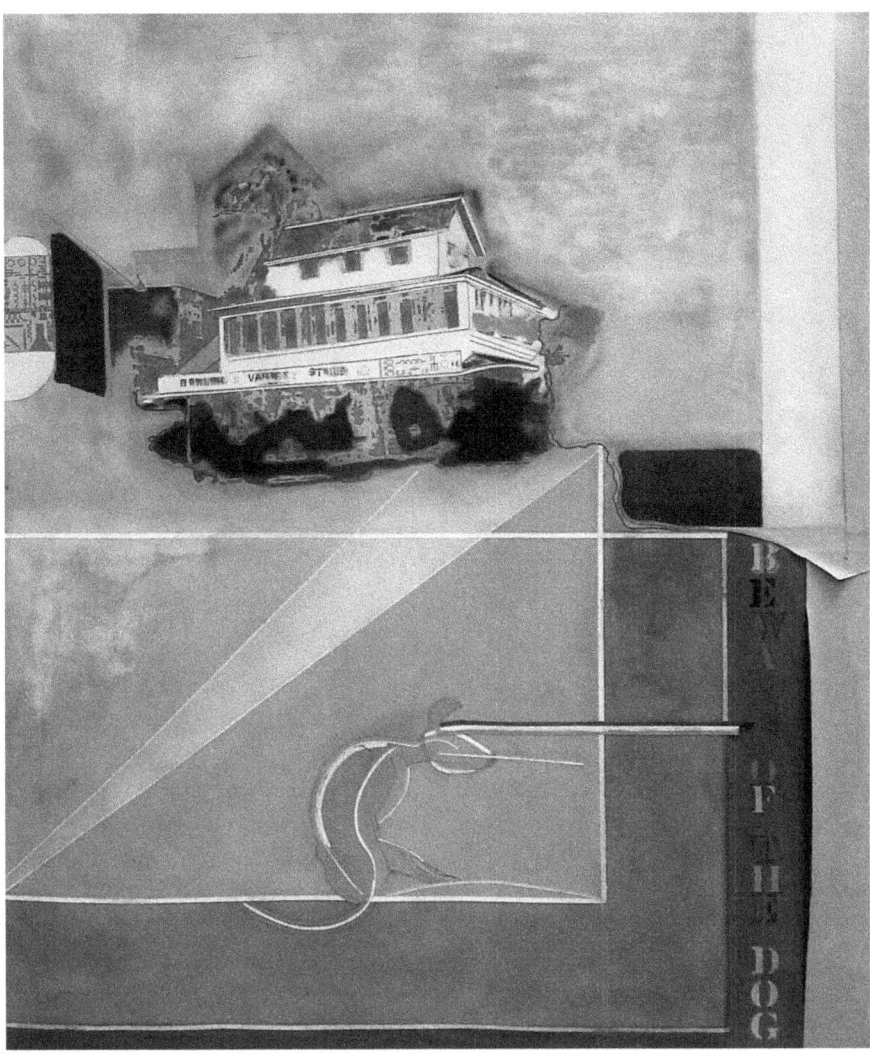

Frank Bowling, *Beware of the Dog* (1966), acrylic and oil on canvas, 120.7 × 78.7 cm. **12**

painting. By way of this biographical trope, he had succeeded in showing solidarity with other Carterian 'graduates of hunger'. These works make explicit Bowling's place in a more political story of transatlantic art practice. For the artists of British Pop that he left behind, this was only ever an armchair interest, or sublated in their domesticated brand of belatedness – for example Derek Boshier's flags piece *Situation in Cuba* (1961, figure 13), a coded vote of protest against the US invasion of the Bay of Pigs.

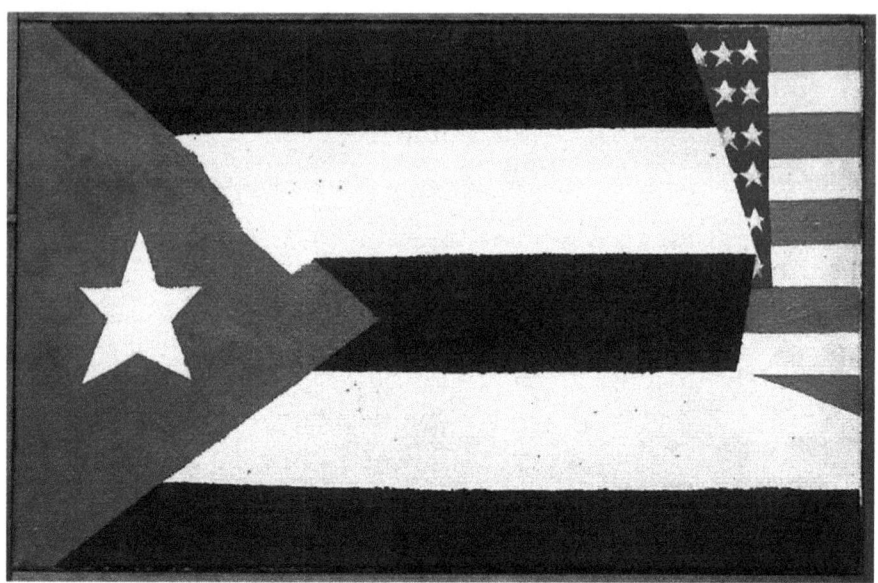

13   Derek Boshier, *Situation in Cuba* (1961), oil on canvas with wood frame, 33 × 51 cm.

On the surface of *Mirror* is a coating of gold leaf whose reflective surface has been impossible to convey in any reproduction of the painting. It provides the shape of the ironwork structure of the pictured staircase. Like the furniture in its painted kitchen, this quality combined with the high colour luminosity of *Mirror* gives an overall illusion of the picture space as a polished surface. It suggests looking back, with the painting, and through the painting, to the body of Bowling's larger output and the concern with mirroring that has overlain his career to date, which he has explained as a feature of his process in the studio:

> Working, as is my practice, loosely on the floor and on the wall. When things are on the floor I reflect it is rather like seeing an image in a clear stretch of water. And after a time taking the piece to the wall. One to one, like looking into and at a mirror, several mirrors and the reflections therein. The truing and faring.[67]

Reflected and dismantled in *Mirror* is the hegemonic narrative of British Pop, based on concerns with temporality and historical remembrance. It treats the anxiety about belatedness that has shaped Pop's historiography, and shows how the attempts to overcome that anxiety have involved a turn to a rather ambiguous resource. The ability to carry an air of provincialism has served as a virtue for most of the artists of Pop: the very symbol of the locality and British-ness of their art is a corresponding, fashionable belatedness. But provincialism and anachronism, when pressed into the service of the historical record, have brought benefits for only some artists of British Pop. The sort of revisionism which would illustrate Frank Bowling's story, and oppose his inscription as a belated outsider, is therefore not enough for understanding Bowling, nor, for that matter, Pop. Bowling's association with the belated outsider remains a stubborn obstacle in his yearning for canonical inclusion, since it is the same association which animates the Pop canon. Backwardness and outsiderness become markers of value in the Pop story, and are consequently all the more sought after, fought over, and protected, with different varieties of belatedness emerging from that conflict. The deeper contradiction is that what contributed to this country's sense of its own redemptive belatedness, as illustrated in the Pop story, is the same process of decolonisation in the Caribbean which brought Bowling to Britain and into its academies of art.

Notes

1 G. Kubler, *The shape of time: Remarks on the history of things* (New Haven and London: Yale University Press, 1962), p. 91.
2 B. Robertson, J. Russell, A. Armstrong-Jones and the Earl of Snowdon, *Private view* (London: Nelson, 1965), p. 283.
3 T. Smith, 'The provincialism problem', *Artforum*, 13 (1974), 54–59, p. 56.
4 This to a large extent also characterises my own, earlier account of Bowling. See: L. Wainwright, 'Frank Bowling and the appetite for British Pop', *Third Text*, 91 (2008), 195–208.
5 J. Baudrillard, 'Pop: An art of consumption' (1970), in P. Taylor (ed.), *Post-Pop art*, trans. P. Foss (Cambridge: MIT Press, 1989), pp. 33–44, p. 33.
6 My interview with Frank Bowling, 28 April 2006.
7 L. Alloway, 'The development of British pop', in L. R. Lippard (ed.), *Pop art* (New York: Thames & Hudson, 1966), pp. 27–68, p. 43.
8 A. Seago, *Burning the box of beautiful things: The development of a postmodern sensibility* (Oxford: Oxford University Press, 1995), p. 138.
9 Seago, *Burning the box*, p. 138.
10 A. Huyssen, 'The cultural politics of pop: Reception and critique of US pop art in the Federal Republic of Germany', *New German Critique*, 4 (1975), 77–97, p. 77.
11 The artist Colin Self (b. 1941), who identifies himself today as a Pop artist, has recalled a feeling of 'anachronism' in choosing to study art in Norwich and at the Slade School of Art: 'I went to Norwich Art School, 8th February 1958, which [*sic*] I'd only just discovered there were such things as art schools. That was a shock! I thought art only belonged in the olden days. And in the olden days you could be a pirate or an artist. And I thought: they still did it? I thought I was a walking anachronism.' C. Self, interviewed on BBC Radio 4, 'Front row', 16 July 2008.
12 Morris's master's thesis approached Brancusi through Kubler's terms. See: A. Reinhardt, 'Art vs. history', *Art News*, 64:19 (1966), 19–21; cf. W. Smith, 'Ad Reinhardt's oriental aesthetic', *Smithsonian Studies in American Art*, 4:3/4 (1990), 22–45. Smithson's connections with Kubler can be seen in: J. Flam (ed.), *Robert*

Smithson: The collected writings (Berkeley: University of California Press, 1996). A detailed examination of Kubler's influence on Smithson is given in P. M. Lee, '"Ultramoderne": Or, how George Kubler stole the time in sixties art', *Grey Room*, 2 (2001), 46–77; P. M. Lee, *Chronophobia: On time in the art of the 1960's* (Cambridge: MIT Press, 2004).

13 D. Summers, *Real spaces: World art history and the rise of Western modernism* (London: Phaidon Press, 2003), p. 16.

14 On the exhibition *Art in 1946 and After*, M. H. Middleton of the *Spectator* predicted that although Britain might be shedding 'the political commitments of a great world power', the country seemed destined 'to hold a position of leadership we have never previously known as the artistic centre of the world'. Three decades later, in 1976, R. B. Kitaj, writing in the catalogue to 'The human clay' exhibition, would return to this theme: 'The bottom line is that there are artistic personalities in this small island more unique and strong and I think numerous than anywhere in the world outside America's jolting artistic vigour.' Middleton is quoted in P. Fuller, 'The Neo-Romantics. London, Barbican Art Gallery', *The Burlington Magazine*, 129:1012 (1987), 472–4, p. 474; R. B. Kitaj, *The human clay: An exhibition* (London: Arts Council of Great Britain, 1976). By contrast, an exhibition of 1987 at the Royal Academy attempted 'to challenge the stereotyped views of the shortcomings of twentieth-century British Art, which for too long has been bedevilled by a reputation for politeness, provincialism and even timidity'. S. Compton (ed.), *British art in the twentieth century: The modern movement* (London: Royal Academy of Arts, 1987). Reinstating such a reputation was a notably impolite, chauvinistically anti-American response to the exhibition from Peter Fuller. He concluded that British art of the twentieth century is best seen for 'those resistances to, and refusals of, the worst aspects of modernity, and Americanism, which had previously ensured the distinctive, conservationist qualities of the British tradition'. R. Shone and P. Fuller, 'British art in the twentieth century. London, Royal Academy', *The Burlington magazine*, 129:1009 (1987), 261–5, p. 265.

15 From among the literature contemporary with Pop see: A. Bowness, 'The American invasion and the British response', *Studio International*, 173:890 (1967), 285–93; Lippard (ed.), *Pop art*; S. Gablik and J. Russell, *Pop art redefined* (London: Thames & Hudson, 1969).

16 There is an even wider literature here, but key examples include: C. Harrison, 'Modernism and the "transatlantic dialogue"' in F. Frascina (ed.), *Pollock and after: The critical debate* (London: Harper & Row, 1985), pp. 217–32; M. Livingstone (ed.), *Pop art* (London: Royal Academy of Arts and Weidenfeld & Nicolson, 1991); J. A. Walker, *Cultural offensive: America's impact on British art since 1945* (London: Pluto, 19980); N. Whiteley, '"Cultural imperialism"? British hard-edge painting in the 1960s', *Third Text*, 22:2 (2008), 209–27.

17 T. Crow, *The rise of the sixties: American and European art in the era of dissent, 1955–69* (London: Calmann and King, 1996), p. 12.

18 Quoted in G. Marcus, 'No money down: Pop art, pop music, pop culture', in M. Francis and H. Foster (eds), *Pop: themes and movements* (London: Phaidon, 2005), pp. 208–10, p. 208. See also L. Alloway, 'Avant-garde, London', *Image*, October 1960, p. 40.

19 D. Robbins, *The Independent Group: Postwar Britain and the aesthetics of plenty* (Cambridge: MIT Press, 1990).

20 L. Deighton, 'Foreword', in Seago, *Burning the box*, p. vii.

21 R. Banham, 'The atavism of the short-distance mini-cyclist', *Living Arts*, 3 (1964), 92; L. Cooke, 'The Independent Group: British and American pop art, a "palimpcestuous" legacy', in K. Varnedoe and A. Gopnik (eds), *Modern art and popular culture: Readings in high and low* (New York: Harry N. Abrams, 1990), pp. 192–216.

22 Associating the period with 'crisis', such disdain is echoed by Peter Fuller, who has noted Britain's 'bewildered recognition of the reality of a decadence, characterised by subservience to empty American fashions, and an understandable dwindling of the public for the newest art'. P. Fuller, 'The visual arts', in B. Ford (ed.), *Modern Britain: The Cambridge cultural history, Volume 9* (Cambridge: Cambridge University Press, 1992), pp. 99–145, p. 99. Like Fuller's, much of the commentary on Pop commiserates with those critics from the period who were convinced of Britain's weakening position in the arts, weighed against irrefutable American leadership. Len Deighton has summarised this view, writing that: '... although the RCA student body – with its ex-service students keen to earn a living – had no time to spare on politics, anti-Americanism was well-established there. Tweedy gentlemen-artists, who resented the thought of American bombers flying over "Constable country" found common cause with leftist students who loudly proclaimed that American design meant only Coca-Cola billboards and large cars with too much chromium.' Deighton, 'Foreword', pp. xi–xii.

23 L. Alloway, 'The long front of culture', *Cambridge Opinion*, 17 (1959); H. Foster, 'Survey' in Francis and Foster (eds), *Pop*, pp. 17–18.

24 C. Finch, 'London pop recollected', in D. E. Brauer, J. Edwards, C. Finch, W. Hopps and N. Rifkin (eds), *Pop art: U.S./U.K. connections, 1956–1966* (Houston: The Menil Collection, 2001), pp. 21–41, p. 21. Brauer *et al.* write of Pop's transatlantic historiography: 'Pop Art has often been considered an essentially American phenomenon, but in fact British artists and theorists in the 1950s were the first to debate and formulate Pop's main tenets. ... Both the British and American artists who were eventually grouped under the rubric of Pop Art looked toward the United States as the primary source of this subject matter.' Brauer, Edwards, Finch, Hopps and Rifkin (eds), *Pop art*, p. 17.

25 Pamela Lee's study is confined to preoccupations with time, but of a different kind: P. M. Lee, *Chronophobia*.

26 N. Rudd, *Peter Blake* (London: Tate Publishing, 2003), p. 7.

27 'Roots are important to Blake. Although locations are seldom specified, his work exudes an overall feeling of Englishness, reflecting the artist's affection for his native soil.' Rudd, *Peter Blake*, p. 7.

28 S. Faulkner, 'Dealing with Hockney', in P. Melia (ed.), *David Hockney* (Manchester and New York: Manchester University Press, 1995), pp. 11–29.

29 D. Hockney, *David Hockney on David Hockney* (London: Thames & Hudson, 1976), p. 160.

30 J. Aulich and J. Lynch (eds), *Critical Kitaj: Essays on the work of R. B. Kitaj* (Manchester: Manchester University Press, 2000), p. 2.

31 The sociological dimension of such definitions of 'modernist/nonmodernist'

production has been examined closely by Janet Wolff. As an illustration of the way in the importance of British art is often dismissed, she quotes the comment made in 1999 by a critic of *The New York Times* that: 'From an art perspective, England has always been ultraconservative and, frankly, a bit of a snore. ... Even since the time of angst-ridden modernists like Francis Bacon and Lucian Freud, British art has remained quaintly tethered to the figurative tradition, *as if everyone wished the 20th century would just go away*' (my emphasis). D. Solomon, cited in J. Wolff, *AngloModern: Painting and modernity in Britain and the United States* (Ithaca and London: Cornell University Press, 2003), p. 167. As I see it, Solomon is also in thrall to an underlying sense of art in Britain as unable to keep up with twentieth-century modernity, as, in a word, belated.

32 Interview with Frank Bowling, 28 April 2006.

33 Bowling, *Birthday* (1961), oil on canvas, 127 × 101.6 cm.

34 Frank Bowling, *The Martyrdom of Patrice Lumumba* (1961), oil on canvas.

35 Interview with Frank Bowling, 28 April 2006.

36 This is the sort of politics that would only begin to emerge in the decade of the 1970s in Britain, carried forward by those Australian writers and curators, notably Terry Smith, who wrote frequently on what he identified as the 'provincialism bind' – 'an attitudinal response of labyrinthine complexity to an externally-determined hierarchy of cultural values'. T. Smith, 'American painting and British painting: Some issues', *Studio International*, 188:972 (1974), 218–23, p. 218. See also: T. Smith, 'The provincialism problem'; I. Burn, 'Provincialism', *Art Dialogue*, 1 (October 1973), 3–11; I. Burn, N. Lendon, C. Merewether and A. Stephen, 'The provincialism debates', in *The necessity of Australian art* (Sydney: Power Institute of Fine Arts, University of Sydney, 1988), pp. 104–26. The Australian beginnings for this discussion were encapsulated in the phenomenon of 'cultural cringe' set out in: A. A. Phillips, *The Australian tradition: Studies in colonial culture* (Melbourne: Longman-Cheshire, 1958). For a related discussion of the exhibition *Australian painting* at the Tate Gallery, London, 1963, see Sarah Scott 'A colonial legacy: Australian painting at the Tate Gallery in London 1963', *Seize the Day*, 1:1 (2008), 1–22.

37 *Image in revolt: Derek Boshier, Frank Bowling*, London, Grabowski Gallery, 5 October–3 November 1962.

38 A. Forge, *New Statesman*, 19 October 1962.

39 The painting was commissioned by the Calouste Gulbenkian Foundation in 1963 to commemorate the Shakespeare Quarto Centenary in 1964, organised by Richard Buckle, and was bought through a Purchase Scheme for new artists.

40 N. Lynton, 'London letter', *Art International*, 6:1–4 (10 December 1962), 42.

41 This has also been a lasting motivation for reassessing subsequent phases of his career, for instance: K. Mercer, 'Black Atlantic abstraction: Aubrey Williams and Frank Bowling', in K. Mercer (ed.), *Discrepant abstraction* (London and Massachusetts: Institute of International Visual Arts and The MIT Press, 2003), pp. 182–205.

42 Bowness, 'The American invasion', p. 290.

43 Letter to the Tate, 1 December 1986.

44 See: Seago, *Burning the box*, pp. 25–32.

45 Interview with Frank Bowling, 28 April 2006.

46 Rudd, *Peter Blake*, p. 7.

47 K. Russell, *Pop goes the easel* (BBC Monitor Series, 1962, 44 mins).

48 D. A. Mellor and S. Watling, *Pauline Boty: The only blonde in the world* (London: Whitford Fine Art and Mayor Gallery, 1998), pp. 4–5. Mellor and Watling have noted such unsurprising sexism in the statistical record of places given to female students (between 1956 and 1965 only 29 per cent of the students at the School of Painting were women) as compared to their attained grades (women achieved 44 per cent of the First Class results). A similar picture pertains to the gendered make-up of the staff, and the initial withholding of degree status from Fashion, the only school headed by a woman.

49 Mellor and Watling, *Pauline Boty*.

50 This is similar to several other instances in which the vocabulary of marginalisation and displacement (focusing on migration, exile and diaspora) has been put to use. The broader historical geography of this appropriation is the focus of the final chapter of M. Sheller, *Consuming the Caribbean: Arawaks to zombies* (London: Routledge, 2004), pp. 174–202. A recent example in the study of literary history is: M. Steven, 'Provincialism and the modern diaspora: T. S. Eliot and David Jones', *English*, 58:220 (2009), 57–72. The potential for this borrowing of terms is a sort of loophole in postcolonial theory. It was left open by the attempts to define the broader possibility for experiencing alienation and 'crisis' as a result of displacement. Consider, for instance: 'The alienation of vision and the crisis in self-image which this displacement produces is as frequently found in the accounts of Canadian "free settlers" as of Australian convicts, Fijian-Indian or Trinidadian-Indian indentured labourers, West Indian slaves, or forcibly colonized Nigerians or Bengalis. … An adequate account of this practice must go beyond the usual categories of social alienation such as master/slave; free/bonded; ruler/ruled, however important and widespread these may be in post-colonial cultures.' B. Ashcroft, G. Griffiths, and H. Tiffin, *The Empire writes back: Theory and practice in post-colonial literatures* (London: Routledge, 1989), p. 9.

51 Mercer, 'Black Atlantic abstraction', pp. 184–5.

52 Krauss has gone further than this by suggesting an even closer resemblance between works by Noland, Olitski and Caro (which for Greenberg and Fried had stood as examples of advanced modernist abstraction) and Pop. See R. Krauss, 'Theories of art after minimalism and pop', in H. Foster (ed.) *Discussions in contemporary culture* (New York: DIA Art Foundation, 1999), pp. 60–1. See also C. Harrison and P. Wood, 'Modernity and modernism reconsidered', in J. Harris, F. Frascina, C. Harrison, and P. Wood (eds), *Modernism in dispute: Art since the forties* (New Haven: Yale University Press, 1993), pp. 170–260, p. 181.

53 C. Greenberg, 'After abstract expressionism', *Art International* (25 October 1962), 24–32, p. 32.

54 Lippard (ed.), *Pop art*, p. 9.

55 Interview on 'Front row', BBC Radio 4, broadcast 19 May 2006.

56 F. Bowling, 'Untitled: Is black art about colour?', in R. L. Goldstein (ed.), *Black life and culture in the United States* (New York: Crowell, 1971), pp. 302–21, p. 321. The essay opens with the following: 'The pressure of cultural nationalism on a global drift has given rise in the United States to a passionate, confused, but fashionable black nationalism, and with it a justified if shrill cry for cultural distinctiveness.

The dilemma of adequately defining differences and giving them concrete form in aesthetic terms cannot be overstated, and is formidable due to confusion, urgency, and historical nearness. Objectivity about art is always a tall order, but a vested interest by whites and blacks in black art deepens the situation to near opacity. In any attempt to shed a little light on the sweeping generalizations about cultural distinctiveness that are currently being disseminated, such generalizations and the position taken by their proponents must be seen for what they are: sincere attempts to define blackness, but not within the context of sculpture and painting. The question still is, Is black art to be appraised for its blackness or its artistic merit?' F. Bowling, 'Untitled: Is black art about colour?', in R. L. Goldstein (ed.), *Black life and culture*, p. 302.

57 Four further attempts to grant Bowling membership of the Royal Academy would follow before final success in 2005.

58 See, for instance, the numerous accounts of Pop given by Marco Livingstone, many standard reading on the topic. These began life as a Master's thesis at the Courtauld Institute of Art (M. E. Livingstone, '"Young contemporaries" at the Royal College of Art, 1959–1962: Derek Boshier, David Hockney, Allen Jones, R. B. Kitaj, Peter Phillips' (University of London, 1976). There Livingstone argues that Bowling is of less interest than other artists of Pop because of the proximity of his works to Bacon, and thereby labels him imitative, or at least derivative. From then on, Bowling is absent from Livingstone's writings. Livingstone's judgement is rather coloured by the description given by Robertson *et al*, in 1965, in the widely circulated book of photography, *Private view*, which includes reflections on the London art scene: 'Bowling's main stimulus has been the example of Francis Bacon. He first saw Bacon's work at the time of the paraphrases of van Gogh; the possibilities which Bacon's agonized vision opened up for him were a source of energy and confidence, and made him realize that a tragic sensibility could engender a commensurate use of paint and handling of colour. Bowling seems now to be finding an increasingly independent means of expression.' Robertson *et al*, *Private view*, p. 283.

59 Interview with Frank Bowling, 28 April 2006. This concurs with Lynton's account of 1962: 'He is a convinced admirer of Francis Bacon and many critics have represented him as a Bacon imitator. To me, admitting Bowling and rejecting most of Bacon, the differences seem so great as to overwhelm the similarities. It is true that he borrows from Bacon some manners of applying paint, but while in Bacon they are used to decorate a painting that in its essential already exists, here they are integral parts of the subject/mode-of-vision/matter compound.' Lynton, 'London letter', p. 42.

60 See, for instance Duchamp's *Tu M'* (1918), Yale University Art Gallery, New Haven; B. Fer, 'Eva Hesse and color', *October*, 119 (2007), 21–36.

61 As cited earlier, this was the group of three pieces including *A Mirror, Three Windows*, and *A Door*, of 1962.

62 This was not without the efforts of curators such as Bryan Robertson who attempted to make art in Britain more international through his innovations at the Whitechapel Gallery.

63 See Walmsley, 'Chronology'.

64 Bowling, *Bartica Born II* (1969), acrylic on canvas, 132 × 112 cm; *Bartica Born I* (1968), acrylic on canvas, 92.75 × 48 cm.

65 Discontinued in 1961, the journal was revived in 1984. A special issue in tribute to Martin Carter was published in June 2000 (*Kyk* 49/50). S. Brown (ed.), *All are involved: The art of Martin Carter* (Leeds: Peepal Tree Press, 2000).

66 M. Carter, *Poems of resistance from British Guiana* (London: Lawrence & Wishart, 1954).

67 Artist's statement, 2006.

3 Mutual temporal ground

Us and them

A rough survey of art in the Caribbean and its diaspora might result in the conclusion that much of the twentieth century, and the present situation, is dominated by a debate on art canons and canonisation. This would be evidenced in the vocabulary of the range of artists who have declared themselves pushed to the margins of art history, those seeking 'inclusion' and 'remembrance', and demanding 'visibility'. This practice goes further than the drive to set oneself up as an artist, with an audience and patrons, and other markers of achievement. It is distinguished by a concern with the terms of canonicity: the simultaneously physical and visual collecting of art and artists in a way that confers status upon them. To be included in the canon, and situated at its centre, is to occupy the place of the best and most representative known to the history of art. But all such places are temporary and not without contestation.

Indeed, the canon as a mechanism for legitimising the artistic past has become prone to intensive critique in art history as a discipline. After the deluge, such concerns have recently lessened in Britain where I teach and research art history. There is a general sense of the 'canon debate' as something that has already happened, and so deserves little further attention. This is an attitude I became conscious of when preparing to speak in the Caribbean on the topic of art canons in 2004.[1] Colleagues then saw me about to make a long journey only to deliver a paper focused on an apparently rather outdated inquiry. It was probably meant to be supportive, encouraging even, when I was told that however anachronistic the canon debate may seem now, nonetheless *they* [academics and artists in the Caribbean] have to go through that, just the same as *we* did'.[2]

It would be too easy to accept from this passing remark that countering or even 'firing' the canon should be passé for some people, and yet pressing news for others. So it is worth unpicking the supposition that debating the canon is something that has already happened in the discipline of art history, that it is over and done with, and should not need revisiting. That attitude hints at where and when art history is thought to be centred as a discipline. It is a parochial suggestion that a brief tendency shown in Britain is representative of the life of the discipline as a whole, while those discussing canons of art today with any seriousness, should simply catch up.

A larger picture may be drawn of art history and the Caribbean on the basis of this attitude to canons. I have begun to assemble this by way of some objections, which are derived from the detail presented in this chapter. First, there is a need to reject the view that canon debates in Britain led to concrete achievements, and that they resemble a success story and a kind of great leap forward worthy of praise. The overall view that I present of British 'multiculturalist' progress in art history at least, is to be treated much like any other myth of progress. Exploding that myth of success in British art has to be tempered by the need to defend multiculturalism, or 'convivial multiculture' as Paul Gilroy has named it, from the current criticism to which it has been subjected.[3] As such, I am at pains to make transparent that older patterns of exclusion from the art historical canon, even after the event of substantial even turbulent critique of the canon, are capable of being reproduced. Techniques of exclusion and marginalisation are in the habit of reappearing in new, perhaps less easily contestable forms. If this undermines faith in canonicity itself as some sort of lasting, once-and-for-all 'redemption' of the marginalised, and leads to questions about suitable alternatives, then so be it. A second objection I would lay at the notion that art history of the Caribbean is dragging behind the times. This is the unacceptable view of Caribbean anachronism that I have broached throughout this book – as though debates about canons of art had never taken place in the Caribbean before now. Not only does this set up an 'us and them' divide, of two art histories with nothing much in common, but it is also a distinction too casually made, and without the benefit of comparing the regions of the transnational Caribbean where struggles around canonisation have condensed.

This chapter aims to unsettle these perspectives of absolute difference and anachronism by emphasising the historical pervasiveness of concerns over canons in the transnational Caribbean. I ask what is at stake when the canon idea is put at the centre of analysis. This is a matter about why concerns over canonical inclusion emerge at all – an attempt to explain why there is a desire for self-definition in British and Caribbean settings: why the 'canon drive'? In each space it is linked to the mobilisation of difference as a political category and a perception that canonicity is equal to the overcoming of exclusion within democratic space. As I show, it is good to know what special character this has taken comparatively; how it might be changing; and how it may be changed. The presiding motivation is to tackle the assumption about a time-lag or delay between the two regions – the Caribbean and Britain – and to see this ideology for what it is. An authentic transnational art history may only emerge after killing off this distorted temporality. The idea that 'we've been through that' is hardly neutral. It rehearses the questionable notion of Britain's academy forever taking the lead. Considering this to be a problem about historical time will allow a view of the possibilities and obstacles around the historical remembrance of artists in both settings. A simple swapping of notes, from one region to the next, and back and forth in time, has implicit benefits for investigating how canon questions about art history and the Caribbean have been raised.

I do not attempt to reconstruct a Caribbean art story in toto. Rather, I am drawn to a particular moment when art history as a discipline was first seriously regarded as a crucial part of the institutional apparatus of Caribbean nation building. Discourses of nationhood are associated with racial and ethnic difference in both the Caribbean and Britain and so provide a running thread. In the immediate period of Independence in the English-speaking Caribbean, concerns about cultural representation, diversity and inclusion took centre stage. The context of the late 1960s and 1970s Guyana is instructive for what happened in Britain in the 1980s, and up to the present. On each side of the Atlantic there are formations that broadly articulate canon debates to matters of national identity. Theirs is a shared analytical space for canonising processes. From a transatlantic view may be spied those contemporary interests in the discipline where attempts to assemble inclusive canons of art history are tried and critiqued. It shows where some important comparative territory lies in a field of political thinking which entwines the transnational Caribbean.

The meeting that I attended in Trinidad was a forceful introduction to why proposals for an understanding of the 'cross-culturalism' of Caribbean cultural practices are so fraught. They have firm antecedents in practices of resistance to colonial rule, and the desire for national and often regional community, which are sublimated to questions of culture.[4] I am concerned to show that canon debates for art of the Caribbean and its diaspora are likely to carry on being fraught, and not only for historical reasons. Revising or reassembling a canon – a new canon, even a counter-canon – necessarily involves a process of selection that is also a process of exclusion. The representation of historical time in the form of the canon operates as a legitimation of artists and artworks, and the ability to control it is a locus of power for the discipline. A politics of time must be concerned therefore to show how the canon is appropriated, and under what conditions the struggle for control of the canon takes the form of resistance and acquiescence. If the canon derives its power from contingent historical conditions, then an art history of the transnational Caribbean is bound to the task of making these conditions transparent. Consequently, the question of whether there is a canon for art of the Caribbean is perhaps less significant than the need to understand the circumstances under which this has come to be at issue, and for whom. The presentation of any such canon has to go along with the will to justify how it is assembled, according to what priorities and pressures, and against what difficulties and what obstacles.

But even more is demanded of a transparent self-evaluation of canons in the field of the transnational Caribbean. As I have argued, this focuses on the anachronistic character imputed to the region's art history. There is a well recognised need to untangle the complexity of cultural, ethnic or racial difference in the negotiation surrounding art canons generally. An additional demand on analysis of canons is to highlight the agency of time, which is a crucial agent in the differencing that takes place through canonisation. Canons are assembled on the basis of temporal parameters. The supposition that the Caribbean and Britain are disconnected, and that the former is anachronistic for the latter, is one such example of how historical time is appropriated as a marker of value. The effort to reverse this situation is concerned with seeing the Caribbean and Britain as coeval, and as not only situated in the same time, but also in the same space. It is a problem of transnational contingency: a problem of seeing more clearly the line or axis that serves as the mutual ground between the Caribbean and Britain.

Denis Williams and post-Independence art history

A long-running, intense interest in the concept of creolisation in the Caribbean offers a strong record of concerns with the canon – concerns that emerged only in the mainstream of art history elsewhere during the later twentieth century. At the level of scholarship, accounts of creolisation have amounted to a description of the diverse racial, ethnic and cultural elements that distinctively comprise the Caribbean. Yet they also address a liberal concern for representation of this diversity that is familiar from critiques of the art historical canon. Accounts of creolisation were initially fixed on distilling the cultural character of the Caribbean as a geographical zone, comprised of territories that held certain affinities that went beyond their de jure status as colonies. These were located in aspects of a diverse heritage drawn from common patterns of displacement and localisation. Notably, art making was not considered as significant, since this was associated more with European cultural values, rather than everyday scenes of resistance and the negotiated forms of culture in plantation societies. When scholarly models of creolisation were articulated to political visions of nation building, their critical function was enlarged and the category of fine art was inserted. During decolonisation, the notion of cultural community – which was embedded in models of creolisation – was increasingly envisaged as a political goal. In the process, culture and the models on offer for explaining its Caribbean forms, became a political commodity. The idea of 'creole nationalism' emerged at the intersection of the study of culture and the political desire for an independent Caribbean.[5]

Chapter 4, focusing on the South Asian diaspora in the Caribbean, explores how official stipulations for 'creole nationalism' would elevate some forms of difference – namely reified ethnic ones, identified for their African origins – to be more contextually valuable and legitimate than others. This chapter, however, begins with a look at what preceded this discontent. The designation of roles to ethnicity and difference in the building of anti-colonial, creole nationalism closely informs the cultural politics of art historiography after Guyana's Independence in 1966. In attempting to distil aspects of this art historical debate that bear relevance for the canon, it is worth identifying the contribution of one thinker in particular. Denis Williams was remarkable in granting extended attention to questions of difference in the context of art historical method. In this particular context of ideas about the architecture of a post-Independence art history for the Caribbean, Williams's work may be drawn into a larger discussion of canons of visual representation that moves forward to also consider Britain.

Denis Williams was both an artist and an art historian and, professionally, occupied a range of further roles. Only the most scant details of his career were known to me before I first went to Guyana in 2005.[6] I knew of his training at London's Camberwell School of Art during 1946–48, before working as a painter and fine art teacher from 1950 at the Slade and the Central School of Art (now Central St Martins). I had also read about his success in 1955 when he was a prize-winner after Lucien Freud in the Daily Express Young Artists' Exhibition.[7] That Denis Williams was well respected in Britain is suggested by the early support he received from the painter and writer, Wyndham Lewis, who secured for him a solo exhibition in 1950 at the prestigious gallery, Gimpel Fils, and wrote admiringly about his work. The biographer Paul O'Keeffe claims that Lewis also found Williams his job at Central,[8] stepping out of character to extend him an extraordinary favour: 'Rarely did Lewis act in anybody's exclusive interest but his own.'[9] A more detailed account of Williams's career in London would show how he interacted with a range of figures of the post-war art establishment – Herbert Read, Roger Hilton – and how he shared a studio with Francis Bacon, even painting on his cast-off canvases.[10]

The scantiness of the surviving record on Denis Williams is not peripheral to understanding and historicising him. Histories of the life and work of such Caribbean subjects are characterised by their thin coverage, their fragmentation through division into national borders, by discrepancies of regional emphasis, and by blind spots and silences. Williams's move away from the colonial metropole in 1957 to the Sudan and then to Nigeria, at the beginning of an academic career in archaeology and anthropology, hardly explains why mainstream art history has seemed to evade the matter of his importance. It also fails to account for why an artist well known in London in the 1950s should so suddenly have become absent from memory of that decade. More specifically, I am concerned with how Williams's contribution to art historical writing in the Caribbean has been overlooked. In the area of considerations around the themes of culture, difference and artistic, as well as national community, Williams found ways to show how such themes intersect with historiographic ones common to the discipline more broadly as he saw it.

His work in this area can be read principally in the series of four lectures that he gave in Georgetown, Guyana in January 1969. They carry a serious argument on the historical contingency of cultural forms, encapsulated in the following suggestion:

> Guyanese society might be seen, then, as a complex plurality in continual process of achieving a complex singularity – a singularity which is always itself open to change. By virtue of the action of the several catalytic elements ceaselessly modifying and qualifying it, the nature of this singularity cannot remain static. This could hardly be otherwise, since the effects of the various elements which at any moment determine the content and fabric of this singularity can never be predicted.[11]

Williams's general claim was that 'the nature of the human presence … changes, and with this also changes the nature of the culture generated'. He emphasised 'the human presence' as a transformative, constitutive element of historical change, made possible by the division he saw between the human subject and culture. He therefore recommended that the cultural ought to be 'bracketed' or 'reduced', that is, thought about through what Husserl had called the phenomenological *epoché* – the suspension of reflective knowledge of the world in favour of a 'presuppositionless' 'science of essences' (*eine Wesenswissenschaft*).[12] This required that he fix his attention on what Husserl termed the 'zero-point' (*Nullpunkt*)[13] of experience, taking the body to provide the only means by which human being is possible at all, and the starting point and ground for all thought. It was a means for Williams to put aside assumptions about the make-up of Guyanese society and to get behind the hegemony of colonial ideas about its failure to constitute a sovereign society. This was a fundamental turn to ontological questions about the human bodies that peopled the Guyanese reality, and by extension the larger decolonising Third World. As he would write about the role of the artist in Third World countries, 'In so far as the Third World is a substantial reality, it is a reality without a distinctive or pervasive cultural presence.'[14] In so doing, Williams worked toward Husserl's famous declaration to 'return to things themselves', or as Merleau-Ponty took to mean:

> to return to that world which precedes knowledge, of which knowledge always *speaks*, and in relation to which every scientific schematization is an abstract and derivative sign-language, as is geography in relation to the countryside in which we have learned beforehand what a forest, a prairie or a river is.[15]

Williams went on to disseminate his ideas on the value of phenomenological 'bracketing' to audiences in early 1970s Guyana. The breadth of his
thought can be measured by the range of possibilities he suggested for cultural
interpretation. A closer reading of culture would follow after freeing the
concept from claims of immanence (in which categories of culture and being
are conflated), and in the face of cultural and racial essentialism. On this basis,
he theorised a sense of what might be understood of culture once the term
is detached from 'presence'. The general theme of Williams's writings became
that of how to articulate the dynamism of bodies as agents of historical and
cultural change by virtue of their differences of ancestry. This led to a descrip-
tive interest in the material presence of the peoples who had occupied Guyana
prior to European contact, and the complex interactions that might be had
between this and the ancestry of its many ethnicities.

By foregrounding the distinctions between ancestry and culture in particular, his lectures on the arts were designed as a beacon for illuminating the
challenges and dilemmas of the newly created state of Guyana, focusing on
the accepted wisdom of the nation as a territory or 'land of six peoples'.[16] Once
formal Independence had been achieved, the sorts of inter-ethnic tension that
Guyana had always faced, often condensing as political violence, took a new
shape. In this uncertain setting, Williams's sought to historicise the period's
prevalent anxieties, and to signal its political future through analysis of
creativity and the arts. One example of this is the way he tackled the question
of modernity through the study of the prehistory of the geographical area of
the Guianas. In his posthumously compiled and published study *Prehistoric
Guiana*[17] he stressed that different prehistoric groups lived together peace-
fully, largely along the north-west Guiana coast, and would exchange ideas
and technologies.

If the general picture Williams presented was a kind of idyllic multiculturalism, then this has to be explained against the background of Guyana's
struggle to contain fragmentation along ethnic lines, under the sign of a
'co-operative republic'.[18] At the same time, the complex edifice of archae-
ological procedures represented by Williams's book held a single, critical
purpose: to gather the resources and to grasp the precursors for a national
unity of 'ideas and technologies'. However remote in historical time were those
early Amerindian societies, Williams nonetheless would emphasise what he
called the 'spiritual ancestors', in whose footsteps, he wrote, 'There simply is
no alternative route to a national self-image.'[19]

During the 1960s in Guyana, that path had led through the notion of
culture, with the meaning of the term itself undergoing an evolution. Its
status changed from a political commodity and normalising concept during
the country's seismic shift from colonial dependence to official nation-state,
later to become the floating signifier of a sustainable national future during the

moment of immediate Independence. In a debate about the likely direction of Guyana's cultural development, Denis Williams provided a way of thinking about the critical potential held by difference, in terms of a diversity of historical, ethnic and cultural legacies that would contribute to new forms of social being. Adding to the tally of 'six peoples' a further category of 'non-race', he examined the figure of the many ancestored 'pork-knocker', the name given to independent prospectors for gold and diamonds that frequented the country's alluvial plains in the rural interior. As he explained: 'It is this person who, in the fact of miscegenation, is the symbol among us of that process of cultural catalysis [...] which I hold to be the distinguishing characteristic of all New World societies.'[20] Such pride in what had for so long been accorded the derogatory, even legalistic term, 'miscegenation', stood at the centre of Williams's demand for recognition of the value of Guyana's mixed ancestry. Surveying the path ahead of Guyana's continuing struggle for national unity through the 'cultural catalysis' of difference, he argued that the unfinished project of decolonisation most of all demanded expert study. Toward a futurology of unity and difference he wrote: 'To the naked eye it certainly seems that there is no trace of synthesis on any fundamental level of Guyanese culture; our cultural affiliations remain discrete and disparate – a conclusion which we must accept until such a time as scholarship produces evidence to the contrary.'[21]

Williams's interests encompassed a range of academic disciplines that in complementary ways were pressed into the service of his philosophical aims. How he approached the relation among these with reference to Guyana and the epistemological ground covered by the country's institutional infrastructure is revealing of his priorities. The struggles over nationhood and Williams's endeavours toward an 'indigenous' archaeology of Guyana were enabled and underscored by several institutions of art which he either championed or had a hand in building. It is remarkable that just three of these – the Walter Roth Museum of Archaeology and Anthropology, the Burrowes School of Art, and the National Gallery at Castellani House – provided ample space for the modern apparatus of museology, archaeology, ethnography, anthropology, connoisseurship, curatorship and studio practice. Williams demonstrated technical ability and leadership in them all, but it was his understanding of the work that they shared out that is most significant. As with his lectures of 1969, he sought to clarify how the notion of artistic modernism could be given concrete relevance in a Caribbean setting through the idea of nationhood and 'self-image'. A context was thereby created for certain objects as works of art (for their collection, display, teaching and research), presented as national artistic heritage. Alongside this was the place of the cultural artefact, with prominence given to items of Amerindian origin, as elaborated in *Prehistoric Guiana*. At the Walter Roth Museum, the distinctions between these two were marshalled together.

Williams took a cardinal role in the purposeful objectifying of Guyana's national aesthetic knowledge, ensuring that it was 'ring-fenced' by a common set of institutions. His radicality can be gauged by the way he would encounter the disciplinary divisions within the Old World academy, as he might have termed it, showing these in fact to be at odds with Guyanese interests. In this sense, his work recommends Guyana as an exemplary setting for clarifying the comparative ways in which art history has struck its enduring pact with the nation state. He showed how to privilege the art of the nation, defining its character through the notion of shared heritage, while calling for art historical understanding of the national to recognise the peculiarities of the Guyanese setting. It was an exhortation that has raised some searching questions. Where there is a strident political desire for multicultural community, how might this aspiration inform the intimate relationship between art history and nation building? How can disciplinary practices, archives and modes of collecting, classification and display become articulated to yearnings for nationhood? How might the concomitant practices of art history, anthropology and archaeology serve adequately in imagining modern community? In what important respects does the task of locating these disciplines in Guyana differ historically from their establishment at the former colonial metropole? What contradictions arise in considering the important differences that figure in the Guyanese setting? In designing art historical approaches to the special circumstances of Guyana, what insights and difficulties emerge?

In the face of an inherited disciplinary apparatus, Williams did not simply (re)build or replicate a national infrastructure for art history and its adjacent disciplines. Making a clear distinction between the values of the Old World and the New he seized the opportunity for a deep questioning of their useful-ness, showing the courage to pose questions about the status of art history once transposed to a Caribbean context. The results outline what might be called a sort of 'raceless pork-knocker' art history, which, like the quintes-sentially miscegenated 'human in infinite process of catalysis'[22] evades being defined by way of a single scholarly tradition or intellectual ancestry. This indicates how questions of the roles and possible futures for art history are inseparable from the need to explore perspectives on disciplinary and insti-tutional knowledge production as such. Williams seemed to anticipate the soothsayers of 1980s art history who declared a crisis in the discipline.[23] His rhetorical move was to suggest that if there is a crisis in the nation state, and a crisis in, or of, art history, then the two are rather compatible in understanding one another. In contemplating the moment of crisis that has often been claimed of independent Guyana, Williams had the insight and political will to illustrate art history as especially well suited to the task of thinking through his country's dilemmas and deep uncertainties. It would offer the means for exploring the parallels and connective tissue between that national context and the production of knowledge. He provided a starting point for analysis of the ways in which Guyana and the wider Caribbean might be shown as particularly fertile ground for the task of considering the mainstream of art history in the Western academy.

British Black Art

The questions raised by Denis Williams during Guyana's post-Independence period, found parallels in the cultural politics of the Caribbean Artists Movement (CAM), a generation of West Indian artists and writers in Britain who grouped together during 1966–72. Yet these insights and experience would be hardly registered by the subsequent generation of artists of Caribbean descent in Britain who emerged during the 1980s. It is understandable why Guyanese art historiography of the previous two decades was difficult to recall in Britain, owing to the geographical distance. But it is harder to accept that the developments around CAM, which happened in Britain, could so easily be missed. It was perhaps in view of this omission that Anne Walmsley wrote in 1992 of the need for CAM to be 'fully documented and made public'.[24] Walmsley claimed to have 'deliberately avoided theoretical analysis of CAM, in the belief that this would constrict and distort it'. Taken as a whole, however, the documentation that underwrote her stance is inherently and complexly theoretical. It made transparent how the outlooks and common concerns of CAM members were often focused on the movement's own historiography. This was evidenced in their numerous meetings and correspondence, and was manifest in their art and writing. In this sense, by placing the matter of historical remembrance at its centre, Walmsley's group biography can also be considered a continuation of the CAM project, extending the influence of the movement beyond its 1972 dissolution.

Walmsley's study of CAM offers a starting point for a discussion about the contingencies of historiography and artists' groupings represented by contemporary contexts for negotiating the canon and the art historical record. During the 1980s, in Britain, prior to her account, there was little remembrance of artists of the Caribbean who were active in contesting Britain's post-war art history during the previous two decades. Artists, mainly of the second generation of Caribbean migration, made much of what they shared with artists of several other diasporas – largely those of Africa and South Asia, and to a lesser extent East Asia and the Middle East. Their commonalities were represented in a range of art forms, including filmmaking, photography, performance, painting and drawing, installation and other media. Like CAM, this younger generation was at pains to reflect on their situation within a historical frame, and so invested heavily in historical inscription. Preoccupied with their promotion and recording, around and through their art, they organised together to curate exhibitions, publish, write about art, and to archive the evidence.

It is instructive to regard this broad range of practices primarily as an assault on the art history canon as a record or measure of contents, and given definition by selected elements of the artistic past. For artists of several diasporas in Britain who have claimed exclusion from the canon – which resembles for them the mainstream of a British, national art history – the 1980s has to be considered as the period of the most ebullient statements of this kind. The consequences for the present day, and for a discussion of the Caribbean, rest in the detail of how many of the artists concerned have seen fit to target the 'canonical' art environment, namely the gallery network and art criticism. By so doing, they have taken artistic activity, or what has been called 'arts activism',[25] as the basis for a sort of canon 'counter-formation', as artist Keith Piper explained in 1984:

> You see, today what we are looking for is a Black visual aesthetic, a way of making works that is exclusive to us, in the same way as our musicians have invented many musical forms which are totally 'Black'. We need a Black visual aesthetic because as Black artists we still depend on forms and ideas about art borrowed from European art history. It is that history, and the dominance of its values over us, which we need to reject because they cannot serve us in our struggle.[26]

In Piper's statement, we can identify an artist for whom the authority of 'European art history' had to be discarded, being thought synonymous with a colonising force that entrapped 'Black' artists into dependence, and was a particular obstacle in their 'struggle'. Piper was more intent by contrast on a reverse kind of exclusion, a self-selected one, which shaped the early years of his practice during what became regarded as the 'critical decade' of the 1980s.[27] With fellow artist Eddie Chambers, he organised the first 'Black Art' exhibition at Wolverhampton Art Gallery in 1981,[28] and a year later used the 'First National Black Art Convention' at Wolverhampton Polytechnic in order to form the BLK Group, a collection of art students and recent graduates from the West Midlands that staged exhibitions from 1982 to 1984.[29] They were followed by a run of largely group 'survey' exhibitions of topic- or issue-focused art under the sign of 'Black Art', closely defined as made by black artists to speak to a black community and address 'black issues'. Such events included reference – frequently exemplified in their titles – to an ongoing drive for self-definition, and a sense of needing to drastically intervene against racism. Making this possible was a curatorial concern to name, chart and document an excluded black presence, while highlighting the institutional obstacles in the way of these artists' wider and lasting recognition.[30]

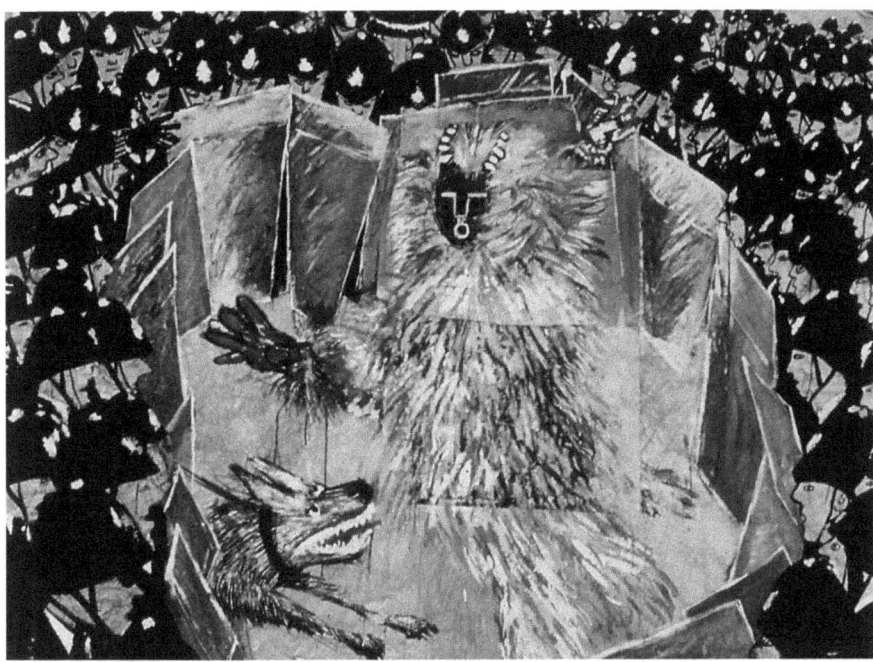

Tam Joseph, *Spirit of the Carnival* (1988), acrylic on paper, 86 × 64 cm.   **14**

'Black Art' stood to emphasise some leading, related themes. It drew its imagery from the facts of racial violence and disadvantage faced by communities of immigrants to Britain and their descendants. In particular, it signalled the fraught matter of national belonging they were having to negotiate at first hand. A single work might touch on one or more of such themes, such as the circumstances of young black Britons, in Tam Joseph's *UK School Report* of 1984,[31] which uncovers the roots of disaffection and 'deviance' in the passage through school and college. His *Spirit of the Carnival* of 1988 (figure 14),[32] responded to mistreatment by the British establishment, visualising a reminder of the police violence and clashes at the annual celebrations in London's Notting Hill.[33]

'Black Art' themes would be handled in other ways, most notably by Claudette Johnson, Joy Gregory, Veronica Ryan, Chila Burman, Ingrid Pollard, Lubaina Himid and others, who led many of the group 'Black Art' shows. A central strand was their robust, often disturbing, introduction of femininity as a complicating aspect of difference, using topics of domesticity and intimacy to confront normative ideas about family, kinship and British nationhood. The complicities of popular imaging with racism and stereotype became a signature concern in the multimedia work of Sonia Boyce, such as her *From Someone Else's Fear Fantasy to Metamorphosis* of 1987 (figure 15).[34] A four-part

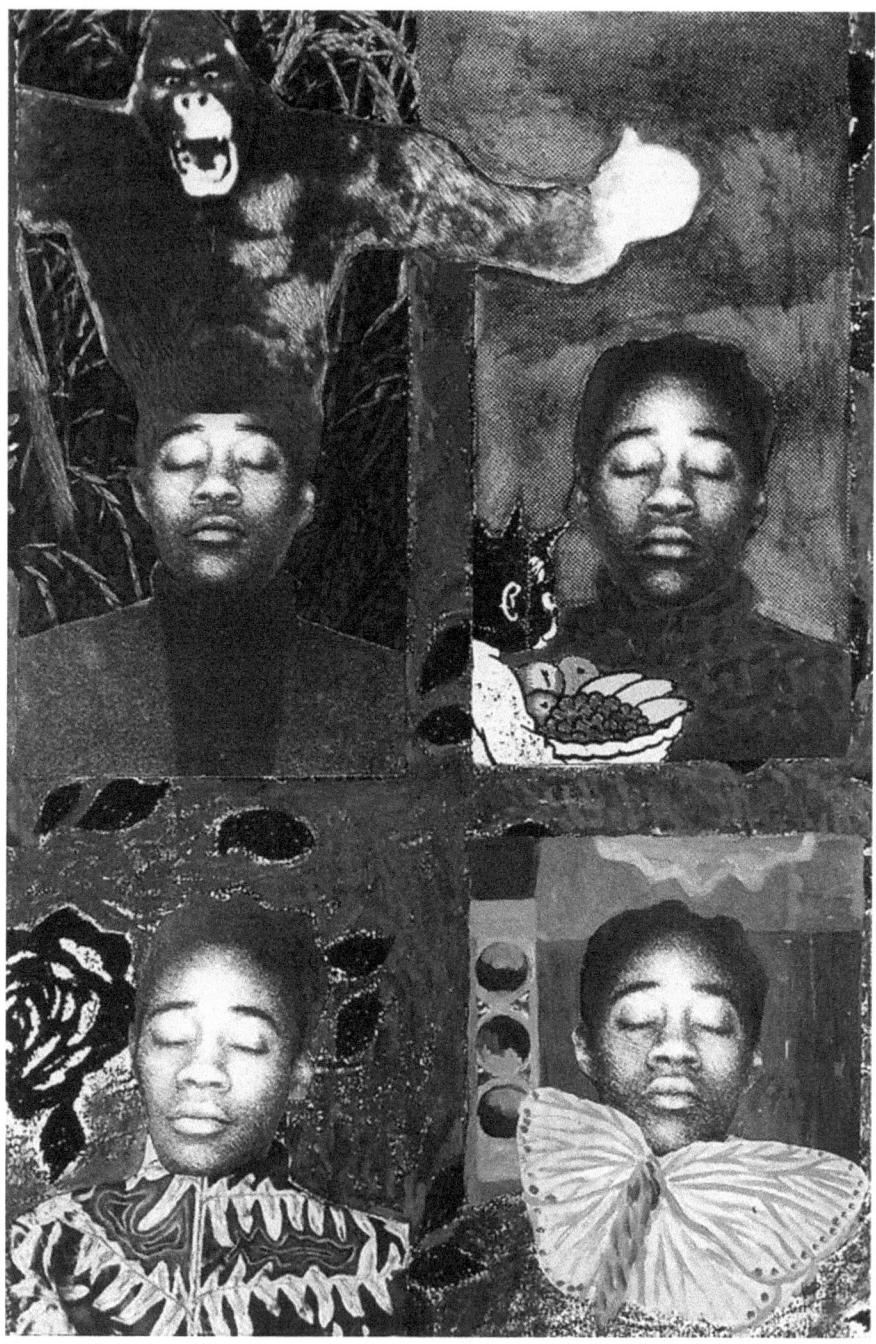

15   Sonia Boyce, *From Someone Else's Fear Fantasy to Metamorphosis* (1987), mixed media on photograph.

self-portrait, with montage and sketched additions, it brought satire to the double oppression of black women by their prevalent fetishism in film, advertising and photography. Boyce's preference at that time for figurative pastel drawing would show how women artists could develop radical positions at variance with those of their male counterparts. The frequently collaborative practices of women refused to replicate the masculinism of those such as Piper and Chambers, questioning their sense of the artist as an autonomous male author,[35] while refusing to rehearse a comparable rhetoric, often drawn from the US Black Arts Movement and Pan-Africanism.[36]

British 'Black Art' had the key characteristic of close involvement with artists of the South Asian and other diasporas,[37] a development that distinguishes the British context from better known formations of artistic 'blackness' elsewhere, such as the United States. It saw the 'Black' concept as a political identity (rather than as an indicator of African descent) being embraced in a widely enjoined critique of the canon. Some of the women named here were of this kind, together with a group that included Zarina Bhimji, Allan de Souza, Shaheen Merali, Sunil Gupta and Sutapa Biswas. The painting and collage by Biswas, *Housewives with Steak Knives* of 1986 became iconic of this 'Asian' participation.[38] Its loose canvas carries a modern-day, multi-limbed *Kali,* with henna-stained hands and protruding tongue, who indicates her status as a goddess of destruction by threatening decapitation with kitchen utensils. A necklace of heads, including the right-wing politician Enoch Powell and other white males, marks out the targets of her aggression (while Margaret Thatcher is conspicuously absent). By way of such 'Indian' references, Biswas made it obvious that 'Black Art', in Britain at least, could come from many ethnic quarters and be a common focus for mobilising a counter-canon.

My interest in artists of Caribbean backgrounds in Britain hinges on this unique assembling of artists of many ethnicities, including those of Asian and African descent. It is instructive, however, to promote a keen sense of the important differences among the voices and positions of that historical moment. Such diversity has generally passed unnoticed. But these artists were not all pursuing the same political goal of a separate 'Black visual aesthetic', as expressed in Piper's statement, and consequently 'Black Art' was far from being an agreed-upon label.

The position taken by Rasheed Araeen, a Pakistan-born member of the Black Panthers and founder of *Black Phoenix* magazine, in which he published a rousing 'Black Manifesto',[39] made this obvious. The publication was later incorporated into the international journal *Third Text*,[40] and with Araeen as its founding editor, its readers could compare his views on the situation of 'Black' artists, with a range of other outlooks, the oppositionalism of Piper and Chambers included. Embracing the term 'Black Art' and arguing forcefully for a militant critique of the canon, Araeen saw 'Black Art' as closely bound up with the history of artistic modernism – indeed as continuous with it – no matter how much this was overlooked in the art historical record. The sort of opposition to the canon which claimed that 'Black Art' came out of a discrete cultural history, somehow removed from a shared modern story, was for him a denial of its provenance and continuing connections. He explained, with a note of concern, in 1988:

> The term 'black art' is now being commonly used by the black community as well as by people in Britain in general. But this common usage is often a misuse, as far as the work that might be called 'black art' is concerned. It may be a convenient term to refer to the work of black artists, but it also implies that their work is or should be different from the mainstream of modern culture. ... 'Black art', if this term must be used, is in fact a specific historical development within contemporary art practices and has emerged directly from the joint struggle of Asian, African and the Caribbean people against racism, and the art work itself explicitly refers to that struggle.[41]

Despite the diversity of perspectives among the 'Black Art' artists, it was common by the mid-1980s for commentary to refer to this community as if they stood, with consensus, for a single purpose. However, an explicit language of resistance, typical of 'Black Art', was not evident in all art made by those who found themselves marginalised. More gravely, given what overlapped about their aims, it was generally ignored that they had only identified themselves as 'Black' in response to their shared circumstances of racism and exclusion from art history. This showed the tendency for canons to oversimplify, to discourage complex, plural or fragmented narratives. It had the consequence that certain artists were being matched with others on the basis of ethnic difference, regardless of their individually held interests, and ultimately led to the frustration of their demands on the canon.

Above all, in 1980s Britain, there were effectively two leading paradigms of 'Black Art' adopted by those who claimed that the mainstream canon was problematic, marginalising and exclusionary. Piper and his immediate colleagues offered the strategy of declaring an absolute separation from the 'European values' which alienated them, declaring their own cultural parameters in the face of exclusion. Araeen's approach, by contrast, was to assert a more nuanced stance. He would claim that the presence of 'Afro-Asian' artists was integral to the art of the twentieth century, and to British modernism in particular. It was not 'different from the mainstream of modern culture', but constitutive of it: a 'constitutive insider' as compared to the outsider or 'other' whose exclusion was essential to defining the main story (on the basis that the canon necessarily excludes). This argument aligned the contribution of 'Black Art' to a tradition of the avant-garde, showing it be part of the same critique of the dominant narrative of canonical modernism that has come to characterise the more plural and fragmented development of art in the later twentieth century. As such, Araeen would voice his discontent with the way that both the 'oppositionalism' of Black Art figures such as Piper and Chambers, *and* the 'institutional indifference' of the mainstream failed to recognise the deeper value of difference. The pressure applied by both of these worked to under-mine avant-garde aims, and to distort art history.

Managing British differences

While there were contrasting positions on the whole question of difference in art history, it was the oppositional attitude, fixed on the 'Black Art' concept, which attracted the most official attention. Through the BLK Group events and Lubaina Himid's show at the ICA, there was generally greater exposure of protest-based work. Yet this offered a line of attack on the canon of British art that was easily incorporated by art institutions. When it was taken literally as a licence to marginalise these artists further, their separatist posture posed a paradox. It encouraged the very spirit of generalisation which had excluded all artists, of whatever 'ethnic' background, from the white mainstream, and in turn had become the focus of artists' protests.[42]

Initially the sort of gallery and exhibition spaces that 'Black Art' was given were mostly separate from mainstream commercial or prominent public galleries. There had been so-called 'community-based' projects such as the Greater London Council anti-racist mural project of 1985,[43] and places like the Black Art Gallery and 198 Gallery with a narrow remit to promote 'ethnic art'. But these were less well known and little accessed by a general art audience and so attracted the criticism that these artists were being deliberately kept apart from their white peers.[44] The support first given in 1988 by the promi-nent Whitechapel Gallery carried the association of its location in an area of London's East End which has traditionally been a place of immigration. Such adaptations by art institutions toward the end of the 1980s, described in the then official vocabulary of 'ethnic minority arts', served to distance artists from other, more valued spaces of national display.

On the surface, blanket promotion of 'ethnic artists', regardless of how they each identified themselves, would seem to suit the oppositionalist attitude. Yet, those like Eddie Chambers were angrily disappointed that the decade of the 1980s was so short-lived, since its properly 'critical' period of bona fide 'Black Art' exhibitions and 'arts activism' ended in 1986.[45] Those with funda-mentally radical investments in 'Black Art' would be grouped together with artists who were not party to such debates through arts programmes and art commentary. And in public life more widely, the growing status of the notion of 'Black Britishness' came to be applied to mean all 'non-whites' in general, thereby losing its meaning as a term of political affiliation. As Araeen had forewarned, when the priority for arts policies became fixed on redistributing resources to minority ethnicities in general, this would frustrate ambitions for wider 'visibility'. Rather than responding to direct arguments about the racial dimension of the art canon, or the conventions of the art system, or the concomitant ethnicising values in national art historiography, the trend became one of misrecognising the constitutive role of black people within art history, and confining their status to an ethnic 'add-on'.[46]

The contribution of academic thought during the late 1980s is, at first sight, an analytical reflection and clarification of the two positions shared among practitioners of 'Black Art'. It was probably conceived in such a way as to reconcile them. It dwelt less on the trope of blackness and particular approaches to art practice, in favour of attention to the field of cultural production in general. Paul Gilroy, writing in 1988 from within the discipline of cultural studies, asserted the idea of a 'diaspora aesthetic', which was developed further by Stuart Hall in connection with Caribbean cinema,[47] by the curator and arts organiser Gilane Tawadros,[48] and academic Kobena Mercer. These thinkers took an ambivalent stance on the matter of difference and ethnicity. They produced what Ien Ang has noted of postcolonial intellectuals as their 'double focus'.[49] The 'diaspora aesthetic' idea was deemed more broadly applicable than 'Black Art', useful for understanding artists of any diaspora whatsoever, and above all designed to engage a positive change in their circumstances.

One line of this approach would find agreement with artists such as Piper. The 'diaspora aesthetic' partly stood for the idea that being diasporic indicates a fixed, easily identifiable experience typical of people of African, Asian and Caribbean descent alike, distinguishing them as a common group, with an essential character, somehow detached from changing circumstances. A second strand was a more properly analytical attitude, emphasising the style of 'diaspora culture' as a far more ambiguous phenomenon. This usage fleshed out Araeen's arguments about the more complex conjunctive role of diaspora subjects in the formation of artistic modernism. Yet the vocabulary chosen was unfamiliar to art history, and more at home in cultural studies and critical theory; its coming popularity and the lack of an alternative was a symptom perhaps of the relative neglect by the art history profession of artists of diverse backgrounds. This sense of the 'diaspora aesthetic' referred to the 'dialogic strategies and hybrid forms'[50] of diasporas, and 'the hybrid, transitory and always historically specific forms in which questions of "race" and ethnicity are articulated'.[51] Such commentary thereby turned away from essentialism, in order to characterise the diasporic as itself heterogeneous, and formed by contingency with history.[52]

Those initiatives from cultural theory altered the landscape of discussion by intervening in the factional schisms among the 'Black Art' interlocutors.

They also broke from the mechanistic, official language of 'ethnic minority arts'. Indeed, academic advocacy exerted particular influence on national organisations such as the Arts Council of England, as well as the national landscape of galleries and museums. It was a development that first caught my attention in 1995 as a student concerned to know what influence the academy might have on its adjacent institutions. I would ask how and why the 'diaspora aesthetic' concept achieved such currency. One observation is that it was deemed more satisfactory than the 'Black Art' idea, as the key to a more textured definition of social experience. The political and historical circumstances of those creative individuals who felt shunned by art institutions seemed to find recognition in the layers of writing that grew around this newly introduced concept. It articulated a rationale for their practices, affirming their value as products of their artists' biographies of migration, settlement, exclusion, resistance and continuity. As an intellectual development, talk of a 'diaspora aesthetic' promised a systematic look at what various creative people were making in their chosen field of cultural production. Further, it seemed to work as evidence and affirmation of their 'diaspora' lives. Artists, arts organisers, theorists and critics alike were now able to speak broadly about 'Black' cultural practices, from fine art to music, dress and popular culture, as all bearing a familial resemblance under the umbrella of 'diaspora'.

In the wake of this popularity among artists, public art institutions were quick to absorb criticism about exclusion and marginalisation. They began to consider more openly how best to grant artists support. By the 1990s, and with the founding of the publicly funded Institute of International Visual Arts (inIVA) in 1995,[53] the official language of promotion had dispensed entirely with the notion of 'ethnic arts', in favour of a firmly multiculturalist emphasis on 'diversity' and recognition of 'difference'.[54] It was similar to what had been around during the previous decade through the work of the Institute of Contemporary Arts,[55] and the connotations of the 'diaspora aesthetic'.

However, there was also apprehension about the nascent institutionalising of multiculturalism. This is nowhere better framed than in Valerie Brown's photo and graphic work, *Encounters* (figure 16), in which a white hand caresses some black buttocks above a fringe of enjoined hands.[56] I first wrote about this image as a visual comment on the fear of 'inter-racial' sex, and of miscegenation as the possible basis for a historical colour bar.[57] I should have taken into account that the icon that repeats along the fringe of the image is borrowed from the publications and letterhead of the (now defunct) Commission for Racial Equality. Brown's piece has far more to do with the suspicion that equality struggles in the arts would fail, so long as black artists move into the grasp of white-dominated institutions, only to become fascinating in a very one-sided way. *Encounters* hinted at how other artists felt about the official vocabulary of arts funding and promotion by the early 1990s. The associations

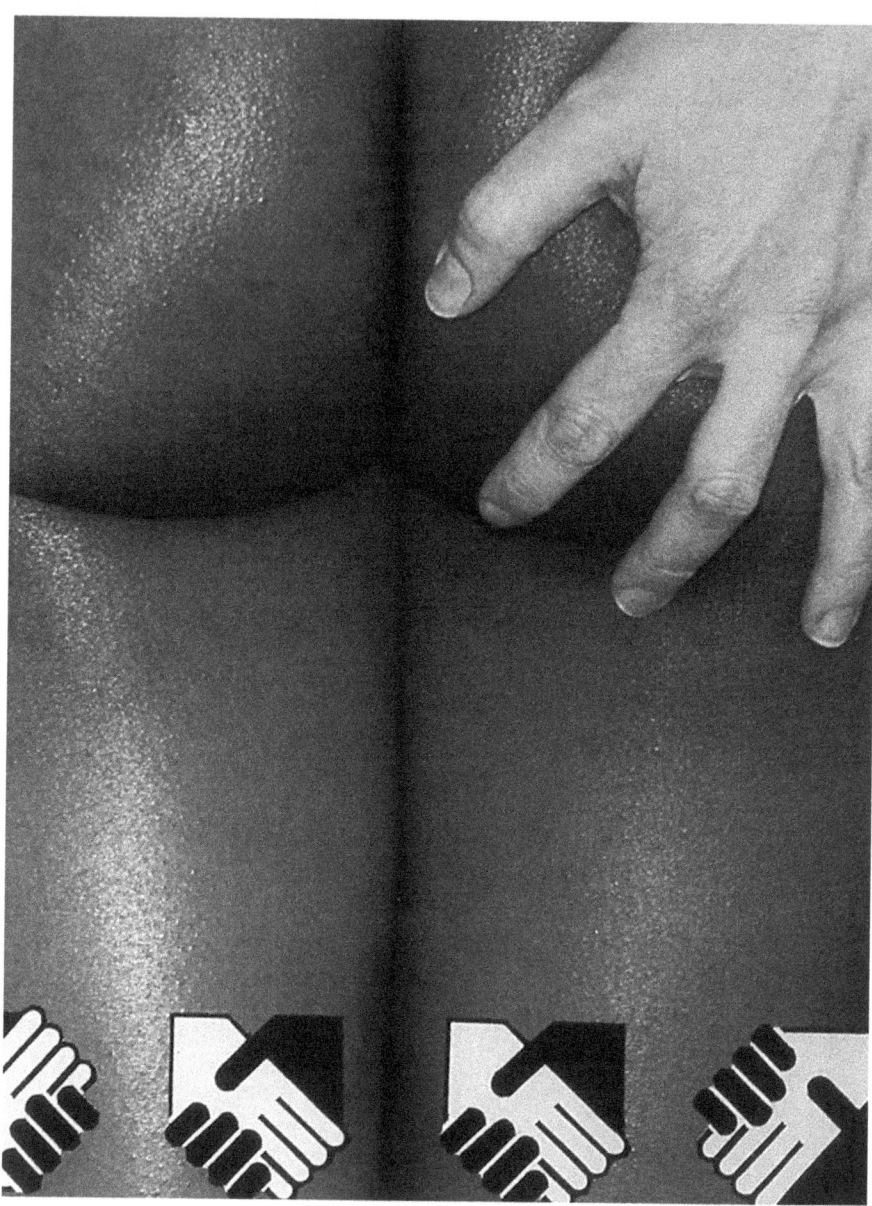

16   Valerie Brown, *Encounters* (from the series) (1991), colour photograph/montage.

around the 'diaspora aesthetic' concept were put to uses that failed to match up to the political ambitions of the 'Black Art' moment. It was an outcome that Araeen observed in 1994, writing that:

in the West, [multiculturalism] has been used as a cultural tool to ethnicise its non-white population in order to administer and control its aspirations for equality. It also serves as a smokescreen to hide the contradictions of a white society unable or unwilling to relinquish its imperial legacies. In this context one can understand the British fascination and celebration of cultural difference.[58]

By the following decade, multiculturalist agendas in the arts were widely institutionalised. They had become a priority for the renamed Arts Council England (ACE), under the policy that 'cultural diversity' with 'specific reference to ethnicity' ought to feature among the funding and job opportunities for artists and curators. Various studies by ACE and by independent scholars have documented this pattern since the year 2000, with a view to setting new policy goals. The largest venture in the post-millennium decade for ACE was begun in May 2003, when a national network of organisers was put in place to launch Decibel, an ACE initiative that lasted into 2008. It was directed to 'ethnic diversity resulting from postwar immigration, with a focus on arts and artists from African, Asian and Caribbean backgrounds' and which promised 'to profile arts practice … and to develop opportunities for increased access into the mainstream'.[59] But like the proposed ACE 'Year of Cultural Diversity', postponed from 2001 to 2002, rebranded as 'The Big Idea', and then subsequently scrapped, Decibel's agenda met with the criticism that it marked a 'current tendency towards a segregated visual arts sector'.[60] Despite its declared aims to ensure that 'the landscape is changing',[61] one critic noted that it 'has failed to spark debate about art world pathologies' typical of the 'institutional racism'[62] signalled in the 1999 Macpherson Report on the Stephen Lawrence Inquiry and the Race Relations (Amendment) Act.[63]

A less specifically targeted critique has been raised to address the sort of institutional change in Britain, experienced by artists of African, Asian and Caribbean backgrounds. One suggestion is that such change is proving to be little more than the refinement of the ability to 'manage' difference and artistic production, and to limit the possibilities for how artists may identify themselves. Kobena Mercer has suggested that such 'multicultural managerialism' and 'multicultural normalisation'[64] had fully taken hold by the end of the twentieth century. Then, ideas of diversity, heterogeneity and hybridity became accommodated under institutional conditions in which 'the subversive potential once invested in notions of hybridity has been subject to pre-millenial downsizing'.[65] Along supporting lines, artist and researcher Sonya Dyer has described in her report on 'artistic autonomy', written for the campaign group The Manifesto Club, '… the unhealthy pressure on artists and curators from non-white backgrounds to privilege their racial background above all else in relation to their practice'.[66]

Dyer's report adds to broader concerns about the adverse outcome of apparently radical sorts of cultural analysis in the area of art history. They seem to have achieved a more popular currency without any ensuing, substantive change. Out of sensitivity to this critique, major curatorial projects can be seen to have backed off a little, and greater care is being shown over privileging the 'racial background' of artists. Instead, exhibitions seem to be more about calling on artists to act as analysts of the problem that curators have encountered. They are given the platform to author a visual commentary on the curatorial pitfalls that may follow in challenging exclusion and marginalisation in the hegemonic spaces of art display. Artists are being asked not to foreground or embody 'race' so much as to highlight and undermine racism. Yet this preferred purpose for artists may also been seen as another, if lesser 'unhealthy pressure'. There appear to be fewer exhibitions that decouple artists from concerns with racism and 'race' altogether.

This situation is no different in kind from what Rasheed Araeen has described of the historical continuities that rest beneath the apparent reinvention of Britain's art system in recent decades. He detects a 'tyranny' located in ideas and modes of viewership which:

> have very little to do with the specificity of art and which have now been appropriated by art institutions that use them to reinforce their colonial idea of the Other. This has helped them redefine postcolonial artists as the new Other, but also predetermine their role in modern society. With the result that any art activity which does not conform to or defies this new definition is looked upon as inauthentic and is suppressed.[67]

On this view, the expectation that certain artists make works that are cultural evidence of their diaspora or postcolonial experience has utterly undermined their value. There is continued demand among mainstream audiences for evidence of a separate tradition of art-making, an Other to European modernism. The role of curatorial practice in formulating these relationships has been of central importance. When staged in terms of a multiculturalist approach to the issue of historical exclusion, curatorial contexts have succeeded in reinstating the ethnic and racial hierarchies that have historically configured the barriers to inclusion of much art discourse.

Araeen's intervention is compelling and a suitable measure for assessing the history of artists of Caribbean backgrounds. Their ambitions have time and again been frustrated by the infelicities and circumscriptions that follow from the contemporary language of display and remembrance. This leaves open the question of how art might offer a way of claiming sovereignty – how it might requisition some space of its own, despite the landscape of over-determined visual meaning that artists of the transnational Caribbean inhabit. It is increasingly difficult for artists to see how they might succeed in staging or prompting such resistance. In the art community more broadly, one response has been to simply speak out and make it clear that the multi-cultural 'mainstreaming' of attention to art is not the same as more widely reaching social, political and economic change. Winner of the 2003 Turner Prize, artist Grayson Perry has indicated that: 'There seems to be a very New Labour idea that if we rigorously ensure a numerically fair proportion of BME (black or minority ethnic) practitioners, then that will automatically facilitate social justice in the wider society. Hmm.'[68] Meanwhile, academics in the field of cultural policy studies have reduced their intervention to scepticism about whether the arts – more specifically arts funding – should have a conveniently measurable 'impact' at all.[69]

Canons and futures

Questioning the dominant canon of art history is a continuous project, and revealing of the still embattled beliefs invested in the discipline as a critical path for a wider social transformation. Whether these beliefs have been realised can be assessed on the basis of the recent shift away from interest in debating the canon. Both the Caribbean and British contexts present examples of the motivations and pressures for seizing the intellectual resources on offer to assemble canons, or counter-canons, and for contestation through art and its historiography. During the 1980s and early 1990s, these were much more conspicuous in Britain than they are at present. Nowadays, exhibition organisers, curators and critical commentators are generally less inclined to try and name a stable corpus of art practices. There has been an end to the 'survey' show designed as a selection of artists coherently grouped by shared outlooks and aims. If artists of diverse backgrounds in Britain no longer focus their energies on 'becoming visible' as such, but more on the terms of their visibility – the manner in which they are promoted and received – this is some indication of the shifting, yet constant demands over representation in art and its histories. But canonising the work of artists of African, Asian and Caribbean backgrounds in Britain has not been without its mixed outcomes and discontents. The canon debate has happened without delivery of the guarantees of acceptance and understanding sought by the artists and artworks of recent decades, and we are left with some harrowing difficulties for writing a history of this art. Clearly, canons have a troubling presence; living with and without a canon are equally as problematic, and never tenable for all of the time. Any proposed canon for a diverse community of identities has to stand up to persistent negotiation, and the double-bind of emphasising contested ideas about ethnicity, nation and culture as the grounds for affinity.

In light of this shifting territory and the apparent instability of canons, it seems useless to wonder about future canonical scenarios that will operate beyond the reach of contingency and change. Instead, the more pressing question concerns what the alternatives are to the apparently ceaseless jockeying for position, the preoccupations with visibility and canonisation, and the part that art historians have played in advocating for one sort of canon or another. A genealogical interest in such developments, especially a better sense of the history of failures around canonisation, would better establish the grounds for this sort of departure. The canon debate is both enabling and yet so problematic. The advantage of knowing its history is in locating and learning from its problems: it is about how to have a canon that is not only self-reflexive, accepting of its temporality, and aware of its exclusions, but also transforms the structure of universal and particular that positions the canon's dominance.[70]

One such route to self-reflexivity has been opened up by the recent critique of the way artists of diverse backgrounds have been represented, namely through curating and scholarship. This has focused on the historical influence of cultural criticism and the manner in which critical theory has presented the art object and the artist. Regardless of claims that 'Black cultural politics insists upon the ascendancy of a broader aesthetic and political project',[71] the weight of interest has rested unmistakably on the latter. This is perhaps what one might expect of a consciously, politically-led initiative to contest the dominant narratives of art history. But under these circumstances, alternative understandings of the histories of art remain very difficult to elucidate. The artist Juginder Lamba has put it, simply, that: 'The work itself has become secondary.'[72] Gabrielle Hezekiah has suggested, commenting on a similar situation in the Caribbean region, that the outcome is 'the subsequent relegation of the work itself to relative obscurity and isolation in the midst of so much rhetorical fluff'.[73]

The basis for these complaints includes the way that methods of cultural analysis have been applied to the art of the African, Asian and Caribbean diasporas. This is exemplified in the use of the 'diaspora aesthetic' idea, in particular when it is invoked to elucidate actual works of art. In such cases, it is becomes difficult to see what distinguishes one work of art from another, since each serves, quite interchangeably, as evidence of the 'diaspora aesthetic'. The caveat widely issued among commentators is that the valuable ambiguity of artworks, their 'surplus' of meaning, is never lost from view. Like the artists they describe, such artworks strike 'postures of indiscernibility'[74] thought to be deeply enabling of a 'diasporic' politics of knowledge and representation. For Hall in particular, they are germane to the emergence of a potentially redemptive notion of ethnicity and identity formation,[75] capable of renewing our sense of the importance of the diasporic as an intellectual construct. But this raises the question of whether artworks are then being pressed into the service of a larger project of self-definition and 'identification', while a more rounded picture of artistic practice and reception is overlooked. The 'diaspora aesthetic' names conventions of picturing held to have wider implications for the symbolisation of 'race', difference and nation. Yet the ambition for this counter-canon of art making may also be frustrated by the theorising of artworks according to their quality of communicating or symbolising in the manner of visual texts and signs.

In the discussions around canonicity and artists of several diasporas, it is this vocabulary – drawn from the 'linguistic turn' in the study of culture – which has gained most prominence. And it is within this context that a certain discontent has emerged. The linguistic and textuality paradigm would suppose that art objects have the ability to codify narratives, or to offer a didactic 'voice' in a wider political struggle, each of which requires the command of a visual language in which art does the work of a signifying cultural text. Hal Foster recognised in his essay on 'The artist as ethnographer?' that this renders the practitioner of art as 'a paragon of formal reflexivity, sensitive to difference and open to chance, a self-aware reader of culture understood as text'.[76] Yet for artist and critic Jean Fisher, thinking in this way tends to suggest that 'art is more a cultural product than a dynamic process or complex set of immanent and sensuous relations',[77] a complaint enlarged by Rasheed Araeen: 'As for the dominant discourse, it is so obsessed with cultural difference and identity, to the extent of suffering from an intellectual blockage, that it is unable to maintain its focus on the works of art themselves.'[78] The *aesthetic* in 'diaspora aesthetic' operates as a blanket term for styles of visual meaning and how they are conveyed – that is, in a hybrid, syncretic or creolising way.[79] It thereby indicates the process of signification and communication, rather than aesthetic experience as perceptual or phenomenological 'sense'. In such a scheme, representation threatens to render the notion of aesthetics obsolete, so that artworks become nothing more than media: encoded signs (of nation, ethnicity, culture, or diaspora) ready to be decoded.

Such criticisms usher in a larger project of investigating the implications for the art history canon of the theoretical attitudes that condensed around concerns with blackness and diaspora. An overemphasis on the textuality of visual objects has brought some adverse outcomes for artists such as Piper and his peers, and this is salutary for methodological choices available to the discipline more broadly. Their works have been made into signifiers, named as cultural products, transformed and translated into signs and representations. That this elaborately skirts around art objects themselves becomes obvious when the constructed, discursive objects of art criticism (the objects of post-structuralist thinking) predominate at the expense of attention to the tactile and visually apparent physical ones which emerge under the hands of artists: art objects with a material dimension, with textures and colours. Indeed, canonical claims have risked becoming complicit in what Barbara

Stafford sees as the 'ruling metaphor of reading', 'the intellectual imperialism of collapsing diverse phenomenological performances, whether drawings, gestures, sounds or sense into interpretable texts without sensory diversity'.[80] As the historian of philosophy Martin Dillon has remarked, 'One way not to see the world is to read it as text.'[81]

The more recent histories of art in the Caribbean and in Britain both emphasise the textual codification of racial, ethnic and colour difference. As a result, it would appear that the vitality and material presence of art, and the experiences and ambitions of contemporary artists, have remained largely undisclosed. Commentators have preferred instead to debate canonisation in the currently familiar ways I have been describing. Granting value to the art of certain individuals or communities requires considerable energy to be maintained in the face of the shifting, hegemonic territory of art display, reception and commentary. A general challenge is how to conceive of a role for art historiography which is transparent about its stakes in the current environment: one shaped by common, often competing claims of exclusion and marginalisation. Without that transparency, the groups involved in commentaries that unquestionably support campaigns for counter-canons risk reaffirming the status of the very 'mainstream', 'centre' or 'norms' that they set out to critique.

From present to past

If there is a general trend in art history to move away from the practices of its 'linguistic turn', in favour of the distinctly phenomenological attitude outlined, then discussions of art of the Caribbean should be recognised for their part in making this shift. In that setting the search for a self-reflexive criticality in the study of artists of diverse backgrounds has led to some innovative approaches for the discipline. This could be extended on the basis of certain precedents in the context of post-Independence Guyana. Indeed, I gestured to how these might deliver some clarity in considering the present predicament of canonisation. In Denis Williams's writings, the theme of difference predominates in a way that gives them a familiar air of contemporaneity – although Williams's conclusions steer toward very different possibilities from those currently on offer. Williams in this sense signals a locus for meditating on the present, and it is worth bringing him into dialogue with some salient contemporary concerns. As shown, in the global climate at the time of writing, difference is increasingly traded as a commodity although not in the same sense that Williams had experienced during the anti-colonial movement. Practices of objectification, evidenced by the rise of the 'xeno-' or 'ethno-spectacle' in the art marketplace, have circumscribed difference through a market-driven pastiche that creates the semblance of a conflict-free space of commerce.[82] The result has been described as 'the carnival of hetero-culture now at large in the metropolis',[83] an embrace of difference misrecognised.

Artist, curator and writer Olu Oguibe has described how in this climate a new role for difference has emerged, which presents particular challenges for artists who are otherwise excluded from dominant metropolitan narratives and spaces of display and historiography:

> At the turn of the twenty-first century, the struggle that non-Western contemporary artists face on the global stage is not Western resistance to difference, as might have been the case in decades past; their most formidable obstacle is Western obsession with and insistence on difference. As some have already pointed out, it is not that any would want to disavow difference, for we are all different one way or another, after all. The point is that this fact of being ought not constitute the crippling predicament that it does for all who have no definite ancestry in Europe.[84]

It should be noted that difference in this obsessive form is entirely inauthentic when measured against the place of difference in the dramatically conflictual zone of Williams's Guyana. However, a comparison between them reveals Williams's framework as offering a critique of such trends toward an inauthentic incorporation of difference – the 'insistence on difference' in such a way that would go against the interests of those excluded. The 'obsession' that Oguibe has noted of the global art marketplace, as it plays its 'culture game', is an obsession with difference conceived as a discrete and stable category, capable of being accommodated into the commodity system of the Western art mainstream. But the warning given by Williams is that difference has a creatively disruptive power and is capable of radical historical change; just as the various cultural, ethnic and racial elements in Guyanese society are forever undergoing a process of complex 'synthesis' and 'cultural catalysis'.[85] The Guyana context illustrates how notions of singularity are unstable and forever open to change, since there is, and will always be, difference. But when accommodation of difference happens on hegemonic terms, it foregoes the opportunity of 'miscegenation' in Williams's positive and reclaimed meaning of the word.

A bold line should of course be drawn between Williams's attempts to understand cultural and ethnic or racial differences, and the simulated hetereogeneity of the present day in which difference has become reified. His thoroughgoing argument about 'singularity' as unpredictable and untenable in the field of cultural practice must be read as more than a philosophy of freedom pertaining to the cultural politics of Independence Guyana. He valued the fruitful interactions among elements of a diverse ancestry as the basis for society itself. Williams's legacy challenges metropolitan experience to recognise and maintain difference as creative 'catalysis' rather than commodity. If the insights he offered speak to the endeavour of shaping a more radical future, theirs is a persistent testimony to the important political alternatives that difference offers. They are alternatives which have become less easy to contemplate in the current circumstances, but no less urgent to pursue.

If Williams's conclusions speak to the present it is through the example he set for a more widely engaged form of radical self-reflection in the discipline of art history, which would entail attention to the Caribbean. More broadly, the lives and works of Caribbean artists and thinkers, which are unevenly remembered in art history, deserve bringing into sharper visibility. They form a forceful address to art history's shortcomings in its treatment of the Caribbean as a historical, creative and material presence. A leading priority is to find some way to understand the Caribbean not simply as a geographical region of special interest, but as having a global status that contributes to more widely reaching art historical problems.

An art history of the Caribbean holds pertinence in helping to indicate some key preoccupations about 'the cultural' as they are configured in the metropolitan order. A lesson to take from Williams's experience is to bracket culture after the manner of phenomenology. This is an appealing prospect when we consider how the models proposed for cultural analysis in British art – among Hall, Mercer and others I have named – came to be so problematic. The institutional embrace of notions of cultural textuality and signification, exemplified in concerns with art as a 'sign' of difference, have transformed, or translated artists and artworks into a visible illustration of institutional liberalism and inclusion, and of 'issues' for promotion. By their inscription as themes of primarily ethnic and national discourse, linguistic units and commodities of exchange, artworks as tokens in 'canon wars' have been drained of their aesthetic depth, their visual textures, intentionalities and peculiar phenomenal presence. The discipline of art history in various institutional settings has also followed suit in apprehending artists of Caribbean backgrounds as significant media for communicating the discipline's aspirant globally conscious multiculturalism. With Williams, we could say that the establishment appetite for difference has had the effect of imposing a species of 'singularity' on a field of creativity, which is otherwise heterogeneous and shifting, ever 'miscegenating', and always prone to doing so. The paradigms of difference and diversity instituted in the contemporary art sector serve to fix and undermine this process. The challenge then comes to be one of how to transcend this practice of seeing art and artists as little more than a visual litany of ethnic and cultural diversity.

The really awkward, but nonetheless necessary, question to ask in changing this situation is why art and artists of the Caribbean and its diaspora should continue to burden themselves with self-perceptions of cultural marginality and exclusion. How sustainable is the 'war of position' entailed in canon debates? Zygmunt Bauman's suggestion about 'identity crisis' is that: 'Militant assertion of group identity will not remove the insecurity which prompted it.'[86] This points to the idea that any strategic position on art canons will have to combat the sort of 'oppositionalism' that we saw with British 'Black Art', and its subsequent accommodation. What is needed is a greater awareness of the difficulties of such identifications, and the appreciation that there are other, more effective modes of resort if we are to imagine other futures.

There is political pressure on art history to understand the role of cultural counter-canons and the experience of marginalisation, and yet this needs to be met by vigorous analysis of the range of ways, present and past, to contest commoditised difference. Artists and their works are too easily inscribed – through display and remembrance – as significations of national place, ethnic 'belonging', and cultural difference. Perhaps art history might have a role in revealing a less easily correlated understanding. For instance, it might choose to account for why visual practices continually refuse the status that Denis Williams pinpointed – the singular role of being media of representation, or serving as the communicative apparatus for reconfiguring social relations, and nothing more. There are consequences of struggles around the canon and the terms they have engendered, but they do not point to the conclusion, as examined in my introduction, that we have 'been there, done that'. When taken up for analysis, such struggles show the limits of applying the category of aesthetics as if it were interchangeable with that of political representation. The transnational Caribbean significantly extends the field of inquiry for art history, keeping the question of art canons open, and refusing to relegate to the past the insights it yields. Art historical study, however unable to live with or without canons, has still to arrive at that mutual ground.

Notes

1 This was the conference, 'Cross-culturalism and the Caribbean canon', University of the West Indies, St Augustine, Trinidad, January 2004. Its papers were subsequently developed into an edited volume, including my own preliminary thoughts on the relationship between Britain and the Caribbean. See: L. Wainwright, 'Mutual ground: Post-empire canons of art in Britain and the Caribbean', in B. Lalla and J. Rahim (eds), *Beyond borders: Cross-culturalism and the Caribbean canon* (Mona, Jamaica: University of the West Indies Press, 2009), pp. 116–48.

2 What was in mind was likely to be the enthusiasm among art historians in Britain, typified by Griselda Pollock's study of 'firing the canon' in art history's 'culture wars'. See G. Pollock, *Differencing the canon: Feminist desire and the writing of art's histories* (London: Routledge, 1999). See also N. Salomon, 'The art historical canon: Sins of omission', in J. Hartmann and E. Messer-Davidow (eds) *(En)gendering knowledge: Feminism in academe* (Knoxville: University of Tennessee Press, 1991), pp. 222–36.

3 For an analytical overview of this situation – although not addressed to art history – see P. Gilroy, *After empire: Melancholia or convivial culture?* (London: Routledge, 2004).

4 Lalla and Rahim (eds), *Beyond borders*.

5 I am condensing much here from the extensive Anglophone debate in Caribbean Studies. For an overview and anthology of perspectives, see: V. A. Shepherd and G. L. Richards (eds), *Questioning creole: Creolisation discourses in Caribbean culture. In honour of Kamau Brathwaite* (Kingston: Ian Randle, 2002); E. K. Brathwaite, *Contradictory omens: Cultural diversity and integration in the Caribbean* (Mona: Savacou Publications, 1974); D. Walcott, *What the twilight says: Essays* (London: Faber, 1998); and D. Miller, *Modernity: An ethnographic approach: Dualism and mass consumption in Trinidad* (Oxford: Berg Publishers, 2007), p. 51.

6 I offer an earlier account of my coming to terms with Denis Williams in: L. Wainwright, 'Speaking to contemporary art history: Denis Williams and Guyana', in C. Williams and E. Williams (eds), *Denis Williams: A life in works. New and collected essays* (Amsterdam: Rodopi Press, 2010), pp. 65–75.

7 They were details brought to my attention by Anne Walmsley's, 'He lived his life totally', *Sunday Stabroek* (5 July 1998), p. 21; another version of this article was published as 'Icons of identity', *The Guardian* (4 July 1998), p. 17.

8 See for example: W. Lewis, 'A negro artist', *The Listener* (BBC, 7 December 1950).

9 P. O'Keeffe, *Some sort of genius: A life of Wyndham Lewis* (London: Cape, 2000).

10 See Williams and Williams (eds), *Denis Williams*.

11 D. Williams, 'Image and idea in the arts of Guyana', *The Edgar Mittelholzer memorial lectures*, second series (Georgetown: The National History and Arts Council, Ministry of Information, 1969), p. 33.

12 E. Husserl, *Ideas pertaining to a pure phenomenology and to a phenomenological philosophy, first book*, trans. F. Kersten (Dordrecht: Kluwer, 1983), part 18.

13 E. Husserl, 'Thing and space: Lectures of 1907', trans. R. Rojcewicz, *Collected works VII* (Dordrecht: Kluwer, 1997); see also E. S. Casey, *The fate of place: A philosophical history* (Berkeley and Los Angeles: University of California Press, 1997), p. 218.

14 D. Williams, quoted in 'Role of the artist in Third World countries', *Guyana Graphic* (9 September 1972), p. 3. See also the full text of his symposium address, published as 'Art and society', in 'The literary vision of Carifesta '72: The role of the artist in Third World society', *Kaie*, 11 (1973), 100–15, p. 109.

15 M. Merleau-Ponty, *Phenomenology of perception*, trans. C. Smith (London: Routledge & Kegan Paul, 1962), p. ix (emphasis in original).

16 Writing in the late 1960s, Williams drew attention to Michael Swan's survey from the previous decade, for which Williams supplied the colour illustration on its cover, and twenty-eight ink studies throughout the book. See: Williams, 'Image and idea in the arts of Guyana', p. 15; M. Swan, *British Guiana: The land of six peoples* (London: Her Majesty's Stationery Office, 1957).

17 D. Williams, *Prehistoric Guiana* (Jamaica: Ian Randle Publishers, 2003).

18 N. Laughlin, 'As it was in the beginning', *The Caribbean Review of Books*, 5 (2005).

19 Williams, *Prehistoric Guiana*, p. xxvii.

20 Williams, 'Image and idea in the arts of Guyana', pp. 15–16; see also p. 10.

21 Williams, 'Image and idea in the arts of Guyana', p. 16.

22 Williams, 'Image and idea in the arts of Guyana', p. 12.

23 This cast of characters and its consequences for rethinking the discipline was set out beautifully at the end of that decade in D. Preziosi, *Rethinking art history: Meditations on a coy science* (New Haven: Yale University Press, 1989).

24 Walmsley, *The Caribbean artists movement*, p. xviii.

25 E. A. Chambers, *The emergence and development of black visual arts activity in England between 1981 and 1986: Press and public responses* (PhD dissertation, Goldsmiths College, University of London, 1998).

26 K. Piper, press release (London: Black Art Gallery, 1984).

27 For example: D. A. Bailey and S. Hall (eds), *Critical decade: Black British photography in the 1980s (Special Issue), Ten 8*, 3 (1992), 1–159; I. Julien and K. Mercer, 'De margin and de centre: The last "special issue" on race?', *Screen*, 29:4 (1988), 2–11; P. Gilroy, 'Cruciality and the frog's perspective: An agenda of difficulties for the black arts movement in Britain', *Third Text*, 5 (1988/89), 33–44; D. Chandler (ed.), *Keith Piper: Relocating the remains* (London: inIVA, 1997), and the artist's own writing: K. Piper, *A ship called Jesus* (Birmingham: Ikon Gallery, 1991). These essays partly respond to Piper's photo-text collages: K. Piper, 'Body and text', *Third Text*, 2 (1987/88), 53–61.

28 Wolverhampton Art Gallery, *Black art an' done: An exhibition of work by young black artists* (Wolverhampton: Wolverhampton Art Gallery, 1981).

29 E. Chambers, C. Johnson, D. Rodney, K. Piper and M. Smith, *The first national black art convention to discuss the form, functioning and future of black art* (Wolverhampton: Wolverhampton Polytechnic, 1982).

30 See: Mappin Art Gallery, *Into the open: New painting, prints and sculpture by contemporary black artists* (Sheffield: Mappin Art Gallery, 1984); Creation for Liberation, *Creation for liberation open exhibition: Art by black artists* (London: Creation for Liberation, 1985); L. Himid, *The thin black line* (Hebden Bridge: Urban Fox Press, 1985); Institute of Contemporary Arts, *The thin black line* (London: ICA, 1985); Black Art Gallery, *Some of us are brave, all of us are strong: An exhibition by and about black women* (London: Black Art Gallery, 1986); Black Art Gallery, *From generation to generation (the installation)* (London: Black Art Gallery, 1986); E. Chambers (ed.), *Black art: Plotting the course* (Oldham: Oldham Art Gallery, 1988); E. Chambers and T. Joseph (eds), *The artpack: A history of black artists in Britain* (London: Haringey Arts Council, 1988); R. Araeen, *The essential black art* (London: Chisenhale Gallery and Kala Press, 1988); Stoke on Trent City Museum and Art Gallery, *Black art: New directions* (Stoke on Trent: Stoke on Trent City Museum and Art Gallery, 1989); E. Chambers (ed.), *Let the canvas come to life with dark faces* (Coventry: Herbert Art Gallery and Museum, 1990). A wider context for these exhibitions can be gathered from: L. Wainwright, 'Bibliography', in D. A. Bailey, I. Baucom and S. Boyce (eds), *Shades of black: Assembling black arts in 1980s Britain* (London and Durham NC: Duke University Press and the Institute of International Visual Arts, 2005), pp. 307–18.

31 T. Joseph, *UK School Report* (1984), acrylic on canvas, 358 × 193 cm. Collection of Sheffield City Art Galleries.

32 Also reproduced in E. Chambers and T. Joseph, *The art pack: A history of black artists in Britain* (London: Borough of Haringey, 1988), p. 30.

33 See E. Chambers (ed.), *Us an' dem: A critical look at relationships between the police, the judiciary and the black community* (Lancashire: Lancashire Probation Service, 1994); K. Owusu and J. Ross (eds), *Behind the masquerade: The story of the Notting Hill carnival* (London: Arts Media Group, 1988); Arts Council of Great Britain, *Masquerading: The art of Notting Hill carnival* (London: Arts Council, 1986).

34 Also reproduced in G. Tawadros, *Sonia Boyce: Speaking in tongues* (London: Kala, 1997), p. 43.

35 For further elucidation, see Boyce's own views expressed at that time in J. Roberts, 'Sonia Boyce in conversation with John Roberts', *Third Text*, 1 (1987), 55–64; cf. L. Nead, *Chila Kumari Burman: Between two cultures* (London: Kala Press, 1995).

36 Note, for example, what similarities the earlier quote from Piper bears to Larry Neal's writing of 1968: 'The Black Arts Movement is radically opposed to any concept of the artist that alienates him from his community. Black Art is the aesthetic and spiritual sister of the Black Power concept. As such, it envisions an art that speaks directly to the needs and aspirations of Black America. In order to perform this task, the Black Arts Movement proposes a radical re-ordering of the western cultural aesthetic. It proposes a separate symbolism, mythology, critique, and iconology. The Black Arts and the Black Power concept both relate broadly to the Afro-American's desire for self-determination and nationhood. Both concepts are nationalistic. One is concerned with the relationship between art and politics; the other with the art of politics.' L. Neal, 'The black arts movement', *The Drama Review*, 12:4 (1968), 29–39, p. 29, reprinted in A. Gayle (ed.), *The black aesthetic* (New York: Doubleday, 1972), pp. 257–74; and in M. Schwartz (ed.), *Visions of a liberated future: Black arts movement writings* (New York: Thunder's Mouth Press, 1989). See also the special issue, dedicated to Larry Neal, of *Callaloo*, 23 (1985). For further British parallels see: E. Chambers, *Run through the jungle: Selected writings by Eddie Chambers* (London: inIVA, 1999), and a concise review of that anthology: N. Ratnam, 'Run through the jungle: Selected writings by Eddie Chambers', *Third Text*, 48 (1999), 78–80.

37 See for example the overview in A. Ghosh and J. Lamba (eds), *Beyond frontiers: Contemporary British art by artists of South Asian descent* (London: Saffron Books, 2001). For listings by artist and year, see: M. Keen and E. Ward, *Recordings: A selected bibliography of contemporary African, Afro-Caribbean and Asian British art* (London: Institute of International Visual Arts and Chelsea College of Art and Design, 1996).

38 S. Biswas, *Housewives with steak knives* (1985), oil, pastel and acrylic on paper and canvas, 243 × 274 cm. Bradford Art Galleries and Museums, reproduced in Chambers and Joseph (eds), *The art pack*, p. 8; and M. J. Beauchamp-Bird and M. F. Sirmans (eds), *Transforming the crown*, p. 29.

39 R. Araeen, 'Preliminary notes for a black manifesto', *Black Phoenix*, 1 (1978), 3–12; reprinted in R. Araeen, *Making myself visible* (London: Kala, 1984).

40 The nature of this incorporation is explained in R. Araeen, 'Why "Third Text"?', *Third Text*, 1 (1987), 3–5.

41 R. Araeen, *The essential black art*, p. 5. Araeen's definition can be compared with the larger pattern of political organisation outside the art community, evident from an earlier statement by the Organisation of Women of Asian and African Descent (OWAAD): 'When we use the term "Black" we use it as a political term. It doesn't

describe skin colour, it defines our situation here in Britain. We're here as a result of British imperialism, and our continued oppression in Britain is the result of British racism.' *Race and Class*, 27:1 (1985), p. 32.

42 This clash of priorities and what could be discerned of their immediate effects is set out in one of the most valuable documents of this period: R. Araeen and E. Chambers, 'Black art: A discussion', *Third Text*, 2:5 (1988), 51–62.

43 Greater London Council (GLC), *Anti-racist mural project* (London: GLC Race Equality Unit, 1985); Greater London Council, *New horizons: Exhibition of arts* (London: GLC Ethnic Arts Sub-Committee, 1985).

44 R. Araeen, 'A history of black artists in Britain' (Unpublished papers, London: GLC Race Equality Unit, 1986); R. Araeen, 'From primitivism to ethnic arts', *Third Text*, 1 (1987), 6–25. These contributions from Araeen respond to, as well as anticipate, the prevailing official outlooks and practices typified during the period from Khan, 1976, until 1989. Some primary and secondary sources include: Arts Council, *The arts and ethnic minorities: Action plan* (London: Arts Council of Great Britain, 1985); K. Owusu, *The struggle for black arts in Britain: What can we consider better than freedom* (London: Comedia, 1986); Owusu and Ross, *Behind the masquerade*; R. Cork, B. Khanna and S. Read, *Art on the South Bank: An independent report* (London: Greater London Council, 1986); M. Fisher, 'Black art: The Labour Party's line', *Modern Painters*, 2:4 (1989), 77–8.

45 See Chambers, *Emergence and development*; and E. Chambers, 'The black art group', *Artrage*, 14 (1986), 28–9.

46 R. Araeen, 'The success and the failure of black art', *Third Text*, 18:2 (2004), 135–52.

47 S. Hall, 'Cultural identity and cinematic representation', in H. A. Baker, M. Diawara, and R. A. Lindeborg (eds), *Black British cultural studies: A reader* (Chicago: Chicago University Press, 1996), p. 220.

48 G. Tawadros, 'Beyond the boundary: The work of three black women artists', in Baker, Diawara, and Lindeborg (eds), *Black British cultural studies*, p. 240.

49 I. Ang, 'Identity blues', in P. Gilroy, L. Grossberg and A. McRobbie (eds), *Without guarantees: In honour of Stuart Hall* (London: Verso, 2000), pp. 1–13.

50 S. Hall, 'What is this "black" in black popular culture?', in G. Dent (ed.), *Black popular culture: A project by Michele Wallace* (Seattle: Bay Press, 1992), p. 29.

51 D. Morley and K. H. Chen (eds), *Stuart Hall: Critical dialogues in cultural studies* (London: Routledge, 1996), p. 9; compare with S. Hall, 'New ethnicities' in K. Mercer (ed.), *Black film/British cinema* (London: Institute of Contemporary Arts, 1988).

52 Hall's use of the 'diaspora aesthetic' term was tied to these two perspectives. On the one hand, he advocated critical work that 'allows us to see and recognise the different parts and histories of ourselves, to construct those points of identification, those positionalities we call a "cultural identity"'. See: S. Hall, 'Cultural identity and Diaspora', in J. Rutherford (ed.), *Identity: Community, culture, difference* (London: Lawrence & Wishart, 1990), p. 237. On the other, Hall concurred with Mercer's observation that, 'across a whole range of cultural forms there is a "syncretic" dynamic which critically appropriates elements from the master-codes of the dominant culture and "creolises" them, disarticulating given signs and re-articulating their symbolic meaning … [a] hybridising tendency'. Quoted in Hall, 'Cultural identity', p. 220.

53 Established in 1995, the Institute of International Visual Arts (inIVA), based in London, is largely funded by Arts Council England, to provide a continuing programme including publications, exhibitions, education, a web presence, commissions of artwork, art writing, artists in residence and open lectures.

54 Arts Council of Great Britain, *The arts and cultural diversity* (London: Arts Council of Great Britain, 1989); R. Lavrijsen (ed.), *Cultural diversity in the arts: Art, art policies and the facelift of Europe* (Amsterdam: Royal Tropical Institute, 1993); S. Walker, 'Black cultural museums in Britain', in E. Hooper Greenhill (ed.), *Cultural diversity: Developing museum audiences in Britain* (Leicester: Leicester University Press, 1997); Black Arts Alliance, *Black arts alliance report* (Manchester: Black Arts Alliance, 1999); Greater London Authority, *Without prejudice? Exploring ethnic differences in London* (London: Greater London Authority, 2000).

55 See for example: Institute of Contemporary Arts, London, 1985; D. A. Bailey and K. Mercer (eds), *Mirage: Enigmas of race, difference and desire* (London: ICA and inIVA, 1995); H. Bhabha (ed.), *Identity* (London: Institute of Contemporary Arts, 1987); K. Mercer (ed.), *Black film/British cinema*.

56 Also reproduced in *Four x 4: Installations by sixteen artists in four gallery spaces* (Preston: Harris Museum and Art Gallery; Wolverhampton: Wolverhampton Art Gallery; Leicester: The City Gallery; Bristol: Arnolfini, 1991), p. 16.

57 L. Wainwright, 'Canon questions: Art in "Black Britain"', G. Low and M. Wynne-Davies (eds), *A Black British canon?* (Basingstoke and New York: Palgrave Macmillan, 2006), pp. 143–67, p. 150.

58 R. Araeen, 'New internationalism, or the multiculturalism of global Bantustans', in J. Fisher (ed.), *Global visions: Towards a new internationalism in the visual arts* (London: Kala Press, 1994), p. 9.

59 R. Hylton, 'The politics of cultural diversity', *Art Monthly*, 274 (2004), p. 20.

60 Hylton, 'The politics of cultural diversity', p. 20.

61 Arts Council England, 'Decibel', on www.decibel-db.org (accessed 1 November 2009).

62 Hylton writes in 'The politics of cultural diversity': 'The notion that some people are more culturally diverse than others is as spurious as it is to consider some people as being more ethnic than others. ... "Ethnic minority" and "culturally diverse" are terms that privilege a limited notion of difference based on race. Such euphemisms are unhelpful because they presuppose normality to be white and everything else to be diverse' (p. 22). See also R. Hylton, *The nature of the beast: Cultural diversity and the visual arts sector: A study of policies, initiatives and attitudes, 1976–2006* (Bath: Institute of Contemporary Interdisciplinary Art, 2007) and M. Hargreaves McIntyre, *Take away the label: Artists' views on ethnicity, practice and career support in the UK* (London: Axis, 2005).

63 Her Majesty's Stationery Office (HMSO), *The Stephen Lawrence inquiry: Report of an inquiry by Sir William Macpherson of Cluny* (London: Home Office, 1999); Commission for Racial Equality, *The Stephen Lawrence inquiry: Implications for racial equality* (London: Home Office, 1999); Home Office, *Race relations (Amendment) act 2000: New laws for a successful multi-racial Britain* (London: Home Office, 2001).

64 'To the extent that the postcolonial vocabulary, characterised by such terms as

"diaspora", "ethnicity" and "hybridity", has displaced an earlier discourse of assimilation, adaptation and integration, we have witnessed a massive social transformation which has generated, in the Western metropolis, what could now be called a condition of *multicultural normalization.*' K. Mercer, 'A sociography of diaspora', in Gilroy, Grossberg and McRobbie (eds), *Without guarantees*, p. 234; S. Hall and S. Maharaj, 'Modernity and difference: A conversation between Stuart Hall and Sarat Maharaj', in S. Campbell and G. Tawadros (eds), *Stuart Hall and Sarat Maharaj: Modernity and difference* (London: Institute for International Visual Arts, 2000), p. 46.

65 By 'downsizing', Mercer indicates the systematic absorption and circumscription of initiatives to promote diversity by public and other institutions, a meaning given special inflection by this borrowing of vocabulary from a corporate ethos of productivity and efficiency. See Mercer, 'A sociography of diaspora', p. 235.

66 To quote Sonya Dyer in full: 'Today, the institutionalisation of diversity policies means that art is being sidelined, and in many cases black artists are first and foremost regarded as black. This is clearly shown by the unhealthy pressure on artists and curators from non-white backgrounds to privilege their racial background above all else in relation to their practice. Black artists and curators are often expected to produce projects that are geared towards attracting a black and minority ethnic audience. One young British Asian curator I spoke to about this said that he had never felt "othered" until he began working in public galleries. It goes without saying that white artists and curators do not generally feel the same kind of pressure to appeal specifically to white audiences.' S. Dyer, 'Boxed in: How cultural diversity policies constrict black artists', Manifesto Club's Artistic Autonomy Hub together with *a-n* (23 May 2007), on www.manifestoclub.com/aa-diversity, p. 11. See also: S. Dyer, F. McAuslan and T. Gausi, 'Why are the arts so white?', *Time Out* (17 October 2007), pp. 19–30; and M. Mirza (ed.), 'Rethinking Race', *Prospect Magazine*, 175 (22 September 2010).

67 R. Araeen, 'A new beginning: Beyond postcolonial cultural theory and identity politics', *Third Text*, 50 (2000), p. 11.

68 G. Perry, 'Positive discrimination patronizes black artists', *The Times* (30 May 2007), p. 16. The artist Martha Rosler made a similar assessment of the United States during the 1990s, where pressures for cultural inclusion have increased too: 'an art world version of multiculturalism (and where more appropriately situated than in the realm of culture?), necessary but sometimes painfully formulaic, which produces a shadow constellation of the identities of the wider society but without the income spread'. M. Rosler, quoted in J. Stallabrass, *Art incorporated: The story of contemporary art* (Oxford University Press, 2004), p. 21. The first chapter of Stallabrass's study explores in further depth correlations between neo-liberal agendas such as these in the arts and those of the wider political economy. See also: L. Wainwright, 'Art (school) education and art history', in R. Appignanesi (ed.), *Beyond cultural diversity: The case for creativity. A Third Text report* (London: Third Text Publications, 2010), pp. 93–103.

69 E. Belfiore and O. Bennett, *The social impact of the arts: An intellectual history* (London, Macmillan, 2008).

70 This is the ground that was approached for instance when assembling a canon of

African American literature, as Henry Louis Gates Jr wrote: 'I am not unaware of the politics and ironies of canon formation. … The canon that we define will be "our" canon, one possible set of selections among several possible sets of selections'. H. L. Gates, *Loose canons: Notes on the culture wars* (Oxford: Oxford University Press, 1992), p. 32. This self-declaration of the necessary contingency at the site of canon production has been closely surveyed by Anna Bryzski and contributors to her recent anthology. She speaks of 'partisan canons' as 'multiple, historically situated canonical formations, that is, of different canons, produced at different times and in different geographic locations by individuals, groups, and institutions pursuing at times very different agendas'. It is not clear whether Bryzski's chosen category approximates to the strategic and self-reflexive engagement with 'the politics and ironies of canon formation' that Gates described, and what role therefore the politics of difference has to play in the 'situated' and contingent formation of 'partisan' canons. It is certain that there is at least one further possibility that neither thinker entertains. For all the arguments about the need to pay attention to the particular in trying to understand and overturn the dominant canon, we are still faced with the persistence of universalism. What I have been arguing is that appealing to the particular leaves de facto the dominant canon intact, and indeed it elaborates not only a secondary but a complementary discourse. This emphasis brings the central canonical ground no closer to reassessing and transforming the terms of its inclusions but may indeed compel it to find more novel ways of reproducing itself, through and not despite difference. A. Brzyski (ed.), *Partisan canons* (Durham and London: Duke University Press, 2007), p. 3.

71 Tawadros, 'Beyond the boundary', p. 274.
72 S. Rizvi, 'Here and now 2: Juginder Lamba in conversation', in Ghosh and Lamba (eds), *Beyond frontiers*, pp. 255–8, p. 256.
73 G. Hezekiah, 'Conceptualising the boundaries of nation-space: Some thoughts on art, criticism, and the creation of a canon', *Small Axe*, 3 (1999), 79–80.
74 Tawadros, 'Beyond the boundary', p. 274.
75 S. Hall, 'On postmodernism and articulation: An interview with Stuart Hall', in Morley and Chen (eds), *Stuart Hall*, pp. 131–50; also: S. Hall, 'New ethnicities', in A. Rattansi and J. Donald (eds), *Race, culture and difference* (London: Sage, 1992).
76 H. Foster, 'The artist as ethnographer?', in Fisher (ed.), *Global visions*, p. 14.
77 Fisher (ed.), *Global visions*, p. 33.
78 Araeen, 'New internationalism', in Fisher (ed.), *Global visions*, p. 9.
79 See: L. Wainwright, 'History as a topic for visual thinking: British art of the Caribbean diaspora', *Wadabagei*, 1:4 (2000), 44–76; L. Wainwright, 'Perception and presence in British art of the African, Asian and Caribbean diasporas' (School of Oriental and African Studies, University of London, 2003), unpublished doctoral thesis; and L. Wainwright, 'Solving Caribbean mysteries: Art, embodiment and an eye for the tropics', *Small Axe*, 25 (2008), 133–44.
80 B. M. Stafford, *Good looking: Essays on the virtues of images* (Cambridge: MIT Press, 1995), p. 8.
81 M. C. Dillon, *Semiological reductionism: A critique of the deconstructionist movement in postmodern thought* (New York: State University of New York Press, 1995), p. 104.

82 See, for instance, the discussion given by Slavoj Žižek, 'Multiculturalism, or, the cultural logic of multinational capitalism', *New Left Review*, 225 (1997), 28–51.

83 P. Gilroy, 'Foreword', in H. Raphael-Hernandez (ed.), *Blackening Europe: The African American presence* (London: Routledge, 2004), p. xix; P. Gilroy, *After empire: Melancholia or convivial culture?* (London: Routledge, 2004).

84 O. Oguibe, *The culture game* (London and Minneapolis: University of Minnesota Press, 2004), pp. xiv–xv.

85 Williams, 'Image and idea in the arts of Guyana', 15–16.

86 Z. Bauman, *In search of politics* (London: Polity Press, 1999), p. 197.

4   Emotional chronology

Earlier chapters show how artists such as Aubrey Williams and Frank Bowling have provided us with a more complex picture of the way that the Caribbean is integral to changes within modernism and the transition toward a more global understanding of the histories of art. This chapter examines a moment in the post-Independence Caribbean when similar issues of participation came up against new sorts of obstacles – in the more recent search for a suitable mode of art practice in the aftermath of decolonisation. One artist in particular, the painter Shastri Maharaj, sought inclusion in the art community of Trinidad yet that aspiration was stalled by what became normative for art of the Caribbean. He found that the results of his art training abroad met with little interest, even discouragement and failure, and that the overall focus on ethnicity within the imagining of national culture would come to present an abiding barrier.

In 1980s Trinidad, to be an artist with international or 'outside' associations was to find oneself on the wrong side of the preferred story of national art making. Maharaj had come to understand, through his foreign training, that certain approaches to painting, such as realistic figuration, were deemed to be anachronistic in the canonical history of artistic modernism. It is remarkable that an artist trained in post-conceptual techniques and critical approaches to painting would, with time, abandon these altogether. He would 'return' to realist figures and landscape scenes, often working in direct references to Hinduism and stereotypes of Indian dress. Initially, these were received gladly by the art community in Trinidad, allowing the artist to feel in demand and enjoy a sort of ready success. But this would soon change, owing to the contention over what would make for a legitimate artistic subject in a context of continuing concerns with 'the nation'.

The historical pressures felt by an artist of Maharaj's East Indian background illuminates a larger scene in the post-Independence Caribbean in which art and ethnicity have been made to intersect. As in Chapter 3, on the similarly problematic links between creativity and 'difference', I am concerned to show up the considerable discontent brought by this intersection. The choices that Maharaj has made as an artist have produced far from favourable outcomes for him. Through his practice, he purposefully identified his East Indian ethnicity, only to find that this would eventually frustrate his goal of becoming an artist of continuing national importance in Trinidad. The circumstances in which he has practised have offered a narrow field of choices for how he would paint. Regardless of what may be said of his national 'success', in another sense his works are entirely contextualised by discourses of the Caribbean nation, and with somewhat devastating results.

This chapter therefore enlarges on my ongoing account of how articulations have been made between art and ethnicity against an unstable ground of hegemonic social conditions. In the multiculturalist promotion of 'diversity' and 'difference', and with the concept of the 'diaspora aesthetic' in Britain, such articulations have proved to be enabling at one historical moment, yet circumscribing at another. Artists' attempts to occupy mainstream 'visibility', conceived as the goal of inclusion in a national art canon, have in the British setting meant identifying with diasporic 'difference'; a critical point of leverage for exposing myths of national inclusiveness. I am interested in how this may have taken shape during the same period – of the 1980s to the present – in Trinidad, plotted in the biography of an artist whose striving for national canonisation has used related means, and met with similar limitations.

Maharaj's attempt to recuperate anachronistic forms in his paintings has brought him relative success. He is troubled by the difficulties of working within the confines of Trinidad's particular landscape of ethnic differences, specifically what is associated with East Indian ethnicity. Clearly, there is a deeper problem here for the historiography of art in the Caribbean. In trying to expose the overemphasis on ethnicity for this artist, it is tempting to focus only on the cultural politics of representation, thereby reproducing accounts of 'difference'. One way through this territory is to evaluate this context by looking at the emotional dimension of this artist's experience, finding ways in which emotions may be unfolded from his career and so serve to complicate the more familiar critical approach to historicising conditions of marginalisation. If, as argued, the tendency must be resisted to read ethnic difference from the signifying surface of works of art, then an 'emotional chronology' of Maharaj will show how he has suffered such readings, and what deeper historical and aesthetic experience is being concealed by an over-exclusive concern with 'difference'. The emotionality around Indo-Caribbean presence is relevant to the discontented relations between ethnic difference and painting, but goes beyong this by occupying a distinct analytical space. How such feelings change – the temporality of the emotions – are contingently related to the discursive context of a Caribbean nation such as Trinidad. My overall aim is therefore one of opening a channel for thinking beyond the circumscriptions of that setting for one of its artists.

In Trinidad, roughly equal numbers of people identify with South Asian (or 'East Indian') as with African backgrounds, while the remaining population embraces a growing spectrum of mixes. Trinidad's large community of East Indians are descended from those who came shortly after Emancipation as indentured labourers, alongside an equally large number of the descendants of enslaved Africans. Against the background of this unusual demography, Trinidadian nationhood has become a space for the production of ethnic signifiers which condense in various forms of official 'culture'. Cultural policy in the immediate years of Independence set out a rationale for art making in particular. It was thought to serve as a 'foundation' on which to raise a national cultural consciousness after independence from British rule. Thus it became incumbent upon artists to loudly proclaim ethnic differences within an ideological programme of 'unity through diversity'. During the most vigorous moment of anti-colonialism, in an attempt to unlock the country from its colonial past, such interests condensed in the official culture of 'creole nationalism'. This would include fine art and 'craft', and other fields such as carnival, music, theatre and literature.

It is worth paying attention to the continuing legacy of the post-Independence expectations of art practice. Indo-Trinidadian or 'East Indian' practices may be explored against this background, not simply in the areas of image-making, but also in aspects of celebration and performance. The official emphasis in Trinidad on culture as a chief agent of decolonisation, has contributed to the way conceptions of 'Indianness' have operated within an emotional field. The role assigned to art in building the independent nation can be read in the question of the commercial success of artists who identify themselves as Indian and then compared to how 'Indianness' is being renegotiated in popular contexts. This throws light on the matter of the counter-hegemonic ownership of cultural practices within contemporary diasporic communities and the emotional field in which this operates.

Image-makers, wedding performers, and the singer-songwriters of chutney and other identified 'East Indian' musicians, offer alternatives to the prevailing ideas about 'Indianness' that were instituted in Trinidad during decolonisation. In this regard, such artists are makers of knowledge, in their role as producers of cultural objects (and by virtue of their ability to speak and to offer accounts of their own experience, as in the interview material included here). My central concern, therefore, is to examine what these individuals and their practices reveal about the relative and shifting historical landscape of postcolonial emotions, memory and political desire. Much research in anthropology and visual and material culture studies has insisted on framing cultural objects as significations of national place, transnational connection, political position, or ethnic 'belonging'. But we have yet to confront the ways in which diaspora culture is commoditised – the way in which its aesthetic forms are taken to be representative of one or other ethnicity or diaspora, and taken as 'signifying' visual media. The alternative is to pay due regard to a broader sense of 'the cultural' beyond this 'representational' status.

A closer discussion of the aesthetic presence of such forms in relation to the emotions indicates a more complicated status for 'the cultural'. What results is a better understanding of the complex intersections of cultural practices and the emotions and an alternative basis on which to historicise them. As such, I have taken a specific approach to what Raymond Williams once termed 'structures of feeling', by relating to how Caribbean subjects engage with a vocabulary of the emotions, and the relation between this and their cultural objects. Williams identified 'characteristic elements of impulse, restraint, and tone; specifically affective elements of consciousness and relationships: not feeling against thought, but thought as felt and feeling as thought: practical consciousness of a present kind, in a living and interrelating continuity'.[1] Aspects of memory and remembering, and visual, musical and performed practices, offer the basis for extending such existing approaches to the analysis of 'feeling'. I do recognise that cultural objects are the conveyers, or media, of political and social meaning. Even so, I would suggest that cultural production is at the same time important for generating various sorts of 'positioned' historical presence that involve an emotional dimension, which is itself a structuring agency. Being implicated in this emotional field, the historical and cultural context of the Indo-Caribbean leads us to question the status of the emotions rather than to take them for granted. The Caribbean setting demonstrates the operations of the emotions, and brings us to the point of challenging the conditions of that setting by way of an analysis of what here I have called 'emotional chronology'.

Transit, transition, transformation

The continually shifting emphasis given to ethnicity – its frequent rearranging in temporary ways – through cultural practices in Trinidad, takes place within a complex emotional economy. The prefix 'trans-', as in 'transit', 'transition' and 'transformation',[2] may be used instructively to emphasise the dynamic status of art and cultural production – and the production of social interactions and political positions – in this setting. Notably, such interest in the 'trans-' prefix extends beyond the paradigm of translation, a concept shown in Chapter 3 to be central in the treatment of works of art as text, and once a key strand of postcolonial cultural and literary criticism, especially the study of coloniser–colonised relations under conditions of empire.[3] Rather than settle on looking at the theme of translation, however, I would suggest going further, by evaluating how cultural practices and the emotions intersect. Cultural practices are not in this sense 'translations' of emotional conditions or concerns. Rather, they are critical transformations that exist across contemporary globalised, diasporic spaces and fail to be captured by models of cultural texts as instances and sites of translation. With their material foundation in view, I suggest that we can understand more deeply how artists and art practices of the Caribbean are located in time and space, and entangled in an emotional life that has otherwise remained undisclosed to art history.

What interests me is an expanded analysis of the production, circulation and reception of cultural phenomena – with attention to their locations in time and space through their entanglements in the emotions. Of course, the historical legacy of imperialism may also be seen in the postcolonial Caribbean. The colonial past is entwined with the present inequalities of global power in the twin-island Republic of Trinidad and Tobago. This entwining is suggested by the centrality of continuing attempts to overcome the divisions of colonial rule, such as by appropriating the concept of national identity and a multi-ethnic society, and by working toward an ideal of Independence. The belief invested in this unfinished project of national freedom, and in particular the yearning for cultural autonomy, is evidenced in the attempted separation of the country's national art market from the international networks of contemporary artworks and artists. This operates in tension, however, with the localisation of those art discourses which are drawn from contact, communication, and experience and training overseas. I would suggest that this is an indication of the globalising processes in the Trinidad context – processes of attempted detachment from the 'outside' and 'the international' that nonetheless happen under their abiding influence.

This transitory quality of Trinidad can be explored further in the relationship between creativity, ethnicity and the emotions. It is useful to see how the key 'trans-' concepts interact with one another. For instance, the contemporary transitions and transformations that the island is undergoing can be traced and understood with a mind to its history of transit, the long-standing patterns of the movement of subjects and objects. I very often heard during fieldwork some historical narratives of the transit of enslaved Africans and indentured South Asians, and the Chinese, Europeans, and those from the Middle East who moved to the Caribbean, as well as the indigenous subjects who were displaced and whose lives were disrupted. These accounts were offered largely on the premise of being a useful introduction to the island for any foreigner. However, their deeper significance is that their central theme of cultural 'origins' holds a role in rethinking and transforming present-day social relations. Narratives of geographical movement were relayed to me as if they 'explained' Trinidad's present-day ethnic differences. But this rather 'scripted' historical present was coupled with much anxious debate about the need for the country to transform and develop beyond its historical past.

One such transformation is the growing prospect of an emerging national or 'creole' identity which may be capable of collapsing and reconciling older ethnic differences. During my time in Trinidad, I became aware of how this has particular consequences for those people identified as Indo-Caribbean. It may not be helpful any longer to speak of an Indo-Trinidadian identity as a dynamic cultural category at all. Individuals of this group, particularly of the younger generation, frequently declare themselves more comfortable with a Trinidadian creole identity than an Indian one.[4] Despite what we may understand to be the motivations for Indian and Hindu nationalisms, this creole or Trinidadian identity is increasingly assured across ethnic divisions. It is less common to find that the current generation feels marginal or victimised and so less likely to identify with an 'Indian' or 'Indo-Trini' label. This is even the case in rural central and southern areas of the island, which are widely identified as East Indian. Indo- contact and settlement with Afro-Trinidadians has contributed to an overall heterogeneity on the island. During fieldwork I stayed in an Indo-Trinidad household in Claxton Bay, where all the plots of land along one side of the road had been distributed by my host's grandfather to each of his nine children. Despite their ownership of this area, daily contact with Afro-Trinidadian neighbours and shared contact points such as the local shops, at work, schools and the public transport stand, made for constant mixing. A large ashram sited at the end of the road had become a place for Hindu, Muslim and Christian prayer. Hindu *satsangh* was held there on Christmas morning and Eid-ul-Fitr celebrated. There was also a wide range of places for Christian worship – Seventh-Day Adventist and the New Testament Church of God – described locally as 'new churches'.

Metaphors of transit, transition and transformation have a wide significance in the Trinidad setting and illuminate how creative practices and ethnicity intersect. They show creative practices as having processual qualities, which are suited to the dynamic social circumstances that I have outlined. As artists in Trinidad struggle to enter and to shape the island's growing contemporary art milieu, the sort of Trinidad creole that they embrace is very much at odds with its earlier nationalist manifestation, in which creole culture was equated with a Euro-/Afro- blend.[5] In this sense, the creole concept is historical, being subject to change from this earlier manifestation to a more recent one. In recent debates on creativity the distinction drawn between improvisation and innovation is instructive,[6] and may help to convey the character of certain transformations in Trinidad. To quote Ingold and Hallam: 'The difference between improvisation and innovation, then, is not that the one works within established convention while the other breaks with it, but that the former characterizes creativity by way of its process, the latter by way of its products.' The creole concept is an officially mobilised 'improvisation' of sorts in the face of historically imperial attitudes toward Trinidadian cultural value and distinctiveness. What has yet to be addressed is how the 'innovative' – as compared to 'improvisatory' – cultural practices of Indo-Caribbean artists and musicians may be located and assessed. Since Trinidad is both a context for improvisation in creative production, as well as innovation, then the task is to show how these are to be differentiated. Ingold and Hallam's improvisation vs. innovation appears to break from the influential distinction made by Michel de Certeau – the contrast he drew between strategies and tactics,[7] and thereby his emphasis on what is broadly speaking the spatiality of resistance. Even so, it would be worthwhile to ask how analysis of the politics of temporality, given throughout this book, and the emotional dimensions of improvisation and innovation may complicate these preoccupations with both the material (in the shape of 'process' and 'product') and the spatial.

Finally, a specific focus on Indo-Caribbean identities is revealing for the contextual study of creative practices in the Caribbean region more broadly. Historically, problems of creativity have largely been aligned along a Euro-/Afro- axis, such as in the formation of political consciousness and discourses of national belonging. But this only misrecognised creative practices, taking them to be instruments of social and political change alone, at the expense of a more transformative conception of culture. It was an outcome perhaps of nation-building discourses and historical revisionism in the post-war Caribbean. The following section shows, in the case of a single artist, how a creative practitioner has lived with constraints of this political kind (alongside other, largely career-related constraints) and why this experience should be registered historically through the emotions.

An emotional chronology of 'Indian art' in Trinidad

I came to know the artist Shastri Maharaj (b. 1953) in 2004 and began to see his biography and his art as significant for understanding Trinidadian concepts of 'Indianness'.[8] The 'Indian art' he is known for – he is often referred to as an 'Indian artist' – connects to Trinidad's anti-colonial history and a wider discussion of the Indian diaspora in the Atlantic world. Maharaj's career as an artist illustrates how Trinidad's changing demands for ethnic difference are constructed visually. A surprising detail of his career is that such demands cannot be sustained. Not only has the artist struggled to cope with the contextual need to be 'Indian', and to offer 'Indian art', but that need has turned out to be shifting and cannot be relied upon as a source of commercial success or critical acclaim. Maharaj's art and experience therefore show up the alleged rewards of the emphasis on ethnic difference and the incompatibility of an assumed relation between visual creativity and ethnicity.

Shastri Maharaj lives in the town of Chaguanas in central Trinidad, and at the time of my interviews with him he was occupied during the working day with teaching in the visual arts at the nearby Valsayn Teachers' College.

In 1972, he studied mathematics and physics at the University of Winnipeg collegiate in Canada, and went on to achieve a Bachelor of Fine Arts at the University of Manitoba. Maharaj told me about his time in Canada when he was taught by the installation and performance artist, Jeff Funnell (b. 1940). Another art teacher made an impression on him once he returned to settle in Trinidad in 1981: Alexander King, who had been taught by a student of the Fauvist-Cubist, Georges Braque. After his education abroad, Maharaj worked

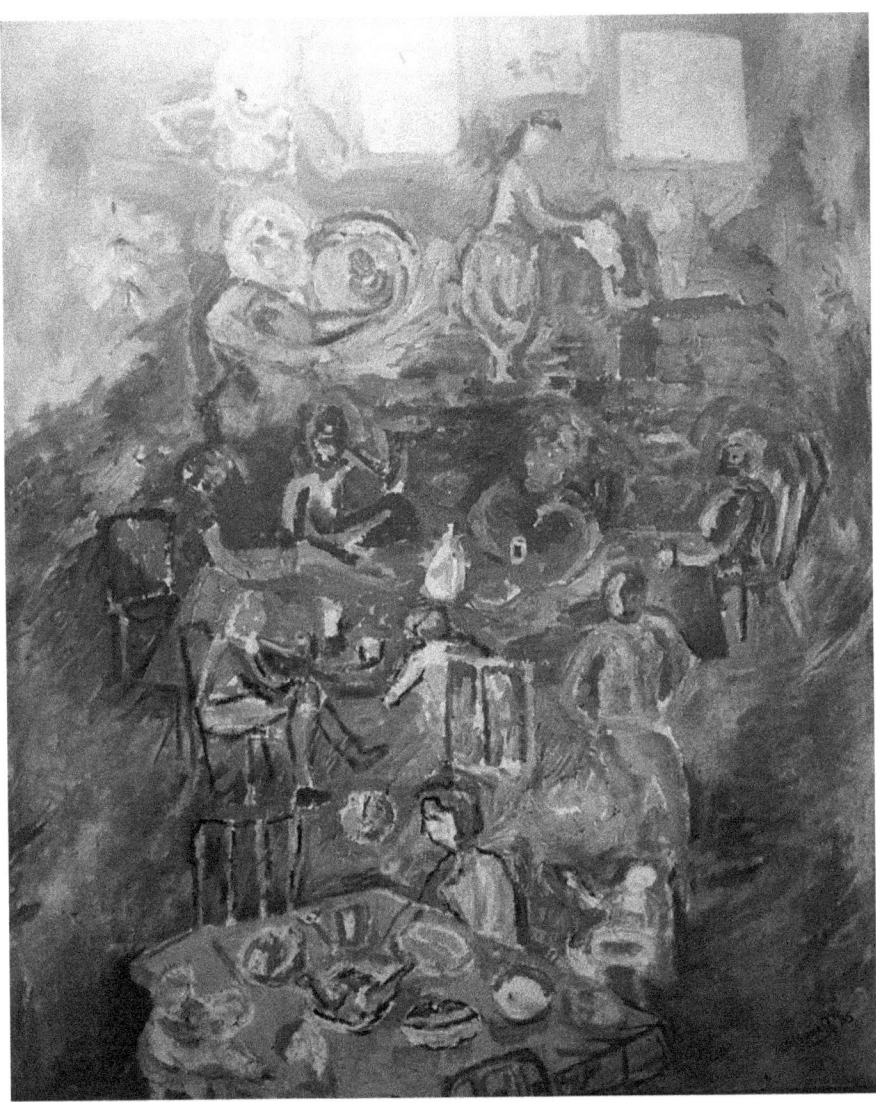

Shastri Maharaj, *Sunday* (1990), acrylic on canvas, 152.4 × 106.7 cm.   **17**

to establish himself in Trinidad as an artist, doing (in his own words) 'new wave shit, postmodernism, all that'. His aim was to 'visually assault society', as he put it, 'just like Dubuffet, Schnabel and Miró'– an eclectic choice of those artists that had impressed Maharaj during his art training.[9]

Subsequently, during the 1980s, Maharaj avoided making the sort of visual images that had satisfied political interests in the arts in Trinidad during decolonisation (figure 17). He sought to ignore the officially championed approach taken by M. P. Alladin and artists of a previous generation, seeing that this would position his art as Indo-Trinidadian or as made by a Caribbean 'East Indian'. As he described in his weekly newspaper column, 'Art is Life': 'The themes of his [M. P. Alladin's] paintings documented the cultural and social traits and customs of the East Indians. … elements of design and colour that speak of the presence of the East Indian.'[10] Bravely refusing to emphasise an East Indian 'presence', Maharaj aimed for a contrary position. The impact of his painterly, figurative practice can be seen in press reviews of the time. These indicated Maharaj's foreign education and the welcome sophistication that he brought to the Trinidad art scene. In one of his weekly columns of 1983, 'On the art of life', William Gordon, staff writer for the establishment newspaper *The Trinidad Guardian,* responded to a solo exhibition by Maharaj staged in the Trinidad capital:

> This show reflected those influences rather than the typical concerns of 'Third World Art', of art as a vehicle for personal discovery rather than as an applied craft with firm rules and clear basic presumptions. …Shastri has been able to accept the challenge of avant garde art influences in North America.[11]

Such high praise – of the local youth whose exploits overseas had earned him the accolade of artist – was not typical of the sort of encouragement that East Indian artists were given in Trinidad after Independence.[12] Indeed, beyond critics such as William Gordon, Maharaj would find that his ambition to 'visually assault society' had a rather limited following. There was pressure from official bodies to represent 'East Indian life' and the pursuit of 'craft', such as the National Council of Indian Culture. In 1983 the Council sponsored a painting competition on the theme 'East Indian Life-Styles – One Face of our Nation', with a first prize of a three-week visit to India. A call went out for original works 'including subjects such as family life, ceremonies, festivals, work, music, dances, etc., both of past and present times'.[13] Staged to inspire competitors, visitors to the shopping plaza West Mall – in a wealthy North West suburb of the capital – were invited to view the work of Rajiv Kaushik, an artist brought specially from India, whose 'high standard of traditional painting and batik wall hangings show the fastidious conventions and subtle colour sense of classical Indian Art. [...] Jewel-like Rajput pieces and all the

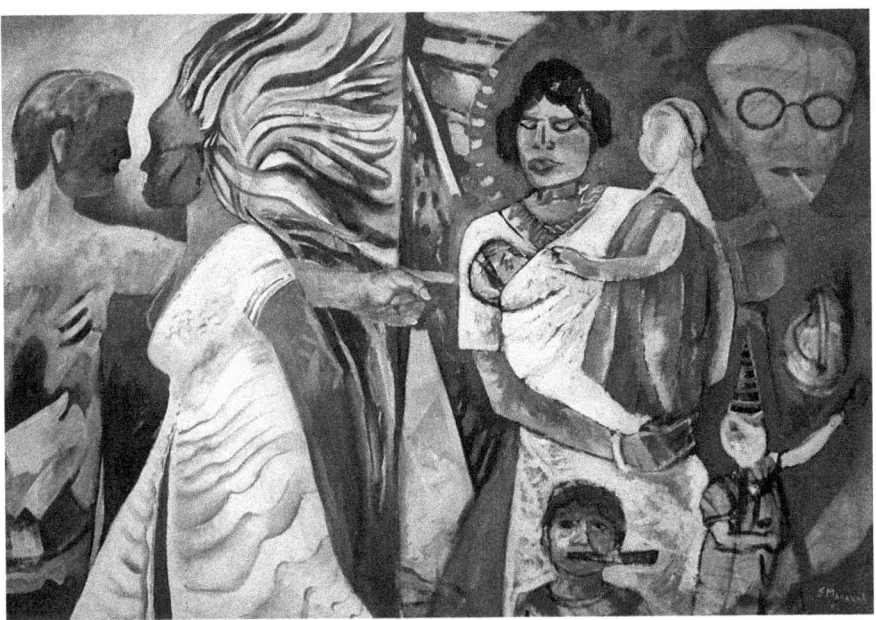

Shastri Maharaj, *Symbiosis* (1992), acrylic on canvas, 182.9 × 104.1 cm.　　**18**

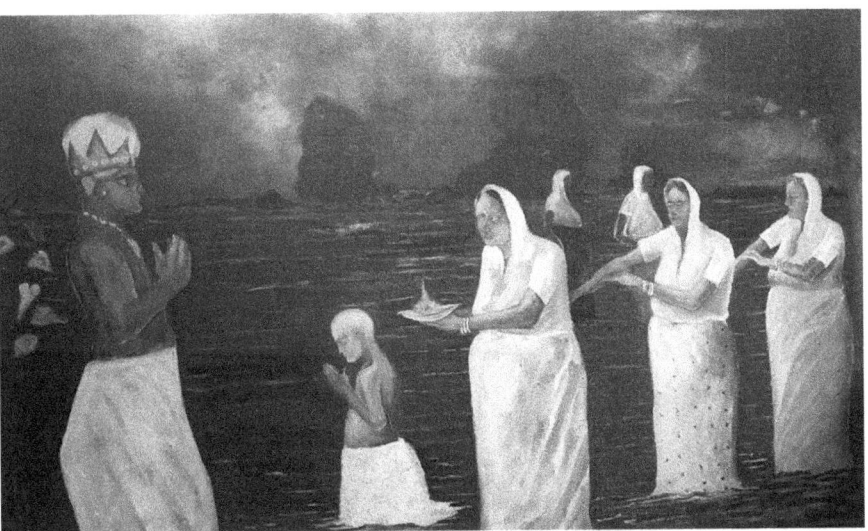

Shastri Maharaj, *Janeo* (1998), acrylic on canvas, 121.9 × 76.2 cm.　　**19**

enchanting plays of Lord Krishna and the gopis, show a whole world in flat stylised spaces of richly patterned charm."[14]

Maharaj, feeling undervalued and misunderstood, saw his only opportunity for gaining local patronage to lie in a compromise. As he reflected: 'The Indo-Trinidadian amidst a very Eurocentric approach to culture, in terms of music, song, dance and dress, realised that the proliferation of his arts forms had to be presented in a form that would be appealing to its followers to ensure their continued support.'[15] By the end of the 1980s, his attitude to imaging had changed (figure 18). His pieces began to take up overt indexes of East Indian ethnicity as prescribed by his intended audience of 'followers'. He warmly embraced a creole nationalist formula which involved elaborating on a group of motifs of 'Indianness' and invocations of 'tradition' that were not dissimilar to those being solicited for the competition at West Mall. For much of the 1990s to the present, Maharaj's paintings developed in this way, often with recognisable Hindu elements coupled with details drawn from the local geography (figure 19).

The result was initially an establishment success. With the coming to power in 1995 of the mainly Indo-Trinidadian-led party, the United National Congress, and through support from the ascendant East Indian elite, Maharaj's national status as an artist appeared to be affirmed. However, this assured patronage disappeared when political power reverted to the People's National Movement in 2002, with its traditionally Afro-Trinidadian following. From Maharaj's point of view this led to the demand that he produce images which avoid the references in his works of the mid-1990s. From 2002, his art once more changed track, and he purposefully gave up his earlier treatment of 'Indian' themes.

Art and ethnicity at their emotional limits

When I met Shastri Maharaj he had come to paint images of houses (figure 20). These capture the common pattern in Trinidad, of two-storey frames for domestic dwelling. At one time these were put up in brick and wood, and are now all in concrete, although recognisable still for having only the upper floor enclosed. This leaves a space 'under the house', as it is referred to, for storage, and eventual completion by subsequent generations of the offspring of the household (figure 21). While otherwise common throughout the country, for Maharaj these 'stilt-' or as he suggested 'bird-' or 'spirit-houses' are emblematic of the rural parts of the island. He has produced an open-ended series of these in which the houses are frequently placed in spare, largely defoliated surroundings, jutting above smooth horizons of baked earth. By assigning titles that indicate place names (like *Somewhere in Fyzabad*),[16] to some of these works, he has added a further association to more isolated parts of the country

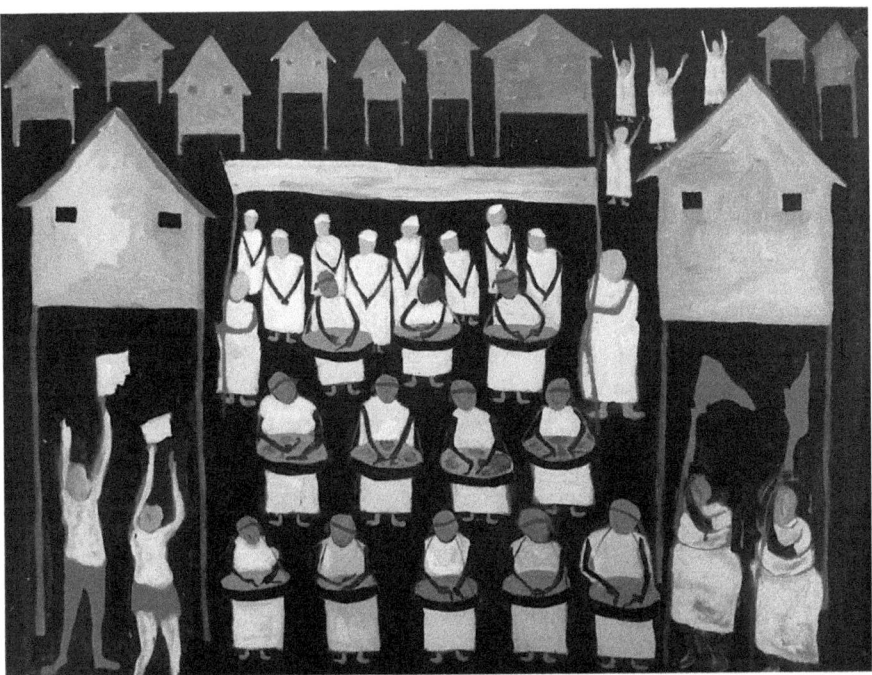

Shastri Maharaj, *Jour Overt* (2000), acrylic on canvas, 61 × 43.2 cm.   **20**

where East Indians have traditionally lived and worked the sugar plantations. Maharaj told me to look for houses like these in Caroni, a sugar-growing area not far from his home.

During our first few meetings, Maharaj told me nothing which would suggest that he was uncomfortable with the expectation placed upon him as an East Indian making 'Indian art'. On the contrary, the ethnic geography of Trinidad indicated by his painted houses seemed to confirm his desire to identify as Indian. He told me of his growing purpose to illustrate his Hindu beliefs, while remaining careful to point out that he does not approach his art in devotion to Hinduism. As he argued, his works are intended as a pointer or channel back to himself: 'they get to the source. I am the source', he told me. He recalled to me a dream of once finding himself in dialogue with a guru, which prompted him to paint an image of the goddess Lakshmi.

Maharaj and I talked about the way in which the theme of Indianness has been present throughout his career and how it is being continually modified through his works. He told me that maintaining an 'Indian art' has required an effort that is difficult to sustain. This is due to the shifting background of interests in ethnicity at the levels of official patronage and the local art market. He complained about feeling disadvantaged to be living in Chaguanas, an area which is generally characterised as an East Indian heartland, despite the high degree of ethnic mixing there as in the rest of Trinidad. His tangible hostility towards other artists who make up the urban elite in Trinidad's capital, Port of Spain, was underscored by an ethnic distinction: 'I'm a Hindu artist. I want to be independent of French creole [urban elite] patrimony, and the vogue crowd. They prostitute art. The Johnny-come-lately artists haven't gone through the test of time. [They are] upstart artists who have no philosophy behind their work, and paint recreationally.' The growth in newcomers to the vocation is the result, Maharaj explained, of the relatively low commissions demanded by galleries, of around 30–33 per cent. A worse problem for him, however, was the coupling of patterns of patronage with ethnicity. Maharaj no longer enjoyed much public interest nor could he consider his art a viable source of income since, 'Professional Indians don't buy art', he complained.

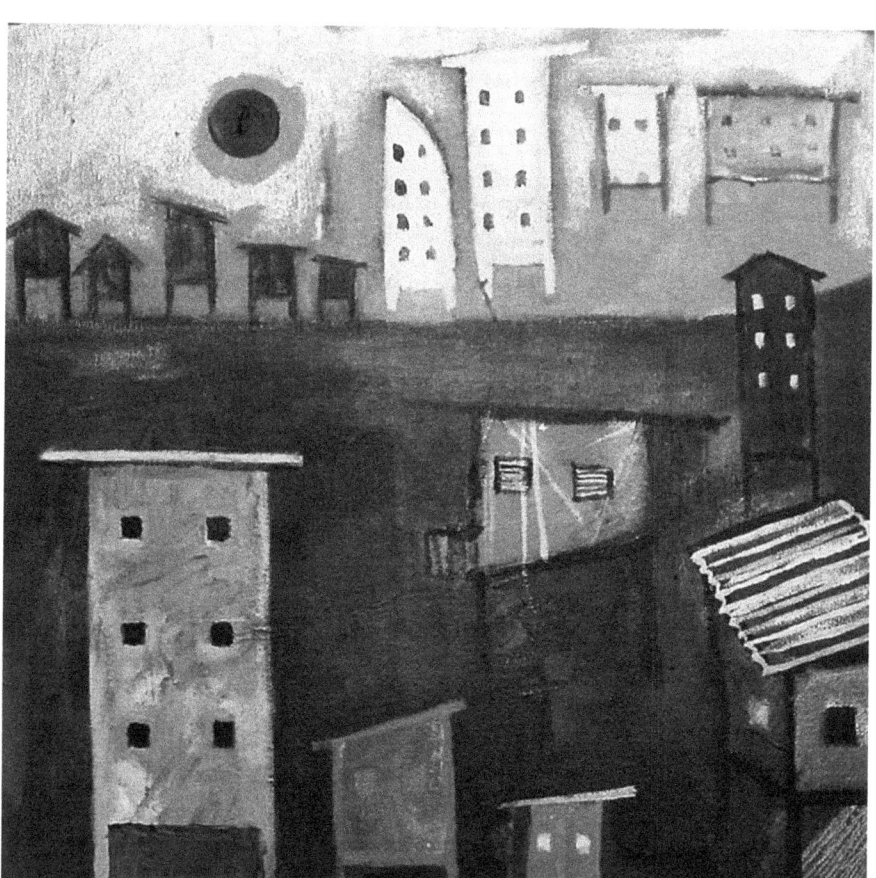

21   Shastri Maharaj, *Barracks* (2006), acrylic on canvas, 61 × 43.2 cm.

This has compelled him to look for buyers from 'across the board, of other ethnicities – architects, lawyers …'

It might be said that Maharaj's feelings demand nothing more than an orthodox historical analysis of 'decline'. This would focus on the theme of a failing career for an artist curtailed by professional rivalries, a state of saturation in the local art market, and an erosion of opportunities for promotion and display. There is plenty here to confirm what the sociology and anthropology of art have identified as a myth of the 'free creator, unaffected by outside influences' – by showing that art producers always operate within professional fields of power, competing for recognition, status and economic gain.[17] This is an extension of the critique brought to bear within the history of art by artists and thinkers of the modernist avant-garde, who have extensively problematised the idea of the artist as an 'authoritative aesthetic spokesman'. Charles Harrison, for instance, has dismantled claims for creative autonomy, by taking seriously that 'what a painting expresses or means *must* be a function of what it is made of and from, culturally, socially, technically, historically, psychologically and morally, independently of the mind of the spectator …'.[18] In the Caribbean case this would lead us to reject the uncritical notion of Maharaj the painter as an 'authoritative *ethnic* spokesman', to rephrase Harrison, and in line with the polemic offered by artists such as Rasheed Araeen.[19]

In putting the emotional aspects of Maharaj's experience into the foreground, the limitations of using ethnicity as an analytical category become clearer. Here we are faced simultaneously with the fallacy of creative autonomy and the inadequacy of the art-as-ethnicity paradigm. As such, it makes sense to disentangle the visual from the category of ethnicity, and to explore creativity within a more 'embodied' history. Recent analysis of the emotions has covered the terrain of both 'the vehement passions' (grief, fear, rapture and so on),[20] and affects and emotions such as shame, humiliation, irritation, anxiety, envy, disdain, surprise, and so on.[21] Having set out the chronology of his emotional experience, it is Maharaj's sense of disillusion in particular which emerges as the ground for another analytical path. Maharaj lives rather uncomfortably with an idea of 'Indian art' that first emerged during decolonisation. It was instituted during Independence through the emphasis on art as a signifier of ethnic diversity within the national community. However, the concept of national culture devised in that earlier period has had an effect that is being felt well beyond such anti-colonial beginnings. The founding moment of nationalism amounted to the reifying of ethnic differences, in a widely enacted objectification and 'commodification of ethnicity'.[22] This has had a lasting significance for art practice. One outcome is that commodification is just as capable of working with as against the agency of visual image-makers. A commodified ethnicity thereby disavows what transformative potential that difference once promised during decolonisation.

With this in view, it is easier to see why Maharaj should feel that his ambition for an art career has been so curtailed. He is marked by a deep ambivalence about the connotations of 'Indianness' around his dwindling art practice. In his studio he showed me attempts to detach his images from any such connections, with arrangements on canvas of geometrical shapes in space rather like Kandinsky's. Another group of his unsold works included large canvases reminiscent for me of those of the Indian painter Bhupen Khakhar, who has also worked to complicate the matter of identity in post-Independence India, namely by emphasising his homosexuality. Maharaj regards this range of visual interests as testament to his uniqueness, and an indication of his potential for perpetual creative development. As he told me: 'I'm not playing with people's expectations, I'm just becoming less ignorant daily. I am sacrosanct, there's no Indian man like me, with family, and painting.'[23] The artist's narrative about his career, told in a vocabulary of the emotions, bears a more complex relationship to difference than is accounted for in the ideology of the multicultural nation. Certainly, he spoke in a way that frequently mixed references to ethnicity and religion, much as the anthropologist Aisha Khan has noted in how Trinidad's South Asian diaspora more generally mixes metaphors of race and religious identity in the ideology of the mixed or 'callaloo nation'.[24] But the horizons of visual creativity and difference have remained at odds in Maharaj's emotional experience. This is despite his ambitions to bind them together by attempting to insert or insinuate his art into Trinidad's hegemonic imaginary of difference.

The notion of 'Indian art' in Trinidad is a starkly historical category. The account given here should illustrate the serious care that is needed to avoid any simple analytical coupling of creativity and ethnic difference. This becomes clearer when tracing out the purposeful adjustments to his practice that Maharaj has made at stages in his career. Some of his works have employed essentialist categories of ethnic difference which he had previously declared as anachronistic from the point of view of his 'avant-garde' training. A leading contradiction of anti-colonial thought was that it often borrowed and restated the official ideologies of ethnic difference that originated during colonisation. Maharaj reproduced this pattern at the moment when he embraced visual motifs of Indianness, which have a precedent in the visual descriptions of India that circulated throughout the British Empire. By choosing to paint these motifs, Maharaj also replayed the hierarchy deriving from European academic conservatism in which painting presides over other media of visual representation. Maharaj's aim was to put these associations to other uses: they were to furnish his faith in the value of constructing an Indo-Trinidadian identity, the promise of finding a market, and achieving national importance. As such, over subsequent years, Maharaj has persevered with the 'Indian art' idea. This is despite his sense of disillusion and the developments in Trinidad whereby ethnicities are commodified and emptied of any transformative value. The artist's emotional experience suggests that there are points when the resource of ethnicity and the connotations of 'Indian art' become circumscribing and reach their limits.

Everyday emotions beyond ethnicity

At about 9 pm I went to Chaguanas, to a large gathering of perhaps 160 people celebrating the night before a Hindu wedding. The ceremony itself was to take place at the Hanuman murti and ashram, but this evening, the bride's parents were hosting 'a night of entertainment' as the master of ceremonies put it at their home, which involved singing, dancing and some comedy. Food was served on large green leaves in a spacious backroom, and with almost the same variety as at that morning's puja. On a brightly lit temporary stage in a large open-plan room, unfurnished save for scores of plastic patio chairs, and balloons, a drummer played on an electronic drum pad, whilst another musician handled an electric keyboard. In the course of the evening they accompanied a string of singers, male and female. Pre-recorded music that played through a PA system formed the backdrop for the children and adolescents who danced in the style of the sequences from popular Indian films, dressed in brightly coloured costumes.

Most of the singers were soloists singing in Hindi or Bhojpuri, which they read from personal notebooks carried with them on stage. The mood of the songs ranged from the melancholy Mr. Amar Ali McDougall, to a more jubilant quintet that included the bride's mother, which began a medley of songs at a moment early in the proceedings when a sacred practice, the 'parching of the *lawa* (rice)' (they sang 'Bhuje de lawa, bhuje de lawa') was taking place over an open fire in front of the domestic shrine. I took a photograph of two women central to the 'parching' engaged in some dancing, 'winding their waists' and 'wining' [rhythmic gyrations of the hips] as they 'parched'. The bride, dressed in sari blouse, skirt and pinned dupatta danced to great appreciation, and I was told that this was an unusual happening at a woman's own wedding celebration. The MC made several reminders between acts that amongst the families of the bride and groom were musicians and singers who formed the majority of the performers that evening. One especially popular singer of chutney songs from outside the family held the stage for about 40 minutes to do a comic set comprising snippets of sung verse in Hindi and Bhojpuri. Their finale was a song with the refrain, in English, 'the cat licked the butter, the cat licked the butter'.[25]

My notes above describe a context in which wedding performances, including those by members of the wedding party, and in this case even the bride herself, carry a persistent identification with East Indianness. The juxtaposition of this private context with that of the art making, display and public reception of Shastri Maharaj, is suggestive of how ethnicity is signified in private and public spaces – since these two contexts certainly speak to that division. It also points to how identifications with Indianness are codified in high art as compared to the popular arts, or popular culture. Further, the space of wedding celebration evidences what Maharaj insists is a running element in his visual practice: the emotionality surrounding the desire for a grounded, or as he put it, 'grass-roots' understanding of his works, evidenced in his treatment of everyday 'East Indian' themes.

The stylistic and iconographic switches in Maharaj's career, in part, demonstrate what David Freedberg has located as 'the effectiveness, efficacy and vitality of images themselves',[26] in that these changes are an embodied response to Trinidad's unfolding political scene. However, I have tried to make clear how this 'effectiveness' compares to the more everyday context of production. This is to draw on Freedberg's suggestion that art historical study ought to attend simultaneously to everyday forms of material production (thereby returning to a much older interest for the discipline, set out by those such as Riégl and Wölfflin).[27] There are tangible links between Maharaj's career and the wedding scene. The emotional aspects of the wedding that I attended are crucial to any assessment of this 'popular' identification with an Indo-Trinidadian community. As for Maharaj's art, they are uncomfortably positioned by the inscription of Indianness as a cultural component of Trinidadian national community.

Another way to explore the dynamics of the production of Indianness is to address an area of practice that sits beyond, as well as within, the national. One such is the field of performances by singers such as Rikki Jai. Through parody

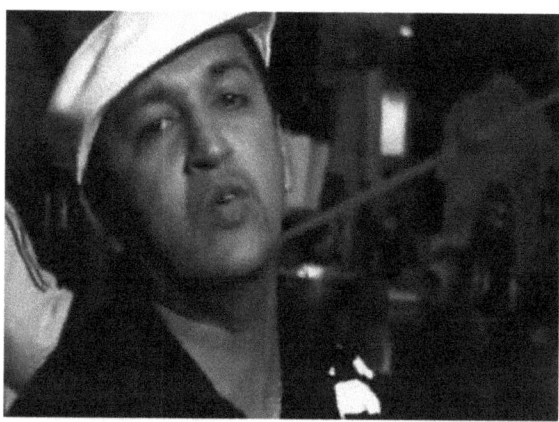

22   Rikki Jai, *Boleh Murugwah*, still image from the music video on youtube.com.

and self-parody they are a complex reversal of the widely marketable Indo-pop culture of Trinidad, and the apparent attachment to the national suggested by the privacy of wedding spaces. Jai (born Samraj Jaimungal, in Friendship Village, San Fernando) emerged as a singer and songwriter in Trinidad with his song entitled *Sumintra* of 1988. The more recent *Boleh Murugwah*,[28] (figure 22), focuses on the ritual of the parching of unpolished rice on the eve of a Hindu wedding, part of the two-day *matti kaur* ceremonies in which women, predominantly, take the lead; and which at other times involves the burying of spices, and suggestive games and role playing thought to serve as the sexual initiation of the bride and bridegroom. Much of the song is sung in Bhojpuri, a language of the Indian state of Bihar from where many of the indentured labourers came to the Caribbean after 1843.

Within Jai's career we can trace a move from his initial role of entertainer for an Indian audience and into an expanded field. His concerts and audio and video recordings enjoy a wide distribution among national and international listeners, those within the Caribbean region and its diaspora. It is notable that Jai is thereby shedding the status of cultural producer for an audience of any single ethnicity, or national space. Even so, it is notable that he has succeeded in retaining each of these publics while reaching out more widely.

The basis for his appeal has been looked at in the style of his performances. Bangalore-based scholar, Tejaswini Niranjana notes that Jai performs chutney, chutney-soca and calypso – labels for a body of music that broadly ranges from folk-derived Bhojpuri lyrics and rhythms to those sung in Trinidadian English and with Afro-Caribbean beats. Jai thereby shows an ability to move among genres with melodic lines which are distinct from one another. As Jai suggested to Niranjana in interview, chutney and Hindi film songs have an 'Indian *gamak*' which distinguishes them from soca or calypso (and which would suggest that for Jai chutney-soca is more like soca than chutney). Jai has explored the relations between these genres by being one of the first singers to hire a dance troupe and a drama troupe to provide the background narrative for his performances – a formula more familiar in soca. As Niranjana writes, 'He felt that the chutney industry was "too dormant" compared with the more interactive performances in the "soca industry." Before he introduced soca performative elements, he said, there were "no hands in the air, no rags, no towels [being waved]".'[29] The younger singer and songwriter Ravi B has extended the address to multiple audiences typical of Jai, and yet with a particular appeal to a new Indo-Caribbean constituency made up of consumers of diverse music styles.[30]

Returning briefly to Maharaj, when the artist spoke about his travels abroad for education in Canada, he would emphasise the international connections in the story of his life and career. This chapter of transit may be matched with an account of transformation: at one point or another, as I have outlined,

Maharaj and Rikki Jai alike had both identified with, and yet de-identified or disavowed, the categories of 'creole', 'Indian', and 'Indo-Trinidadian'. The scope for their success in doing so was set out by constraints that were beyond their influence. These often prevailed upon them from the past. The overall national theme of transition from colonial subjects to inhabitants of a free and sovereign state would suitably provide the wider historical backdrop to these contemporary shifts.

The suggestion here is that attention to the *movement* of objects such as works of art and music may usefully extend an analysis of the emotions and ethnicity. The movement of objects and images valued as fine art – taken to Trinidad from a European context of production and reception – converges in transit with images referring to a notional Hindu identity, such as those painted by Maharaj, or promoted by the National Council of Indian Culture. These latter are appropriated into the ideological category of 'European art'. This has had mixed results for those seeking to reconcile the otherwise divergent historical antecedents of the art of the coloniser and the artefacts of the colonised.

Such objects have become the fraught site of some further, ensuing transitions. Maharaj's art, as with Rikki Jai's music, has at various moments signified Indianness and, at others, a creole identity that bespeaks an association with nationhood. The meaning of these productions then undergoes transition as their significance shifts with time and location. Maharaj's art is neither 'popular', nor for that matter is it, as he suggests, 'elite' – at least not enough to be embraced by 'French creole', middle or upper-class art patrons. Equally, to describe Rikki Jai's works as simply 'popular' music would mean foregoing a discussion about which public or audience his music appeals to, and whether this may be delineated easily by social group or nationality. Even more problematic is whether Jai's music may be described according to ethnicity, since an ability to transition any neat category of ethnic difference seems to be its defining feature.

Overall, these patterns suggest a need to open up the theme of ethnicity and to question its suitability as a foundational category for cultural analysis. Performers such as Rikki Jai complicate the easy assumption that musicians of the Indian diaspora stand at the centre of a network of relations between those seeking to forge an East Indian ethnic community through cultural phenomena. Chutney music is contingent with practices of differencing, which defy the circumscriptions of Indian nationalism and transnationalism. This music cannot be separated from the more complex production of publics within the Caribbean and its diaspora – in other words, those publics and groupings which run across ethnic boundaries. Wedding music also raises the question of whether these performances reproduce 'folk' traditions of celebration in any significantly different way from how music such as Jai's has renegotiated 'folk' signifiers. In each case we are presented with the issue of how mass-marketed music such as Hindi film scores, chutney and chutney-soca are being consumed. There is a parallel here with Maharaj's frequent reconsiderations of such 'ethnic indexicality' – the ostensible visual indication of ethnic or diasporic difference in his art. These reconsiderations are made uncomfortably along the timeline of his career. The changes that he has experienced are an embodied locus of the historical conflicts taking place more widely in Trinidad around the mobilisation of Indianness.

Understanding the relationship between emotions and ethnicity requires an extended look at various options for understanding cultural practices. On the one hand is the emotional 'affect', or the affective elements of cultural practices, and on the other, the field of cultural reception where ethnic and diasporic difference is inscribed onto an otherwise ambiguous phenomenal surface. This is a dimension that critical study of the transnational Caribbean has been unable to contemplate in any depth, largely because cultural analysis itself has contributed to the inscription of difference. It has also routinely elided aesthetics (a particular area of concern within artistic discourse) with theoretical approaches focused on visual signification and, more specifically, an interpretative model of 'culture as text'. In this way, the role of aesthetics has been largely bypassed; there is a tendency to translate the realm of cultural experience into the thematic (and largely post-structuralist) vocabulary of representation.

Adopting a greater interest in the emotionally affective presence of cultural practices might combat this tendency. It would help, for instance, to understand the experience of Maharaj as he busily responds to changes in a local art market heavily imprinted by wider political attitudes to difference. Jai's shifts among musical languages and his enlarging audience would also become comprehensible. The presence of these cultural processes can be distinguished from the changing relations among representation and ethnicity. However, perceptual and emotional questions, such as those under the heading of an aesthetics of diaspora, are actively foreclosed by a methodological approach which 'decodes' the cultural and treats it as nothing more than a component of diasporic differencing (and is, indeed, a form of semiological reductionism). Notwithstanding critical concerns with 'the politics of emotions',[31] we still know very little about how the emotions feature in cultural practices in postcolonial contexts. But this may only arrive with a proper departure from the generic identification of the role of culture in decolonising and diasporic spaces such as the Caribbean.

Such are the dynamic transformations that works of art and music both undergo and entail when they are caught at a locus of contestations between questions of meaning and emotional efficacy. Works of art and music are in one historical instance the condensation of anti-colonial feeling, nationalist pride and ethnic difference. However, whether they are capable of sustaining that status is uncertain, since they are subject to transit, transition and transformation, and become the object of further change.

Finally, this brings me to another 'trans-', as in transnationalism. I have outlined cultural practices as having a more complex link to transnationalism than in the current approaches of anthropology, media and cultural studies and, increasingly, art history, where culture serves as a signification of transnational connection as well as deriving its efficacy from that ability to signify. In that account, cultural forms move between national locations and make transnational links possible – they are the basis for a shared or transmitted sense of ethnic 'belonging' within one or other diaspora. This maps a cultural geography of transnational connectivity. In the setting of the Indian diaspora emerges a picture of how diverse locations relate to other parts of the global diaspora, as well as to Indians in the Asian sub-continent. Cultural practices – including media such as music, film and television – are vital for forming and continuing such lines of contact. In this sense, otherwise overlooked elements of 'the cultural' are thought to offer a symbolic reach, and enable a thriving economy of relations within diaspora communities.

The material in this chapter offers, in part, a response to the usefulness of such paradigms, in their understanding of cultural practices in diaspora spaces as being important most of all for their ability to mediate and communicate. By contrast, I have indicated that the cultural refuses to occupy that status alone, and that this needs to be made clear if we are to resist the allure of a commoditised aesthetic of diaspora culture. By paying attention to the emotions, Trinidadian artworks and performances reveal more complex implications for the cultural. Even where ethnicity is so central to understanding national and transnational community, as it is in Trinidad, I have shown why cultural practices deserve alternative analytical attention beyond the models of representation, textuality and signification.

Conclusion: ownership and the emotions

I began by indicating that notions of Trinidadian national culture – with art making as its vanguard – were structured along multi-ethnic lines and derived indirectly from a desire for ever-sharpening distinctions between the 'overseas', or 'metropolitan', and 'local' components for cultural production. It was this condition of literal isolation which was thought to be enabling of national distinctiveness in Trinidad, since a major anti-colonial concern was to press cultural creativity into the service of 'domestic' rather than 'outside' interests. A leading proponent of this view was the first prime minister of Trinidad and Tobago, Dr Eric Williams, who expressed the terms of this relationship to the 'outside' in his many addresses, interviews and publications, such as in the following:

Dependence on the outside world in the Caribbean in 1969 is not only economic. It is also cultural, institutional, intellectual and psychological. Political forms and social institutions, even in the politically independent countries, were imitated rather than created, borrowed rather than relevant, reflecting the forms existing in the particular metropolitan country from which they were derived. There is still no serious indigenous intellectual life.[32]

Williams's message encourages the creation of forms and institutions capable of containing or generating indigenous cultural products. This leads me to suggest that it ought also to be read as part of a broader emotional discourse of ownership in the Caribbean. Williams insists on a move away from those products which are 'imitated rather than created, borrowed rather than relevant'. Such ideas have remained hegemonic in the aftermath of Empire and are central to anti-colonial politics. But what is unexplored about them is how they couple ownership and production, and pay little attention to cultural consumption. The 'insiderism' of anti-colonial cultural debate focused on the rejection of 'outsider' ideas and practices – preferring to replace them with 'home-grown' ones. Far less emphasis was given to rejecting colonial patterns of *consuming* 'indigenous' products. In short, there was little confrontation of the categorisation of the cultural (the divisions of art and craft; of fine art, popular arts and 'folk', as M. P. Alladin suggested),[33] which Trinidad inherited at the moment of its Independence. There was also no appreciation that the outcome of commoditising culture as a political resource would mean the disastrous reification of ethnic and racial differences.

Certainly, much may be gained from avoiding such reification, given the sort of experiences among artists and performers that are outlined here. I have suggested that this might begin by reflecting on the emotions as a historical register of what happens when the cultural is employed as a site of differencing. The examples in this chapter suggest a need to unpick such categories of the cultural and to pursue the current turn away from models of cultural representation. In general, the emotional processes described here are part and parcel of political dynamics, such as the desire to create a creole, national identity, independent of the imperial legacy, and the yearning for an Indo-Trinidadian identity as a component of national community. Such emotions suggest how state-sanctioned forms of Trinidadian 'Indianness' are being *felt* as well as renegotiated, in ways that throw light on patterns of counter-hegemonic ownership of cultural practices within diasporic space.

At root, much rests on being able to see the limitations that result from identification with the Indian diaspora in Trinidad. Of course, these need to be evaluated alongside the benefits and opportunities that such an association has granted in the historical past. In either case, analysis of this context then becomes a matter of the need to pay more direct attention to cultural phenomena. This would avoid what cultural theorist Barbara Stafford has named the 'ruling metaphor of reading'[34] – the apprehension of cultural objects for their representational, signifying and textual qualities. Dispensing with this model – of the legibility of cultural practices – in favour of a chronology of the emotions has particular outcomes on the ground for Caribbean artists and performers. These individuals face demands among audiences for a readable ethnic difference, in a context where readability is germane to the cultural object becoming a commodity. However, once they are shown to be involved in a more complex emotional set of interactions (in which objects and images actively evoke particular emotions, rather than simply lending themselves to emotional demands, as vehicles or media in their service) then a fuller sense of the motivations for cultural production itself emerges.

The pressures, as well as the opportunities, to signify diasporic difference configure a discursive field which artists and performers are obliged to navigate. Why they should choose art making, song and performance in order to do so can be understood from the details of how cultural reception and the emotions intersect. The contrapuntal forms of emotional ownership that operate around cultural practices show how aesthetic experience can be relieved of the burden of discourses of difference. To put this more simply, artists and performers in spaces of diaspora live and work with the obstacles, as well as the opportunities, of ethnic identification and they apply themselves to cultural production in a desire to exceed those limits. Here I have aimed to demonstrate the emotional dimension of that historical search for ownership of one's own cultural practices. Within the overdetermination of ethnicised spaces, cultural products are transformed by the emotions into less confined alternatives.

Notes

1 R. Williams, *Marxism and literature* (London: Oxford University Press, 1977), p. 132.
2 Compare with M. Svašek, 'Improvising in a world of movement: Transit, transition, and transformation', in H. K. Anheier and Y. R. Isar (eds), *Cultural expression, creativity and innovation* (London: Sage, 2010), pp. 62–77.
3 H. Bhabha, *The location of culture* (London: Routledge, 1994).
4 P. Mohammed, 'The "creolisation" of Indian women in Trinidad', in V. A. Shepard and G. L. Richards (eds), *Questioning creole: Creolisation discourses in Caribbean culture. In honour of Kamau Brathwaite* (Kingston, Jamaica: Ian Randle Publishers and Oxford: James Currey, 2002), pp. 130–47.
5 C. Cozier, 'Between narratives and other spaces', *Small Axe*, 6 (1999), 19–37, p. 23. Compare to the observation made by Deborah Thomas in her account of 'folk Blackness' in Jamaica as a prevailing norm of identification. D. Thomas, *Modern blackness: Nationalism, globalization, and the politics of culture in Jamaica* (London and Durham: Duke University Press, 2004).

6 E. Hallam and T. Ingold (eds), *Creativity and cultural improvisation* (Oxford: Berg, 2007), p. 2.

7 M. de Certeau, *The practice of everyday life*, trans. S. Rendall (Berkeley: University of California Press, 1984).

8 L. Wainwright, '"Indian art" in Trinidad? Ethnicity at material limits', *Creative Communications*, 2:1–2 (2007), 163–88.

9 Interview notes, 22 August 2004.

10 S. Maharaj, 'Indo-Caribbean visual arts: Evolution and change', *Trinidad Guardian* (8 October 1992).

11 W. Gordon, 'On the art of real life: In pursuit of real subjects', *Trinidad Guardian* (17 August 1983).

12 P. Scher, 'Confounding categories in the Caribbean art market: Reflections on self-taught artists in Trinidad and Tobago', *Small Axe*, 6 (1999), 37–56.

13 *Trinidad Guardian*, 5 June 1983.

14 *Trinidad Guardian*, 6 June 1983.

15 S. Maharaj, 'Indo-Caribbean visual arts'.

16 For this and further examples, see Maharaj's website: www.smfineart.com/index.htm (accessed 25 October 2006).

17 P. Bourdieu, *Distinction: A social critique of the judgement of taste* (London, 1984); M. Svašek, *Anthropology, art and cultural production* (London: Pluto, 2007), pp. 88–92.

18 C. Harrison, *Art & language* (Birmingham: Ikon Gallery, 1983), p. 12.

19 R. Araeen, 'From primitivism to ethnic arts', in S. Hiller (ed.), *The myth of primitivism: Perspectives on art* (London and New York: Routledge, 1991), pp. 158–84; L. Wainwright, 'On being unique: World art and its British institutions', *Visual Culture in Britain*, 10:1 (2009), 87–101; also: S. Price, *Primitive art in civilised places* (Chicago and London: Chicago University Press, 1989).

20 See: P. Fisher, *The vehement passions* (Princeton: Princeton University Press, 2002); C. Altieri, *The particulars of rapture: An aesthetics of the affects* (Ithaca: Cornell University Press, 2003).

21 S. Ngai, *Ugly feelings* (Cambridge: MIT Press, 2005).

22 K. A. Yelvington (ed.), *Trinidad ethnicity* (London: Macmillan, 1993), p. 10.

23 Personal notes, 7 July 2004.

24 A. Khan, *Callaloo nation: Metaphors of race and religious identity among South Asians in Trinidad* (London and Durham: Duke University Press, 2004).

25 Personal notes, 22 August 2004.

26 D. Freedberg, *The power of images: Studies in the history and theory of response* (Chicago: University of Chicago Press, 1989), p. xvii.

27 F. J. Schwartz, 'Cathedrals and shoes: Concepts of style in Wölfflin and Adorno', *New German Critique*, no. 76 (1999), 3–48.

28 See www.youtube.com/watch?v=ot52acAZlE (last accessed 7 June 2008).

29 T. Niranjana, *Mobilizing India: Women, music, and migration between India and Trinidad* (London and Durham: Duke University Press, 2006), pp. 237–8.

30 See www.youtube.com/watch?v=sUCbWviISuQ&NR=1 and www.youtube.com/watch?v=BGIYUWNHqsI&feature=related. A hit from the 2008 carnival: www.youtube.com/watch?v=mVJnilBYiQc&feature=related (last accessed 7 June 2008).

31 C. A. Lutz and L. Abu-Lughod (eds), *Language and the politics of emotion* (Cambridge: Cambridge University Press, 1990); S. Ahmed, *The cultural politics of emotion* (London: Routledge, 2004).

32 E. Williams, *From Columbus to Castro: The history of the Caribbean, 1492–1969* (London: Deutsch, 1970), p. 501.

33 Indo-Trinidadian, M. P. Alladin (b. 1919, d. 1980), wrote on this distinction in 1975, during his tenth year of office as Trinidad and Tobago Director of Culture, that: 'The art experience in Trinidad and Tobago is substantially the same as that of any other tropical colony or territory which became independent after long rule by a European country. From the point of view of sophistication, the accepted form or type of art expression is Europeanized, as are the materials and concepts employed in its production. This form, in art and life, is considered as being superior, desirable, right and proper. The trained artists of the country have all been schooled in Europe or Canada or the United States. ... There also exists a vast amount of art production at the 'folk' level, which is worthy of consideration. These folk arts are preponderantly of African and East Indian origin. The popular arts are American-influenced. M. P. Alladin, 'Artists and craftsmen', in M. Anthony and A. Carr (eds), *David Frost introduces Trinidad and Tobago* (London: Deutsch, 1975), p. 136.

34 B. M. Stafford, *Good looking: Essays on the virtues of images* (Cambridge, Mass.: MIT Press, 1995).

Chapter 4 examined how the hegemonic status of African diaspora identities in the national context of Trinidad has contributed to the marginalising experience of an artist of the Indian diaspora. This chapter shows how the transnational Caribbean has itself come to be positioned by an art historical understanding of the African diaspora that holds hegemonic status for the discipline. I am drawn especially to curatorial attempts to assemble a history of art for the African diaspora and to offer a more global sense of the connections among artworks and artists on a transatlantic scale.[1]

Several large art exhibitions during the first decade of the twenty-first century were designed to mobilise the African diaspora and to reverse its traditional exclusion from art history and public memory. But this intention seems to be in conflict with the provincialism that has ensued from such representations in their treatment of various sites in the transnational Caribbean. This suggests that the diaspora concept, which once promised fresh possibilities for imagining community beyond the nation, has rather lost its internationalist emphasis and instead become susceptible to political and social priorities located in national settings. There is, in addition, a discernible hegemonic arrangement among these locations. As I argue in this chapter, the predominant uses of the diaspora concept in art history are largely those that connect to US-based realities. Even when their scope takes in regions of the African diaspora outside the United States, such as the Caribbean and Britain, they have less pertinence to a strictly transnational theorisation of art history. Whether such a theorisation is possible at all in the present circumstances then comes to be of issue.

What may be described as a provincialising attitude, grounded in art historical scholarship and curatorial practice, has had an impact on the way that art of the Caribbean and black Britain are remembered and presented. In the treatment of these locations such practices of provincialising can be seen with particular clarity. It is worth speculating on why these contexts especially are so affected. Such anglophone settings stand apart from other European or South American settings for the African diaspora, such as France or Brazil, because they are involved with a generally shared language of curatorial practice and historical scholarship. When US-based attempts to increase the visibility of the African diaspora extend abroad, they penetrate these locations first and most freely. It is a pattern of influence that mirrors the Caribbean's long-standing status as an American leisure resort and a convenient laboratory for US studies of culture and ethnicity.[2]

In Britain, curatorial practices institutionalise the British-American 'special relationship' in the field of the visual arts. They also draw upon the defining conditions and struggles of the North American black experience. One example is the effort to go about 'blackening Europe' by 'making the African American experience primary' in European history. This is a concern with foregrounding the presence of North American ideas and practices – namely in the areas of literature, social studies, politics, film, dance and music – tracing how they have travelled to Europe and changed some of the latter's traditional structures.[3] But if this has anything in common with what Paul Gilroy has noted as an 'Americo-centric discourse', animated by 'its extreme attachments to a reified notion of race',[4] then the prospect of historicising an expanded, circum-Atlantic geography of the African diaspora – traced out in the field of art – is slipping from view.

Art historical interest in Caribbean culture has been generally subsumed into the study of the black or African diaspora. Consequently, the curatorial turn toward the African diaspora has not delivered a fresh framework for thinking about art and blackness in any specifically inter- or transnational way. This is not without the efforts and legacies of those who have shown the courage to challenge the wider art history community for its weak participation in asking how blackness is to be thought about and remembered. There was a moment when attention to 'black popular culture' and subsequently 'black visual culture' seemed to offer perspectives on the African diaspora that bore relevance beyond national borders.[5] Their impact on art history and museum practice opened up entirely new critical areas, a discursive intervention of its time that reversed the critical gaze onto curators and art historians through sustained institutional critique. Yet this has been superseded by a more bounded, far less transgressive sense of the significance of the African diaspora in the context of art and visual culture. In the desire to seek out a definite break between diaspora and nationalism, sometimes, as the anthropologist Aihwa Ong has warned, the 'complicated accommodations, alliances, and creative tensions' that exist between them can be overlooked.[6] The most widely visible frameworks for historicising diaspora have been unable to maintain the separation from the national that is necessary to ensure their analytical and strategic usefulness. This chapter demonstrates that certain spaces of curating are as much in danger of provincialising the African diaspora's diverse geography.

The generation of new 'margins' by this centralising tendency has also been accompanied by attempts to recuperate the status of provincialism. This is continuous with the account given throughout this book of a similar critical purpose that abides in the art of the transnational Caribbean. As we attempt to bring to light the growing global influence of the US's 'domestic script' on race, one can also recognise attempts by artists and curators to turn this orientation around. Even as the display and historiography of art found in the Caribbean and Britain share a familial proximity with the United States, this hegemonic arrangement also elicits some dynamic tensions. The project of reconceptualising a creative (visual) community has taken some novel shapes. This chapter shows how curating and its concomitant practices of documentation hold out a promise of dismantling and disavowing the hegemonic uses to which race and the diaspora concept have been put as founding categories of art historiography. These competing areas of activity are examined from the different perspectives of the Caribbean and its diaspora. This opens on to a debate – taken up in the concluding chapter – about 'contemporaneity', and the extent to which declarations of curatorial 'inclusivity' and 'horizontalisation' in the field of contemporary art may be tested by Caribbean art histories.

An American locus for Africa

What meanings should we draw from a London exhibition in 2005 that declared in its accompanying catalogue that art and visual culture can help in 'the rediscovery of Africa as black America's forgotten cultural locus'?[7] This was the leading premise for a major survey of the Black Arts Movement in the 1960s and 1970s, entitled *Back to Black: Art, Cinema and the Racial Imaginary*, staged at the publicly owned Whitechapel Gallery. Works by forty-seven artists, filmmakers and photographers interacted over two gallery floors, filling the Whitechapel with a rich mixture of film and video, sculpture, print, text and image, photography and painting. The ambition of its organisers – freelance curators David A. Bailey of Britain and Petrine Archer-Straw of Britain and Jamaica, along with the Duke University-based art historian Richard Powell – was to elevate the African diaspora as a shared community of art and visual production, implicating three national locations: the United States, Britain and Jamaica.

A didactic sequence of themes was chosen for grouping the works: *Premonitions, The World is a Ghetto, Tress/Passing, Exploitation/Blaxploitation, One Love, By Any Means …*, and *Lost in Music/Through Space & Time*. The largely black American experiences indicated by these headings, a narrative of black social protest and political struggles and victories, were corroborated best in artworks, film and ephemera from North America. Less in evidence were categories and groupings with a more local relevance to the art from Jamaica and Britain. This was despite the international make-up of the exhibition's curatorial team, its London venue, and the several Atlantic locations from which its artworks were drawn. If, indeed, Africa was the site of black America's 'forgotten cultural locus', as the show's curators argued, then *Back to Black* gave the overall impression that Jamaica and Britain were being assigned their 'cultural locus' in black America.

The press responses to *Back to Black* in Britain were rather mixed. An entirely positive response came from the writer Sukhdev Sandhu in the art magazine *Modern Painters*. For Sandhu, the exhibition demonstrated that British and Caribbean artists of the 1960s to the 1970s were centrally 'formative to the black Atlantic experience'.[8] In contrast, another critic and photographer writing in *New Statesman* confessed that he found the exhibition 'deadly dull' and ridden with 'cliché'.[9] The main reason for his dismissal was that much of the American art shown was already well known through popular reproductions. Many of these works were by the mega-personalities of the American black arts and music scene, and the exhibition featured them heavily in its publicity, in its main room, through a montage of album covers and video shorts, and in a compilation CD on sale in the gallery foyer. The prominence of these figures and works created a conspicuous disparity in emphasis. With much more established symbolic capital in the mainstream representational field, the American material overshadowed the Jamaican or British works and asserted a far greater congruence with the exhibition's overall 'Black Art' theme.

If displaying the American images in the same exhibition space as works from the Caribbean did not achieve the outcome of a transfer of value or capital across the pieces, the same was true of the relation between visual works emphasising elements of Rastafarian iconography and an accompanying verse from Bob Marley's *Redemption Song*, enlarged on a gallery wall. Marley's text only thinly informed viewers of the complex biblical and Yoruba strands in works by the artist Osmond Watson, for example, in his three bas-reliefs in wood: *Madonna of Stony Gut* (figure 23), *Revival Kingdom*, with its very subtly coloured patina, and *Oguon, God of War and Metal*, complete with metal inserts. The iconography of Marley's song also presented the difficulties of associating the exhibition's pieces with a visual record of Rastafarianism shaped much more by mass production and glib promotion. Additionally, if these works have yet to reach the wider attention of international art audiences, that desire was very much in competition with the more common associations viewers were likely to draw between the Jamaican art in the exhibition and tourism. Contributions such as Christopher Gonzales's Messianic self-portrait, with sub-references to the tropes of Zion in his later wood busts (figure 24), and Mallica 'Kapo' Reynolds's paintings, are the sort of items that visitors would easily find imitations of in Jamaica's Montego Bay,

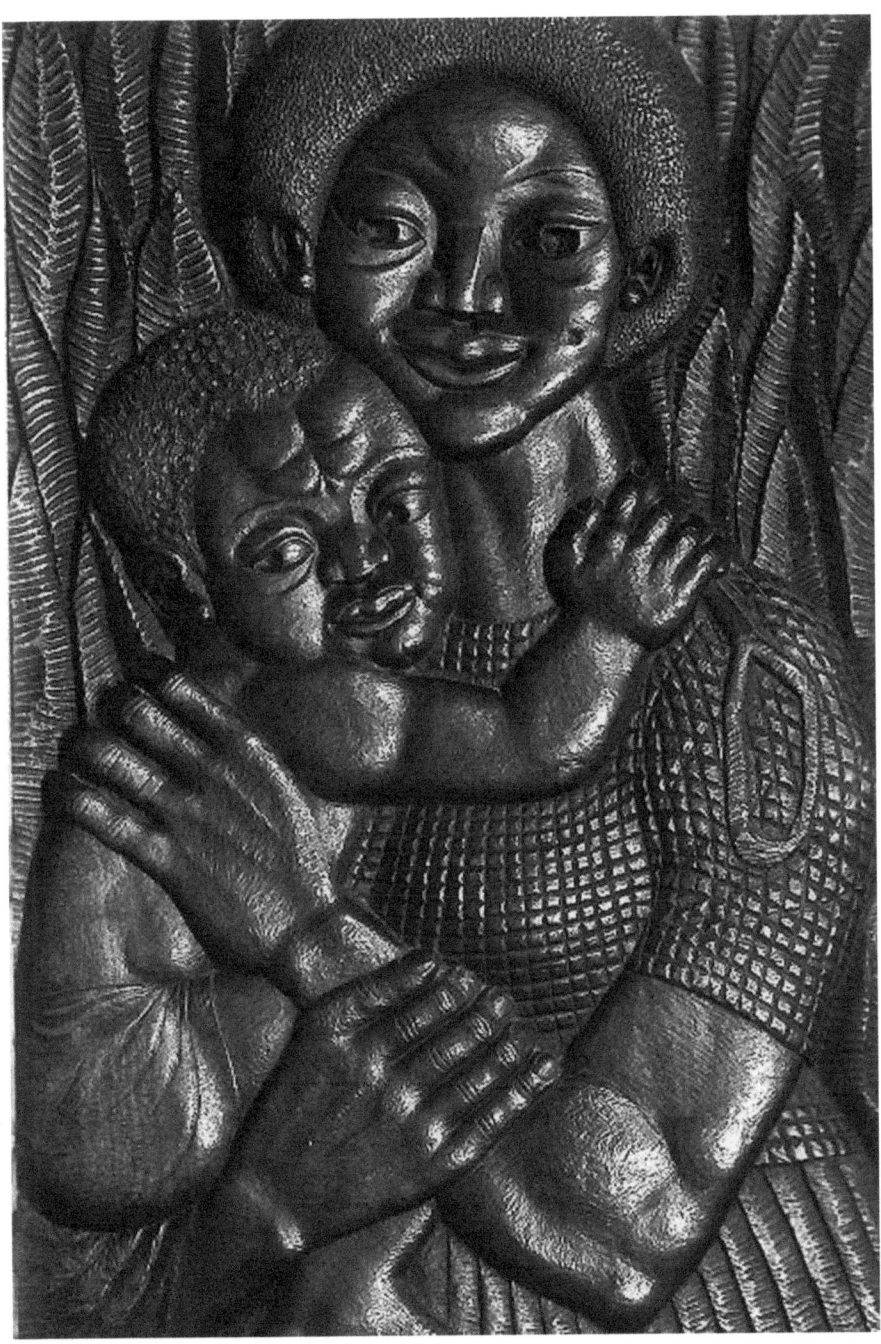

Osmond Watson, *Madonna of Stony Gut* (1971), wood relief, 121 × 59 cm.   **23**

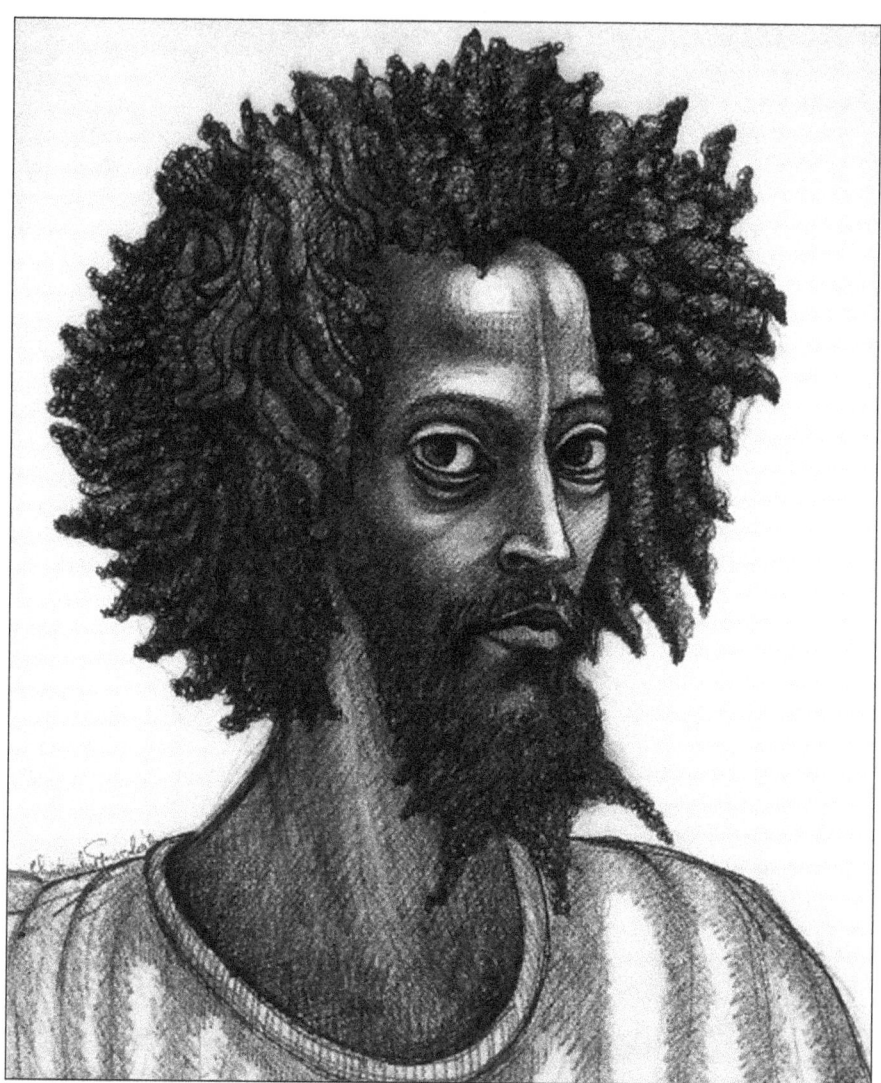

24   Christopher Gonzales, *Self Portrait: Night Spirit* (1976), charcoal on paper, 66.5 ×
54 cm.

Ocho Rios, and various other entry points to the island from Caribbean cruise
ships. The commercial status of these contexts – iconic American 'Black Art',
the market ubiquity of Jamaican musicians such as Marley, and the lingering
resonance between certain artworks and tourist curios – meant that the
Jamaican objects were assembled on an uneven plane.

The treatment of the British images in *Back to Black* failed to differentiate
between British and American black histories. A catalogue essay by Mora

J. Beauchamp-Byrd on Vanley Burke, the photographer of everyday scenes in the inner city of England's West Midlands, explored Burke's contribution in the context of connotations of the ghetto. This ghettoisation both literally and figuratively frustrated the aim of bringing Burke's images out of a forgotten corner of art history. Subsequently, Beauchamp-Byrd's concluding claim was vague: 'Above all, Burke's images reveal, in their startling range of expressiveness, how self-construction, pride and a tremendous sense of place may flourish, far beyond the boundaries marking those realms known (and variously represented) as "ghetto life".'[10] Reading these images from afar with an assumption of their racial exclusivity, Burke's images – scuffed terraces, Old World and penned in – might look just like shots of a ghetto (figure 25). But this analysis alone ignores how black people in Britain have shared their neighbourhoods and poverty with those of many other ethnicities. The Victorian working-class streets that he has photographed are home to less well-off people of all ethnicities; they picture post-industrial slums indifferent to any readable racial geography.[11] Burke's 'histograph' images, as he has called them, are intent on 'capturing the personal, social and economic life of black people as they arrived, settled and became established in British society'.[12] What they show is how those lives were entwined with people of other ethnicities in social spaces that range from the fairground to the workplace.

Back to Black broke from the curatorial custom of asking to what degree might a given artist choose to associate with blackness in their art practice. Equally, it avoided asking why certain artists have historically chosen not to identify themselves with such terms of difference. In so doing, the exhibition left aside conventions of documentation and display that would elucidate a distinction between contexts of visual meaning in the past, and those of the present, as well as from place to place. Drawing on a cultural politics in which a concept of race is present but abstract, it appeared to elide the deep differences between issues faced by African-American communities and those of minorities and imagined communities elsewhere. It chose not to explore why these national histories are, perhaps predictably, mismatched. Instead, *Back to Black* glossed over discontinuities of experience and over-emphasised the centrality of American blackness for Caribbean and British art histories.

If the exhibition *Back to Black* was misleading about the historical significance of the art it included, this loss has to be weighed against the gains of making a display of its scope accessible for the first time in Britain. The exhibition was the first of its kind in Britain to pursue a survey of international parallels in art and blackness, at least since the major exhibition curated by Richard Powell and David A. Bailey in 1997. With few other exhibitions of this scale addressing similar ground, it may be said that the most vigorous and best resourced treatments of art of the African diaspora are those that carry a particular thesis on the artistic geography of blackness. It is one that bears the

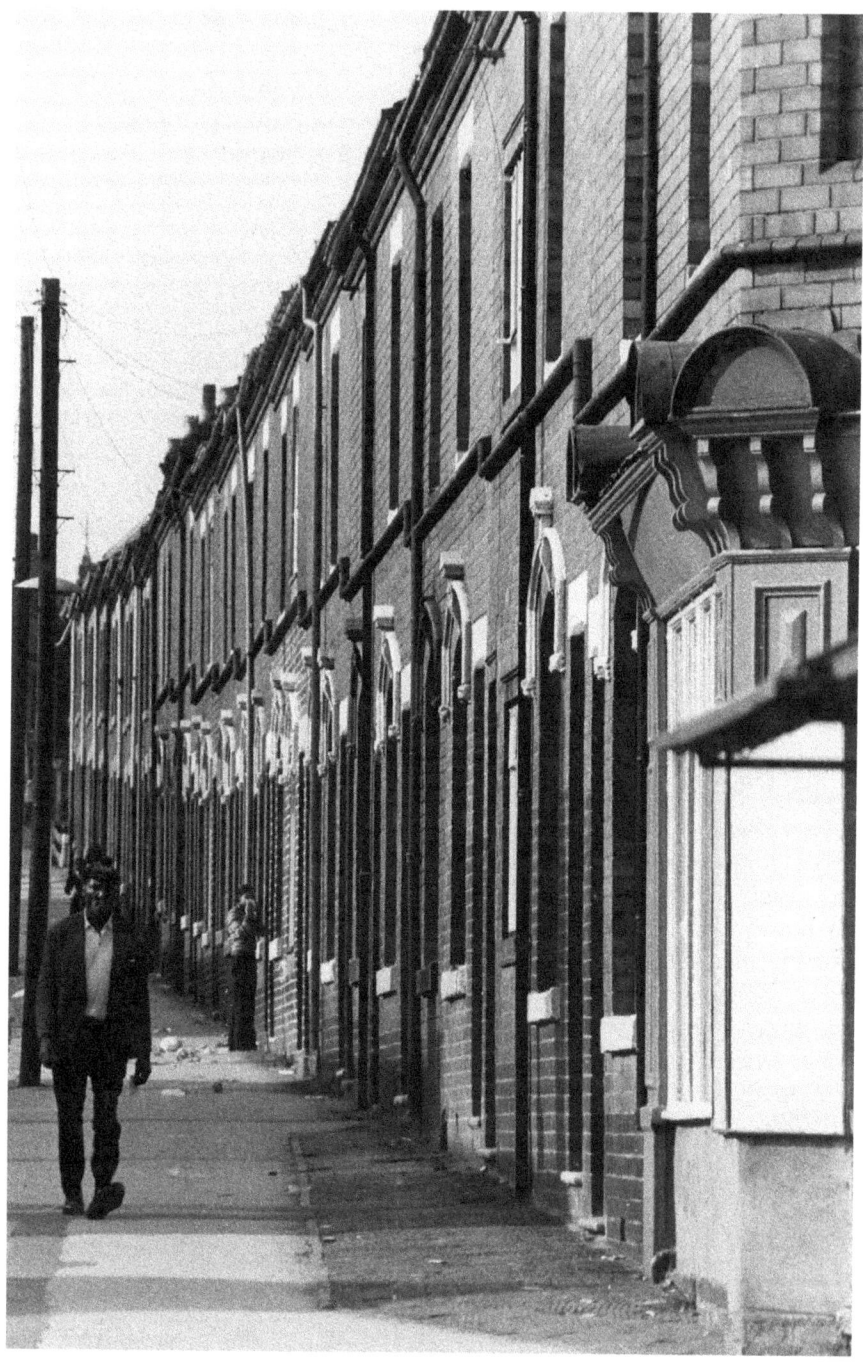

25   Vanley Burke, *Ninevah Road* (c.1970–1979), photograph.

deep imprint of conditions and struggles over race and racism in the United States. These representations are fairly closely matched by a wider trend in the interdisciplinary study of artists of the black diaspora in Britain, where there is a similar routing of British cultural practices through an American framework.

In her account of works by the British filmmaker Isaac Julien, literary historian Louise Yelin has singled out examples that explicitly engage African-American subject matter, such as the films *Looking for Langston: A Meditation on Langston Hughes and the Harlem Renaissance* (1989), *Baadasssss Cinema: A Bold Look at '70s Blaxploitation Films* (2002), and the installation *Baltimore* (2003). It is by virtue of these, Yelin argues, that Julien 'elucidates – and queers – what Stuart Hall identifies as "new ethnicities" and fashions himself as a cosmopolitan, diasporic, post imperial British subject'. Her essay is an attempt to offer anew, within the boundaries of 'African American cultural texts and traditions', a portrait of Julien, yet within the same terms in which he has conventionally been presented and identified himself. Publication of Hall's article on 'new ethnicities' in 1988 took place in the same moment that Julien wrote collaboratively with Kobena Mercer using concepts drawn from black cultural studies. However, Yelin ignores this precedent, choosing not to cite the original publication of such works. Instead she announces Julien, over twenty years after he was first established, as the epitome of a 'cosmopolitan, diasporic, post imperial British subject' who works with film. The distinction is revealing of a tendency to acknowledge this British subject only when he appears to fit within an African-American field of attention.[13] The outcome of developments of this kind is that the national setting of the United States is placed at the forefront of the ways in which the remaining regions of the African diaspora are contemplating their art history. Under the sign of trans-nationalism, American discourses of race and blackness predominate, leaving other regional settings of the diaspora to negotiate their place in this uneven arrangement.[14]

There are further reasons why this approach to historiography, now dominant in African-American art history, according to its logic, cannot engage productively with a more transnational art history. By its rationale, all the most inspiring stories about creativity and difference begin and end in the United States. The *Back to Black* exhibition catalogue made generalisations that during the period of the 1960s and 1970s: 'there was an implicit recognition among most peoples of African descent',[15] and 'messages of national liberation, black power, black beauty and black pride became important all over the world during the period covered by this exhibition'.[16] But the relationships of 'equivalence' between American, British and Jamaican artists of various diasporas are more complex than this portrait allows. By and large, *Back to Black* did not attempt to show blackness when it has been renegotiated to meet local concerns, or when racial self-essentialism encounters serious strategic limits.

One such context, which was overlooked, is the history of 'Black Art' in Britain. As shown in Chapter 3, as early as 1978, the presence of Pakistan-born Rasheed Araeen (a Black Panther, pamphleteer, artist-activist and author of *A black manifesto*) set in train at least a decade of other South Asian 'black' artists for whom the US 'Black Arts' Movement offered blueprints for resistance on British soil. This period showed how the meaning of 'Black Art' can be extended to include works by individuals of the South Asian as well as African diasporas.[17] The British story of challenges to the canon reveals more than the current focus on blackness may allow us to see. The oppositionalism of the British 'Black Art' moment, aligned in spirit to US black nationalism, was only part of the story of how artists of Asian, African and Caribbean backgrounds have challenged the mainstream. They have also done so in an avant-garde tradition (see Chapter 3), as 'constitutive insiders', rather than self-declared 'outsiders' to art history.

This British story holds a wider significance once it is seen against the background of those developments in art of the twentieth century – and into the present – which are characterised by the growing fragmentation of master narratives. This goes above and beyond the black oppositionalism of the US 'Black Arts' Movement, and the strand of similar interest among those who made British 'Black Art'. Assertions of difference are a legitimate and characteristic part of contemporary art. Yet there is a reluctance to accept this broad base of pressure for change, and to favour instead the thesis that identifications with blackness are somehow their own discrete development. The result is to oversimplify what is a much more complex history, and it works to distance certain artists from participating in a common artistic space. To trace out an oppositional story of art and blackness does nothing to combat the market forces and patterns of public patronage that have taken hold since the 1980s, a serious area of concern that I have outlined as a crisis over nationhood and multiculturalism. Instead, representations of blackness that provide recognisable forms of 'cultural difference' and 'diversity' are placed conveniently within a hegemonic order. This has the outcome of reifying 'race' in institutions of art display and remembrance, and *ethnicising* art history. Such oppositionalism fractures the historical bonds of solidarity among artists of many ethnicities who have occasionally come together in an assault on practices of exclusion and marginalisation. More gravely, it detaches the experience of black people from the history of the international avant-garde, and so risks relegating them to the status of parochial, provincialised struggle.[18]

New provincialisms

Certain alternative curatorial approaches to understanding the works and artists of the African diaspora appear better able to describe key aspects of the transnationalism that lies at the heart of this field. They purposefully steer away from vocabularies and terms of evaluation drawn from US-based realities and the portraits resulting from such hegemonic approaches. These emphasise one or more of the following: the history of artistic subjects and artworks which physically connect or entwine the Caribbean and Britain;[19] a mistrust of 'nation based' canons of art history; and a general suspicion about employing the concepts of diaspora culture, ethnicity and difference as if these should suffice as primary explanatory principles for art making and display. Further, these alternatives radically expand the art historical record by transgressing its traditional attachments to nation and geographical place.

Among these curatorial ventures is an interconnected formation located in the Caribbean. A firm alternative to US-based understandings of art and blackness can be found in the work of the Small Axe Collective, with members including the writer Annie Paul and artist Christopher Cozier, who are based in the anglophone Caribbean, and the Jamaica-born political anthropologist David Scott. Positing a 'Caribbean platform for criticism', a leading interest of the collective is to explore the sphere of visual creativity in order to disrupt a rendering of the Caribbean as a provincial zone. Its journal and curated online space have sought to promote an ongoing 'conversation' about the region's postcolonial future, looking beyond the limits of an anti-colonial and diasporic political and cultural architecture.[20] They present the grounds for a refusal to be conscripted as much by local and national terms of historical explanation found within the Caribbean region, as the imposition of paradigms of modernity that would be imposed from without.[21]

In September 2006, the Small Axe Collective met with a public opportunity to examine ways in which art in Trinidad might be brought into dialogue with prevailing attitudes around ethnicity, locality and historical memory. This opportunity came with the launch of *Galvanize* (figure 26), a series of artists' projects and events that happened alongside the largely state-funded, Caribbean-wide exposition, *Carifesta*. *Galvanize* was not part of *Carifesta*, nor in receipt of any of the public money allocated for it. Instead, it made resourceful use of an existing media base, including daily television interviews during the programme's opening weeks, a mutually annotating web of internet sites, designed and written by publishing professionals, and features in globally distributed art magazines.[22] Assuming the title *Visibly Absent* (figure 27), *Galvanize* set out to provoke thought on the strategies of racial and ethnic pluralism that have shaped anti-colonial nationalisms in the Caribbean and which persist through representations such as *Carifesta*, Trinidad's annual

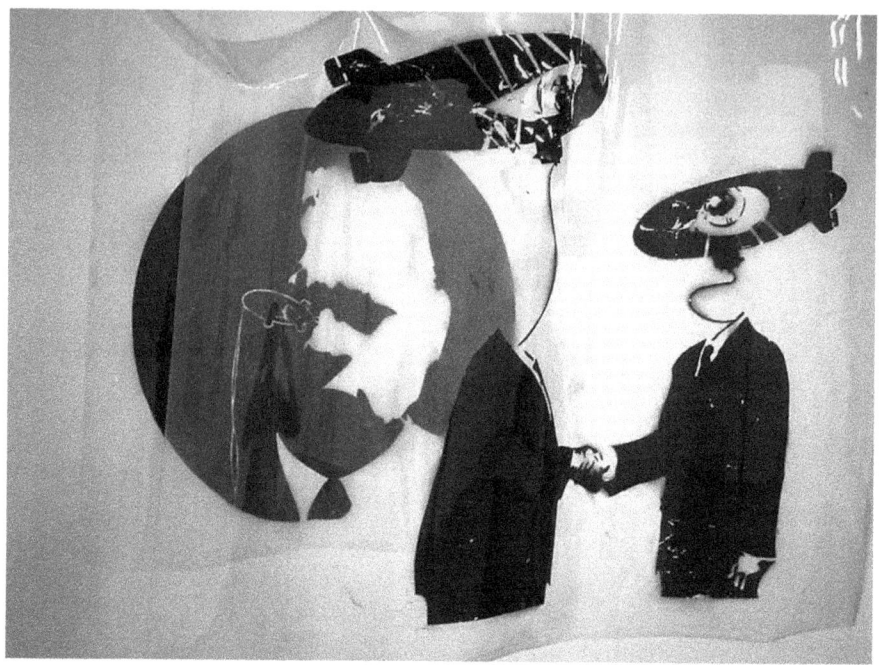

26   Nikolai Noel, detail of *The Black Eye Project* (2006), from a series of twelve, plastic
sheeting, spray paint, aluminium rods, chains, metal clips, 152.4 × 152.4 cm.

carnival celebrations, and the island's local infrastructure for the arts and
education.

A glowing editorial in *The Trinidad Guardian* praised the resourcefulness
and slick organisation of *Galvanize*, drawing a sharp contrast with *Carifesta*
and the debacle caused by its poor execution – a topic which frequently
captured headlines during September of that year.[23] An alternative contribution to *Carifesta* in the visual arts had in fact been debated for some time,
such as the polemic given in 1999 by Cozier, one of the *Galvanize* steering
team:

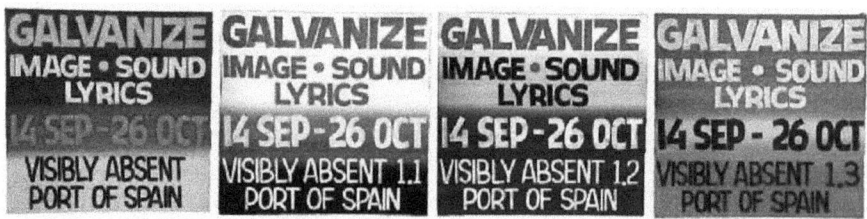

27   Bruce Cayone, *Galvanize* posters (2006).

It has been my experience and view that events such as Carifesta, which were about us coming into being and knowing ourselves after the competitive agendas of the colonial space, have now become tired and exclusive. The idea is perhaps too heavily guided by the agendas of nation building and its cultural programming with its narrative of the 'folk' versus the Afro/Indo Saxon [the educated middle class]. It is, perhaps, now drifting along as either a forum for communal despair or decorative eloquence, or both. Today the poles are different. It may be the 'ownership class' of the nationalist dream versus an unknown internal other that is no longer satisfied to remain as just a voyeur. It is time to support and encourage the participation of new names and ways of responding to this space.[24]

Much of the thinking behind *Galvanize* was done by a group of artists who have explored over the past two decades the divisions of 'inside' and 'outside' that it investigated. Annie Paul's interest in Trinidad, set out in her essay 'The enigma of survival: Travelling beyond the expat gaze', focuses on this group, a community that in a moment of typographical wordplay she calls 'alterNA-TIVES' – namely Christopher Cozier, Steve Ouditt, Eddie Bowen and Irenée Shaw – who, to quote her, 'represent a category of artists from the Caribbean … [who] find themselves on the wrong side of nation stories in opposition to majority groups that assert ownership of the national or Caribbean space'.[25] Travelling beyond the expat gaze (and its expert, 'expatese') means recognising these 'natives without narratives, or perhaps with unpopular or inconvenient narratives', in order to subvert the manner in which: 'In privileging discourse about the self and other exclusively, the expat gaze overlooks identities ostracized or exiled by the national.'[26]

Paul frames this group of artists in the terms of their refusal of expatriate desire – the will of Northern settlers in the Caribbean who have taken up with art making, criticism and curating. Such an observation about the expat overseeing/policing the Trinidad art scene may be less prescient than in the other islands that she has so compellingly written about.[27] Nonetheless, Paul is justified in showing that models of art criticism in the Caribbean region have rested heavily on accounts of the nation and the national, and the indigenous or 'native' anti-colonial. They have thereby denied ground to the experiences and practices of other artists who remain unconvinced about the expediency of such distinctions and have very little invested in the nationalism of their parents' or grandparents' generation. The origin of those terms is less the expat, perhaps, than the strident 'owners' of the Caribbean's national culture, by whose terms the current generation of artists feel limited, or delimited, or 'troped'. As Cozier has put it:

> since the mid eighties in Trinidad, and by the mid nineties in the rest of the anglophone Caribbean, the threat of artist-led initiatives to define or come to

terms with different objectives or responses to the Caribbean space has caused much anxiety. The new enemy of the nationalist has shifted from the colonizer to the perpetual 'next generation' whose allegedly ambiguous relationship to the national space is not understood. At the outer edge of this sacred space is the 'foreign head'. The shift to process and method opens up the idea that the boundary between what is defined as local and what is supposed to be foreign (alien to us) has become unapologetically permeable and that the thematic and conceptual concerns of the artist are not already fixed. So the contemporary space can be interpreted as part of an ongoing evaluative or investigative look at the local, as well as the broader domain of artistic activity globally.[28]

A more recent curatorial project, *La Fantasie* (figure 28), staged in Trinidad during late January and February 2008, further distanced contemporary artists from the ideologies that emerged in the Caribbean during decolonisation.[29] Set in the former middle-class suburb of Belmont, in the capital Port of Spain, the project used a single-storey structure with added facings as an installation site to suggest a modest imitation of the other houses on the same street. Filling its darkened, nightmarish interior with place-specific works that combine photography, painting and sculpture, its group of artist-curators invited visitors to enter at their peril, using a hand-held fluorescent light. *La Fantasie* was installed at 41–3 Norfolk Street, directly opposite the local constituency office of the country's ruling political party, the People's National Movement (PNM), and the title of the work alluded to the official residence of the Prime Minister on La Fantasie Road in nearby St Anne's. These details sharpened its deliberate affront to the liberal-rationalist fantasy of national prosperity that animated the Independence era and PNM ideology: the dream of becoming urban and middle class; of owning a *Fantasie* home of one's own. In addition to the 'underlying engagements with domesticity, settlement, abuse, and violence' of *La Fantasie*,[30] the installation elaborated on the theme of an earlier video sequence created by Christopher Cozier in which repeating images of social housing units are played against a radio broadcast of Trinidad and Tobago's national anthem.[31] Together, these references to the politics of dwelling serve to question the value of Trinidad's 'scripted' national development as a planned racial pluralism, determining how ethnic differences are mapped onto the national landscape.

The contrast in meaning between the images of *La Fantasie* and the photographed streets of Vanley Burke, in which black and white British subjects coexist, could not be more pronounced. Yet such crucial discrepancies between these contexts in the African diaspora would not be noticed by a homogenising gaze, unable to see the diaspora's diversity. Whether in Britain, or in Caribbean locations such as Trinidad, each of these projects indicates how curators and artists remain unconvinced about the usefulness of placing blackness at the centre of art practice. They thereby differ from US-based interventions in mainstream art history, with their insistence on the theme of race. Theirs is a contribution to a more intersectional idea of art history which is missing from accounts of difference as either racial, social, gendered, and so on.[32] They ask what new questions emerge when the commas between these constructions are erased, making for a closer sense of how urgently visual encounters demand comprehension of social relations and historical structures of power as permutated by multiple, conjunctive and layered identities. In a related effort to go through and beyond the national, these initiatives have continued to explore collaborations that transcend the Balkanised political geography of the African diaspora. Above all, they undertake to free art making and display from discourses of essential cultural or racial uniqueness. For instance, they suggest an alternative to the racialised vision of citizenship represented by the 'modern blackness' observed by anthropologist Deborah Thomas, which took hold in Jamaica's public sphere during the late 1990s through youth culture and African-American popular culture.[33] They trace out a more properly transnational geography, which has passed unrecognised by a provincialising perspective.

Before closing this description of contemporary artists in Trinidad, it is important to clarify the extent to which current directions in art practice and curating in the region have moved in dialogue with historical trends around representation and difference. Intellectuals and creative practitioners of the

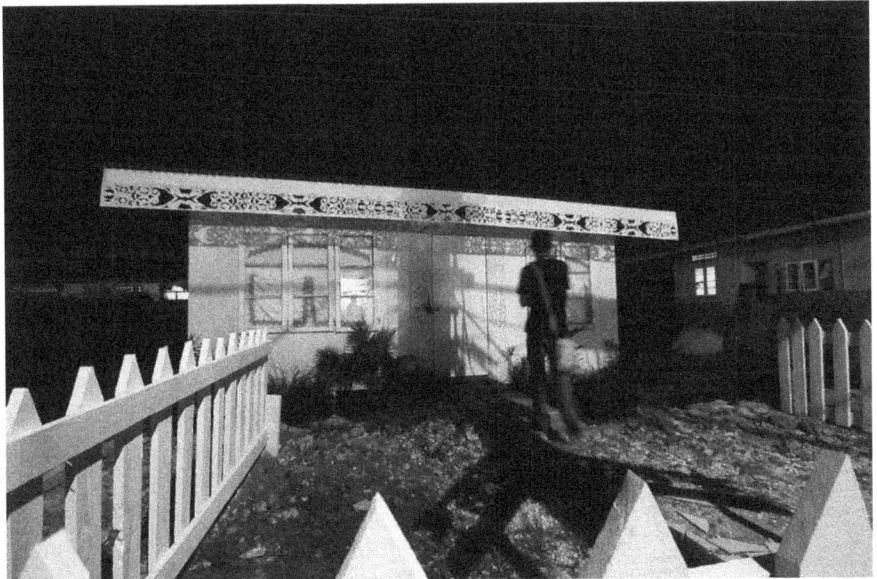

La Fantasie exterior shot of the installation.   **28**

Caribbean have also historically refused to see the region as black, or African alone. What is characterised here as an African-American impulse to include the Caribbean in a wider 'black art history' does not find a comfortable fit with the historical forms of Caribbean pluralism and creole nationalism, Third Worldism and federationism, or indeed any serious attempt to come to terms with the ethnic and racial mix or heterogeneity of the Caribbean during and after Independence. Chapter 3 showed how Denis Williams's art historical writings of the late 1960s and 1970s make explicit the sorts of groups, voices and initiatives that are threatened with chaos by the prospect of the Caribbean being dubbed and essentialised as 'black'.[34] This is some of the background to the lasting suspicion in the Caribbean region of employing ethnicity, race and colour as the founding categories of belonging, creativity and community.

Despite wishing to make a break with the thinking of previous generations in the Caribbean, there is still a remarkable critical interest among younger generations directed to the art of their predecessors. In that sense, the contemporary 'problem space', to borrow a term from David Scott, is historical for the coexistence of several different generations. In Trinidad, it always strikes me that rather than negating the art of, say, Isaiah James Boodhoo, Carlisle Chang, or Leroy Clarke, as emphatically *not* part of the contemporary scene, their art is instead refigured through remembrance in the present. Often long after their artists have passed away, or even when such works have vanished or been destroyed – such as in Chang's airport murals, demolished in the early 1970s – they remain as components in the search for an art of the present. As with Aubrey Williams's experience in 1980s Britain, this may be another instance of what Stuart Hall has called 'passage without supercession, dialogic movement without dialectical overcoming', of 'two moments condensed into one'.[35] If so, then the 'condensation of dissimilar currents' which Hall invokes from Althusser to understand three 'moments' in post-war British history, might be suggestive of the contemporary 'futures past' of art in the Caribbean.

Finally, understanding in greater depth the art of Christopher Cozier, for example, depends on an appreciation of why the artist himself persistently reminds us of the priorities and perceptions of artists from the past (figure 29). In staking out his contemporaneity, they are not forgotten. This parallels the more general fascination in Trinidad for the precedents and roots of artistic modernism on the island, demonstrated by a cultural memory that extends back in time at least as far as the mid-nineteenth century landscape artist, Cazabon (b. 1813, d. 1888).[36] Between Cozier and the broader anxiety to rehearse a 'forgotten' art history, it has become commonplace for emergent artists to talk about their work while invoking what has come before them along a notional timeline of national art history. As keen historians of their own art practice, contemporary Trinidadian artists actively involve past forms

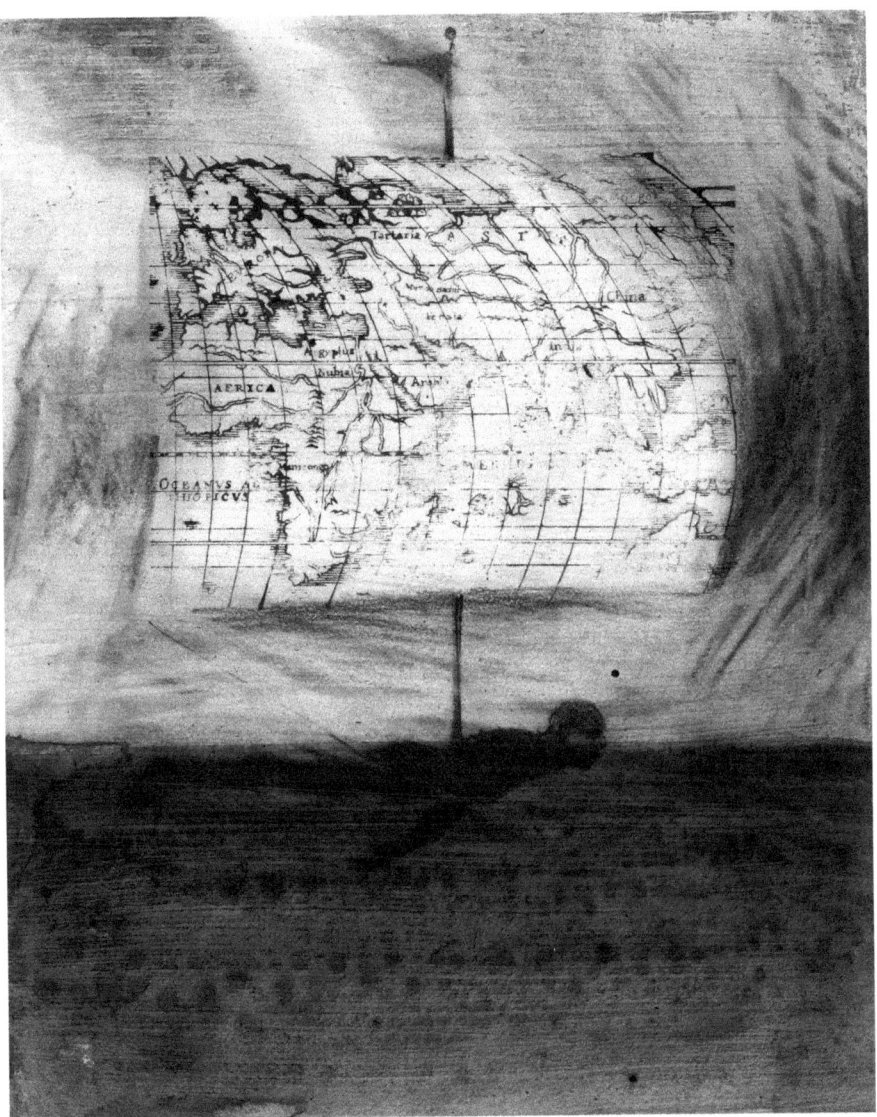

Christopher Cozier, *Castaway* (2006 and ongoing) from *The Tropical Night Series*,   **29**
ink, graphite and stamps on paper, 22.8 × 17.8 cm.

and personalities, drawing them into their contemporary 'conversation'. This is
even the case when the association is made in an attempt at contradistinction,
for instance, the handwritten note left by an older, well-known watercolourist
of landscape at Cozier's first Trinidad exhibition in the early 1980s. According
to the pattern I have described, it simply had to be mentioned that an older

artist had written (reported in the feature article on Cozier, the first ever on an artist of Trinidad to appear in the magazine *Modern Painters*): 'SOME DIRECT ADVICE … you will never be a fine artist. Stick to graphics.'[37]

Certainly such currents begin to undermine the universalising trend in curatorial representation in which certain externally formed conceptions of race, culture and ethnicity are made to appear like a global rule. They represent an attempt to arrest the authority of a US-based paradigm of art and blackness predicated on its claim to a transcendent status. The repercussions of such universalism are being felt across the transatlantic African diaspora and deserve to be better known. Caribbean patterns serve to confront the rhetorical structure of that paradigm by recourse to historical location and specificity, yet without cleaving to provincial 'localism'. Above all, it is the continuing reluctance of diaspora communities to misrecognise themselves in any 'outside' image which animates criticism of the new provincialism of art histories of the African diaspora, and which seems most likely to shape their future within radical curatorial practice and historiography.

Notes

1 I have briefly set out my provisional thoughts on this topic in: L. Wainwright, 'New provincialisms: Curating art of the African diaspora', *Radical History Review*, 103 (2009), 203–13.

2 For a history of this involvement, see the final chapter in M. Sheller, *Consuming the Caribbean: From Arawaks to zombies* (London: Routledge, 2004).

3 See, for example, H. Raphael-Hernandez (ed.), *Blackening Europe: The African American presence* (London: Routledge, 2004), pp. 1–12.

4 P. Gilroy, 'Foreword', in Raphael-Hernandez (ed.), *Blackening Europe*, p. xvi. Gilroy's contribution to this volume is all the more fascinating for its cogent critique of the overall approach of the book. It develops his earlier observations about nationalist tendencies among black American intellectuals: P. Gilroy, *The black Atlantic: Modernity and double consciousness* (Cambridge: Harvard University Press, 1992).

5 See Gina Dent (ed.), *Black popular culture: A project by Michele Wallace* (Seattle: Bay Press, 1992; G. Doy, *Black visual culture: Modernity and postmodernity* (London: I. B. Tauris, 2000); M. Harris, *Colored pictures: Race and visual representation* (Chapel Hill: University of North Carolina Press, 2003); P. Farris-Dufrene (ed.), *Voices of color: Art and society in the Americas* (Atlanta Highlands: Humanities Press, 1997); bell hooks, *Art on my mind: Visual politics* (New York: The New Press, 1995); cf. B. H. Edwards, *The practice of diaspora: Literature, translation, and the rise of black internationalism* (Cambridge: Harvard University Press, 2003).

6 A. Ong, *Flexible citizenship: The cultural logics of transnationality* (Durham and London: Duke University Press, 1999), p. 16.

7 P. Archer-Straw, D. A. Bailey and R. Powell (eds), *Back to black: Art, cinema and the racial imaginary* (London: The Whitechapel Gallery, 2005).

8 S. Sandhu, 'Say it loud: Going back to black', *Modern Painters* (July–August 2005), 70–3.

9 L. Herman, 'Deadly dull', *New Statesman* (4 July 2005), on www.newstatesman.com/200507040033. Somewhat apart from these evaluations is my review essay on the exhibition: L. Wainwright 'Back to black: Art, cinema and the racial imaginary', *Third Text*, 76 (2006), 115–25.

10 M. J. Beauchamp-Byrd, 'Everyday people: Vanley Burke and the ghetto as genre', in Archer-Straw, Bailey and Powell (eds), *Back to black*, p. 182.

11 M. Sealy (ed.), *Vanley Burke: A retrospective* (London: Lawrence & Wishart, 1993).

12 Sealy (ed.), *Vanley Burke*, p. 12.

13 L. Yelin, 'Callin' out around the world', *Atlantic Studies*, 6:2 (2009), 239–53, p. 239.

14 Again, this has been noted in the social sciences, but has remained unsaid for art history. Clarke and Thomas, for instance, have asked, 'What constitutes blackness in the twenty-first century, and to what extent are American black hegemonies restructuring everyday practices in a range of global sites?' D. A. Thomas and K. M. Clarke (eds), *Globalization and race: Transformations in the cultural production of blackness* (London and Durham: Duke University Press, 2006), p. 4.

15 Archer-Straw, Bailey and Powell (eds), *Back to black*, p. 18.

16 Paul Gilroy, '"No, I do not have the right to be a negro": Black vernacular visual culture and the poetry of the future', in Archer-Straw, Bailey and Powell (eds), *Back to black*, p. 168.

17 See: R. Araeen, 'Preliminary notes for a black manifesto', *Black Phoenix*, 1 (1978), 3–12; reprinted in R. Araeen (ed.), *Making myself visible* (London: Kala, 1984), pp. 73–97. There is also some congruence here with how blackness is used in other settings globally, such as South Africa. In the field of 'incorporative anti-apartheid', as Grant Farred reminds us, this use of the term 'black' includes 'three historically disenfranchised groups, "blacks," "coloureds," and "Indians" – those of south Asian descent'. G. Farred, '"Shooting the white girl first": Race in post-apartheid South Africa', in Thomas and Clarke (eds), *Globalization and race*, pp. 226–46, p. 246.

18 This problem of separation may also be compounded by divergent uses of the term avant-garde to retrospectively define formations of black oppositionalism and black subjectivities, referring generally to the earlier part of the twentieth century. See for instance: E. Harney, *In Senghor's shadow: Art, politics and the avant-garde in Senegal, 1960–1995* (Durham: Duke University Press, 2004); and P. Archer-Straw, *Negrophilia: Avant-garde Paris and black culture in the 1920s* (London: Thames & Hudson, 2000).

19 See *Aubrey Williams*, Hayward Gallery, 1998. Another related alternative is to emphasise a Caribbean history for a (counter)-canonical black American artist. See, for instance: S. Price and R. Price, *Romare Bearden: The Caribbean dimension* (Philadelphia: University of Pennsylvania Press, 2006).

20 See www.smallaxe.net.

21 An account of the wider political history of this relationship with reference to modernity is given in D. Scott, *Conscripts of modernity: The tragedy of colonial enlightenment* (London and Durham: Duke University Press, 2004).

22 The *Galvanize* project made use of a detailed and creatively presented website in the format of a rolling diary of events and documentation (see: projectgalvanize.blogspot.com/). This was cross-referenced at the locally authored site of Caribbean Contemporary Art, 'Art papers' (artpapers.blogspot.com/) and the programme of

film screenings (detailed at: studiofilmclub.blogspot.com/), as well as on numerous other websites globally. P. Sander, 'Talking it through', *Caribbean Beat*, 83 (2007); C. Martin, 'Galvanize, Port of Spain, Trinidad', *Flash Art*, 251 (2006).

23 See 'Editorial: Carifesta must engage artists, not just audiences', *Trinidad Guardian* (August 2006), p. 28; L. Allen-Agostini, 'For the benefit of art', *Trinidad Guardian* (2 September 2006); A. Springer, 'Galvanizing our culture', *Trinidad Guardian* (16 September 2006).

24 C. Cozier, 'Between narratives and other spaces', *Small Axe*, 6 (1999), pp. 28–9.

25 A. Paul, 'The enigma of survival: Travelling beyond the expat gaze', *Art Journal*, 62:1 (2003), 49.

26 Paul, 'The enigma of survival', p. 65.

27 See for instance her comparison of a European expatriate presence in Jamaica and Barbados. A. Paul, 'Uninstalling the nation: The dilemma of contemporary Jamaican art', *Small Axe*, 6 (1999), 57–78.

28 Cozier, 'Between narratives', p. 22.

29 The artists who participated in the project were Jaime Lee Loy, Marlon Griffith and Nikolai Noel, who together form *The Collaborative Frog* (see: http://thecollaborativefrog.blogspot.com/2008/02/la-fantasie.html); cf. N. Laughlin, 'La fantasie', *Caribbean Review of Books*, 15 (2008), 26–7.

30 See http://thecollaborativefrog.blogspot.com/2008/02/la-fantasie.html.

31 This reappears in the documentary by R. Fung, *Uncomfortable: The art of Christopher Cozier* (distrib. www.vtape.org, Trinidad and Canada, 2005); see also R. Fung, 'Uncomfortable: The art of Christopher Cozier', *Public*, 31 (2005), p. 16; and www.digipopo.org/content/uncomfortable-the-art-of-christopher-cozier. Aspects of the video are taken up in later work by the Trinidad artist Dean Arlen, and it is tempting to read Cozier's description of this as a comment on his own initial use of the motif. As he writes: 'Ranks of little generic houses shapes symbolise government-provided housing developments and imply the discomfort of the economically displaced, who also face new, unfamiliar social relations and environments.' C. Cozier, 'Boom generation', *Caribbean Review of Books*, 11 (2007), 21. The images of houses in Fung's documentary, although shot by him, formed a sequence from the collaboration between Fung and Cozier, which resulted in the video installation for the exhibition, *Attack of the sandwichmen*, curated by A. Fontana (Toronto: A-Space and The Canada Council, 16 January–21 February 2004). The video itself is called 'The unspeakable state of sliced bread'. A response to the exhibition, which sketches its relation to Caribbean literature and critical theory is found in: A. Kamugisha, 'Attack of the sandwichmen'. (http://storage.smallaxe.net/wordpress/2007/06/05/%E2%80%9Cattack-of-the-sandwichmen%E2%80%9D/). A review of this work and the panel discussion associated with the exhibition is: H. Ford-Smith, 'Chewing on the mix: Creolization, power and art' (www.canadacouncil.ca/NR/rdonlyres/21507FB9–1C8C–4CE0–ACB5–A7A758DCDD49/0/08_aspaceen. pdf). Neither author notes the striking parallel to certain works by the US artist Dan Graham. In his 1966 series of photographs with an accompanying text, *Homes for America*, Graham pictured large-scale suburban 'tract' housing which 'constitute the new city. They are located everywhere. They are not particularly bound to existing communities; they fail to develop either regional characteristics

or separate identity'. D. Graham, 'Homes for America', *Arts* (December–January 1966–67), 20–1; also D. Graham, 'Homes for America' *Rock my religion: Writings and art projects 1965–1990* (Cambridge MA: MIT Press, 1993), p. 14.

32 They share the approach of a special issue of *Signs* co-edited by Jennifer Doyle and Amelia Jones, which insists on 'the intersectionality of gendered experience as inherently, simultaneously, and irrevocably raced, classed, sexed, and so on'. J. Doyle and A. Jones (eds), 'New feminist theories of visual culture', *Signs*, 31:3 (2006), 607–15, p. 608. A related contribution made in the field of literary studies is H. A. Baker Jr (ed.), 'Erasing the commas: RaceGenderClassSexuality region', *American Literature*, 77:1 (2005).

33 D. A. Thomas, *Modern blackness*. See also M. Hanchard's article in the journal *Public Culture*, in which he distinguishes the 'Afro-Modern politics … of a trans-national "imagined community"', from the 'territorial rudiments Anderson attributes to creole nationalism'. As he writes: '… contrary to Anderson's claims that racism is merely the vehicle through which national chauvinism is expressed and implemented, the political histories of the African diaspora expose the role that racism has played as a constitutive – not an epiphenomenal – feature of national identity'. Hanchard is emphatic in his preference for showing how 'the relationships between race, state, and nation have underscored how race and/or ethnicity have functioned as a foundational – though mythical – element of national identity'. M. Hanchard, 'Afro-modernity: Temporality, politics, and the African diaspora, *Public Culture*, 11:1 (1999), 245–68, 267. See also A. Smith, *The ethnic origins of nations* (Oxford: Oxford University Press, 1986); T. Nairn, *The breakup of Britain: Crisis and neo-nationalism* (London: New Left Books, 1977); E. Gellner, *Nations and nationalism* (Ithaca: Cornell University Press, 1983).

34 Among the literature of the same historical moment, yet not specific to art history, see: R. M. Nettleford, *Mirror, mirror: Identity, race and protest in Jamaica* (Kingston, Jamaica: William Collins and Sangster, 1970); E. Brathwaite, *Contradictory omens: Cultural diversity and integration in the Caribbean* (Mona: Savacou, 1974). Nettleford writes that 'suggestions of racial exclusivity and claims of black "superiority" have found effective opposition from the national commitment to non-racialism and the Jamaican dislike for racism', p. 13.

35 S. Hall, 'Black diaspora artists in Britain: Three "moments" in post-war history', *History Workshop Journal*, 61 (2006), 1–24.

36 See, for instance: G. MacLean, *An illustrated biography of Trinidad's nineteenth century painter Michel Jean Cazabon* (Trinidad: Aquarela Galleries, 1986); The Commonwealth Institute, *Trinidad and Tobago through the eye of the artist: From Cazabon to the millenium, 1813–2000* (London: The Commonwealth Institute, 1997). An excellent critical account of Cazabon is given in: A. Wahab, *Colonial inventions: Landscape, power and representation in nineteenth-century Trinidad* (Newcastle upon Tyne: Cambridge Scholars Press, 2010), pp. 103–58.

37 Quoted in: N. Laughlin, 'Trinidad: Discomfort zone' *Modern Painters* (June 2006), 104–5.

Conclusion:
Caribbean contemporaneity

Chapter 5 outlined how the growing dominance of US-based understandings of the Caribbean and Britain has placed these regions at an outer circle of cultural identifications with the African diaspora. In this visual economy of blackness, a 'diffusionist' model of black history passes unquestioned: a vision of black culture emanating as if from a single place to take seed internationally. It is a scheme of the migration (or even a diaspora) of diaspora consciousness. This implies that certain regions of the African diaspora lag behind in catching up with an ostensible vanguard of black cultural heritage epitomised at an American epicentre. Consequently, curatorial spaces can also be complicit in ordering the African diaspora into reputedly 'leading' metropolitan centres, and belatedly 'backward' and 'secondary' peripheries. Implicit in any such art display is the suggestion that those descendants of Africa who do not live within the United States should consider the advantages of adopting its modes of representation.[1]

We have encountered this spatio-temporal model before. It came to frame the orthodox understanding of the work of those artists of the transnational Caribbean who are explored throughout this book. Its influence has been widely critiqued by many postcolonial theorists, such as Chakrabarty. More specifically, in the case of art, it has become a particular target for the avant-garde, after they came to identify the same diffusionist principle at work in hegemonic narratives of art history and cultural modernity. I have been suggesting that, at the same time, avowedly counter-hegemonic approaches to art history (including those that continue to employ the diaspora concept) may also conform to the myth of a modernising, progressive development, with all its attendant temporal and stagist values.

One would then ask how this situation for the Caribbean and its diaspora – in which a variety of provincialisms and conditions of anachronism inter-related through provincialising pressures – can become any sort of basis for transformation. This would focus on the way that intersections of ethnicity, race and visual creativity can be thought about differently. It would also, ultimately, require a transformation of the structuring principles of art historical thought.

Provincialism as a critical concept has lately re-emerged in discourses of the Caribbean, as I have shown in the Trinidad context, which should be seen along the post-war trajectory traced here. I would suggest that there are ways in which this energises the present-day discussion of contemporaneity in art practice, display and remembrance. Artists of the transnational Caribbean have worked through their spatio-temporal conditions. As such, it is instructive to recall how questions of provincialism in particular have long been addressed in relation to visual creativity.

Chapter 2 discussed George Kubler's interest in the importance of time for the historiography of art, emphasising the political dimension of patterns and shapes of provincialism. It is worth noting that before Kubler there had been an earlier interest in provincialism and creativity, more broadly addressed to literature and philosophy. J. N. Oldham, writing in 1936, for instance, focused on what he termed 'the provincialism of mind which actuated some of the most widely praised contributors to world culture'.[2] He also assessed questions not dissimilar to those that we might now recognise as having to do with cultural identity and place. In his observations on Paris, for example, he wrote that: 'the provincialism of Paris has been distinguished from all other systems of cultural behaviour first as a variety of metropolitanism and secondly as *the* variety of cosmopolitanism'.[3] The notion of provincialism features again in cultural commentary of the 1960s. The abstract painter, Jimmy Ernst, would coin the term 'international provincialism', to describe in rather eccentric terms a reprehensible tendency that he found surfacing with the murder of J. F. Kennedy.[4]

More pertinent to art history, perhaps, is the evaluative association between 'esthetic provincialism' and derivativeness made by Lazare, in a 1939 review of exhibitions of nude paintings by the American painter Thomas Benton, and Salvador Dali. Lazare qualified the perceived impurity of Dali's painterly language as 'patois', and of Benton's as 'dialect'. There is an odd coincidence in the use of such terms, given the later interest in linguistic models in Caribbean cultural studies focused on the requalification of the relation between hybridity and cultural authenticity.[5] But it is more likely that there is no such 'reclamation' of the provincialism here. Indeed, some care is needed to understand the background in the use of the term 'provincialism' in mid-twentieth century literary theory – rather than art history or art criticism – in distinction from an assumed modernist literary cosmopolitanism.

It was not until the early 1970s that the question of provincialism would be raised within the proper context of art theory. Terry Smith drew on examples of mainly Australian artists who had been distanced and positioned by the centralising, even imperialising, geography of the mid-twentieth century art system. Smith addressed how artists were consigned to 'the pernicious destructiveness of provincialism',[6] a condition that had less to do with geographic isolation than an ideology of conformism to dominant materials and principles of 'the metropolitan center' of New York. As Smith maintained, this had implications for an artist's reception at both periphery and centre.

> A cruel irony of provincialism is that while the artist pays exaggerated homage to the conceptions of art history and the standards for judging 'quality,' 'significance,' 'interest,' etc., of the metropolitan center, he has, by definition of his situation, no way of (from his distance) affecting those conceptions and standards. He may satisfy his local audience, but to the international audience he is mostly invisible, sometimes amusingly exotic.[7]

For Smith, the way out of the 'provincialism problem' lay in deeper structural change, such as in exhibition spaces, and when a 'receiving country [the provinces where dominant values are received] has founded an authentic, sustaining culture of its own. Then, they would become enriching.'[8]

Throughout this book I have pursued an interest in the 'provincialism question' in a related fashion to how Smith and others posed it in the 1970s, setting in train questions that have subsequently emerged for a more global art history.[9] These are illuminating for Caribbean artists whose apprehension of the bind of temporal distancing has entailed a working through and renegotiation of the charges of anachronism. The sort of 'unusual degree of reflexivity' in exhibition curating that Smith had called for, over three decades ago, may be what recent exhibitions have tried to achieve, such as Nicholas Bourriaud's curatorial project at Tate Britain in 2009.[10] If the exhibition itself met with mixed reviews and was not a remarkable curatorial project, its accompanying text does repay interest as it is instructive of Bourriaud's ambition for the visual display. Where Bourriaud and Smith might agree is on the virtue of recognising the value of 'heterochronic time,'[11] whose importance was first suggested to Bourriaud in 'the symbolic inauguration of planetary art' that he witnessed in the 1989 Paris exhibition *Magiciens de la Terre*. Out of Bourriaud's search for alternatives, a definition of contemporary art emerges, encapsulated in the neologism 'altermodern'.

The expressed motivation of *Altermodern* was to somehow channel the forces of globalisation for the benefit of artists and art history. This rested on seeing global change as the cause of 'the synchronisation of the historical clock,'[12] a levelling of historical value which would undo the sort of hierarchies of historicism that had attended the writing of modernist art history. As Bourriaud argues:

> With the door thrown open to artistic traditions and cultures other than those foisted on the world by the West, post-colonial postmodernism followed along the trail blazed by the world economy, enabling a re-evaluation from the ground up of our visions of time and space: a 'horizontalisation' of the planet on which we need to build today.[13]

It is significant that this curatorial idea should take shape with the chief aim of dispensing, for ever, with older practices of representation, particularly those that render artists provincial and backward. A presiding definition of contemporary art for Bourriaud, which governed his selection for the Tate exhibition, is the number of artists who today 'operate in a space time' where they insist on 'playing with the anachronistic, with multi-temporality or time-lag'.[14] This concurs with Smith's conclusion about a video by Shirin Neshat (figure 30), in which 'Anachronism *is* relevant, but it is questioned. The very idea that one kind of culture, the modernizing ones, gets to decide that another is anachronistic is questioned'.[15]

Indeed, according to both thinkers, there is a general refusal among artists to allow themselves to be disadvantaged by their respective local contexts, their inquisitiveness about history, or even their attachment to otherwise outmoded forms of art making. In a spirit of subversion, these concerns are instead presented as the basis for a distinctive contemporaneity. As Smith has expressed it: '"Multeity," "altertemporality," and inequity are not only the most striking features on any short list of the qualities of contemporaneity; they are at its volatile core. ... The particular, it seems, is now general and, perhaps,

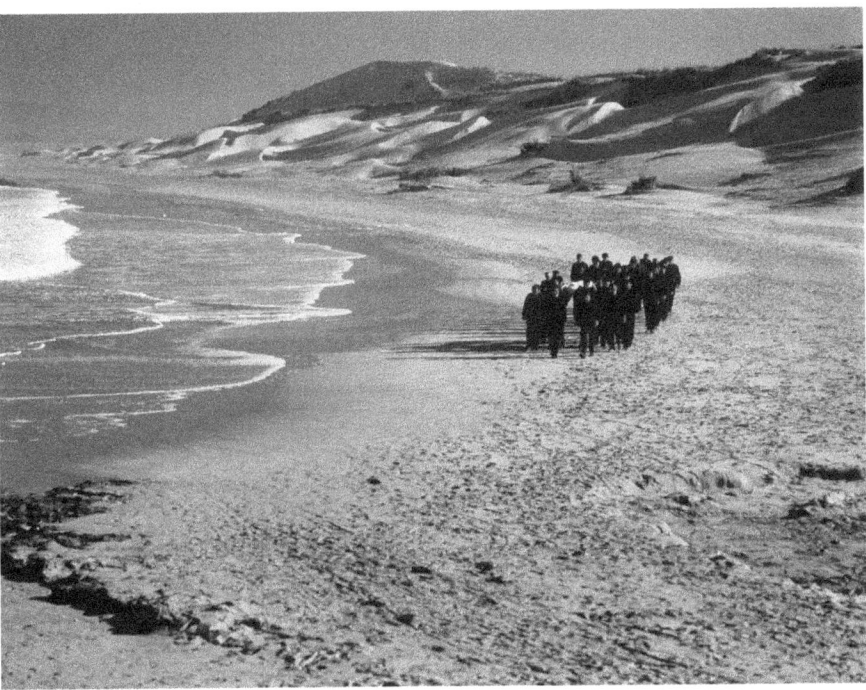

Shirin Neshat, *Passage* (2001), video and sound installation, 00:11:30, dimensions   **30**
variable.

forever shall be.' Expressly, however, this is not 'a recommendation for stand-alone, singularizing particularism; rather, it is an appeal for radical particularism to work with and against radical generalization, to treat all the elements in the mix as antinomies'.[16]

Part of my motivation to explore the ideas that condensed in *Altermodern* was my visit to the exhibition, where I was surprised to see, hanging at the Manton staircase of Tate Britain, Frank Bowling's painting *Mirror* (figure 8). Every visitor to *Altermodern* was obliged to pass this colossal canvas, to see it first from below, and then to move gradually up and along its right side, before proceeding to the exhibition. For me, it was an arresting prefatory note to the exhibition, and invited a meditation on the place of art of the transnational Caribbean in dialogue with the current initiatives to drastically overhaul art history. *Mirror* is a work that, like the Pop phenomenon, sat on the cusp of postmodernism. And yet it serves as a greater testament to the violence of periodisation in art history, since its artist is largely left out of the Pop canon. It epitomises the erasure of Bowling – the painting is, above all, a historical self-portrait of Bowling's marginality – and at the same time it is freighted with the institutionalising of the sometime radical cast of characters comprising Pop. The painting also tests the Bourriaud thesis in a profound way. Hanging in plain sight on a staircase at Tate, *Mirror* was nonetheless outside the defined space of the 'altermodern'.

On the one hand, *Mirror* may be seen as exemplary of the stated rationale of *Altermodern,* even if it was made long before the other works included in the exhibition. Bowling may also be considered a credible ingredient in Smith's 'mix of antinomies'. On the other hand, Bourriaud's scheme of contemporary art seems unable to elucidate the contemporaneity of Bowling. It is a category of the contemporary that is plainly unable to stretch to include him – *Mirror* is left out. Smith writes of the impossibility of periodising contemporaneity as an 'our time' ('… because if the modern were inclined above all to define itself as a period, and sort the past into periods, in contemporaneity periodization is impossible').[17] And yet, this hardly compensates for the categorisation of Bowling's work as not of the same assemblage of antinomies that would make up an exhibition such as *Altermodern*. An artist of the Caribbean has to contemplate when one's art is too anachronistic and too provincial to merit inclusion under even the more 'progressive' definitions of contemporaneity.

In light of the fact that exhibitions such as *Altermodern* commanded this mechanism of temporal differencing, the current claims for having initiated a profound rethinking of contemporaneity begin to sound rather hollow. Bourriaud states that he favours those artists whose aim is to reveal 'a present', those who refuse to conform to an externally imposed measure of a contemporary or 'present' temporality. (This is a self-proclaimed shift of authority from curator to artist. But what calls its bluff is whether it matters that Bourriaud's sense of contemporaneity is not the same as the one that other curators have advocated). The character of contemporary art is thought to rest with an artist's pronounced disregard for measures of historicism – especially those of the dominant twentieth-century labels of modernism and postmodernism. Bourriaud therefore seems to encourage the impulse for self-appointment among artists, imploring them to regain control of their allotted place in the art system and to defy its historical exclusions. An artist may desire to be 'contemporary', to participate in Bourriaud's 'planetary art', and this very desire will acknowledge the need to grant them the importance they seek.

It must be said that this proposal is not without a certain allure. Many artists have found themselves disadvantaged by temporal measures of value. Decisions about the importance of their works are often adjudicated by whether they succeed in being 'up to date', or 'belonging to the present'. Having undergone this experience, the refusal of practising artists to accept a situation of exclusion from contemporary art may indeed be a signal of their contemporaneity. This identification would appear to benefit those artists of the transnational Caribbean who have also staged such a refusal. The goal of revaluing the art of the present is to allow artists to render themselves contemporary, and presumably this may also count for the art of the past. However, it remains undefined how the historical study of art may draw instructively from new ways of thinking about contemporaneity and alterity. It is worth recalling that artists of the Caribbean such as Frank Bowling and Denis Williams, were initially warmly received in their day and arrived as contemporary. As a canon for British art has subsequently formed, that status has been unsettled or lost altogether. It is quite possible that the same will happen with the chosen artists of *Altermodern,* regardless of its 'horizontalising' curatorial vision. Despite every effort to supply novel theorisations and new critical opportunities for artists, are they not always prone to losing their contemporaneity?

It seems right to implore artists to stretch out beyond the conformities of existing art historical paradigms (even if the naming of a category for such aims and attitudes may just as easily become normative and interchangeable with the abandoned ones). This initiative may seem rather optimistic at a time when the extension of global capital into discourses of art has entailed even greater conflict between artists and the marketised art system, further alienating artistic labour. But surely a more pressing challenge is to change the structures of art historical remembrance themselves and to expose its arbiters of value. I have suggested that one such arbiter is the emphasis on the nexus of temporality. This is found in the legitimising processes of canonisation, or the implicit spatiality of art's histories, or indeed, it is evidenced in a bindingly powerful combination of them both in the politics of time.

In this book, I have not set out to argue a definition of contemporary art. Indeed, the present muddle of definitions and claims for contemporaneity is salutary for any such attempt.[18] But I am heartened to see that there is significant current interest in suspending the familiar categorisations of art that emerged in the twentieth century. This is happening in the name of making space for other, perhaps less confining or exclusive, sorts of categories. It may no longer be of particular interest – to those embroiled in the art and contemporaneity debate – to know how a given artwork should be understood on some fixed historical scale. There is growing appreciation that the existing categories of art historical inquiry are limiting, and that they ought to be handled with caution. Consequently, there seems to be a clear political argument afoot, even if few firm methodological or conceptual objectives have resulted from the debate. This is the route to a happy transformation from the concentration of power in the international art system that Smith wrote about in the early 1970s, whereby 'most artists the world over live in art communities that are formed by a relentless provincialism'.[19] Writing in 2006, he has welcomed 'the rich complexities of contemporaneity' which may yield 'more and more insights into adaptable modes of active resistance and hopeful persistence'.[20]

It is with this in view that I take forward a certain optimism of my own about historical understanding of art and artists of the transnational Caribbean. Their presence challenges the sort of centralised power and the related provincialism that is conventionally associated with the art system and art history. This has taken shape over a significant period, as I have shown in my account of its development from the immediate post-war moment to the present. I have asked what new networks of alliance the more recent contributions to this history have established. I have sought to outline what new and old paths and sources of 'creative coping' do these networks offer, and against what order and disorder does their productivity subsist. Overall, I have argued that art of the Caribbean speaks to the wider theoretical concern about the history of art and contemporaneity. This takes place not only when Caribbean works of art disclose an interest in concepts of time. It is there when examining their presence brings us to question what time they are given in the writing of art's histories.

Notes

1 See also Wright's account of his exchange with a bank clerk in Ghana: 'You American chaps are three hundred years ahead of these Africans. It'll take a long time for them to catch up with you. I think that they are trying to go too fast, don't *you*? You see, you American chaps are used to living in a white man's country, and these fellows are not.' R. Wright, *Black power: A record of reactions in a land of pathos* (New York: Harper, 1954), p. 138. See also M. Hanchard's observation that 'it was the march toward technological, institutional, and normative sophistication, a sophistication which Wright himself concurred was needed in order to raise levels of national and continental accomplishment in Africa to those of Europe or North

America'. M. Hanchard, 'Afro-modernity: Temporality, politics, and the African diaspora, *Public Culture*, 11:1 (1999), 245–68, p. 262.

2 J. N. Oldham, 'Anatomy of provincialism II: Provincialism of mind', *The Sewanee Review*, 44:2 (1936), 145–52, p. 145.

3 J. N. Oldham, 'Anatomy of provincialism I: The Nature of provincialism', *The Sewanee Review*, 44:1 (1936), 68–75, p. 73.

4 Ernst wrote: 'A discussion of the artist's traditional quarrel with his social environment everywhere would seem to be of minor consequence in the face of the unspeakable vulgarity of a 6.5 millimeter carbine with telescopic sight. But it is precisely the word vulgarity which best characterizes this global subversion that I have chosen to call "International Provincialism." Under its banner we have witnessed the gradual but very certain consolidation of the anti-humanist left and right into what will soon be recognized as an open Brotherhood of purpose and action'. J. Ernst, 'The artist and the wonderful world of international provincialism', *Archives of American Art Journal*, 4:1 (1964), 12–16, p. 14.

5 As Lazare wrote: 'We find both men shifting experimentation from form to content, resorting to an intensely subjectivized idiom in an effort to humanize their medium (itself become, since Renoir, a machine for escape), failing because of a kind of esthetic provincialism, the Spaniard an unintelligible Freudian patois, the mid-Westerner applying his oils in Missouri dialect'. C. Lazare, 'Review: Art', *The North American Review*, 247:2 (1939), 373–8.

6 T. Smith, 'The provincialism problem', *Artforum*, 13 (1974), 54–9, p. 59.

7 Smith, 'The provincialism problem', p. 56.

8 He continues: 'At present, it seems that the most responsible kind of exhibition would be one that took as its aim, not the supposedly "neutral" presentation of a selection of artworks, but the display of the very problematic which its incursion into a provincial situation raises. This would be difficult, certainly, requiring an unusual degree of reflexivity and some rethinking of the nature of exhibitions, but it is surely not impossible'. Smith, 'The provincialism problem', p. 59.

9 See also: T. Smith, 'American painting and British painting: Some issues', *Studio International*, 188:972 (1974), 218–23; I. Burn, 'Provincialism'; I. Burn, N. Lendon, C. Merewether and A. Stephen, 'The provincialism debates', in *The necessity of Australian art* (Sydney: Power Institute of Fine Arts, University of Sydney, 1988), pp. 104–26. T. Smith, 'Coda: Canons and contemporaneity', in A. Brzyski, *Partisan canons* (London and Durham, NC: Duke University Press, 2007), pp. 309–26; and T. Smith, *What is contemporary art?* (Chicago: Chicago University Press, 2009). Smith has also partnered with Okwui Enwezor and Nancy Condee in tackling related global questions, see N. Condee, O. Enwezor and T. Smith (eds), *Antinomies of art and culture: Modernity, postmodernity, contemporaneity* (London and Durham, NC: Duke University Press, 2008).

10 *Altermodern*, the Fourth Tate Triennial was held at Tate Britain (3 February–26 April 2009).

11 N. Bourriaud (ed.), *Altermodern: Tate triennial* (London: Tate Publishing, 2009), p. 19 .

12 Bourriaud (ed.), *Altermodern*, p. 14.

13 Bourriaud (ed.), *Altermodern*, p. 14.

14 Bourriaud (ed.), *Altermodern*, p. 15.

15 T. Smith, 'Contemporary art and contemporaneity', *Critical Inquiry* 32:4 (2006), 681–707, p. 689.

16 This advances the rather neutral description by Rutz that 'there are different times according to particular cultural constructions placed upon a substratum of duration and sequence and, second, that the shape of time is forged in contests of social power'. H. J. Rutz, 'The idea of a politics of time', in H. J. Rutz (ed.), *The politics of time* (Washington: American Anthropological Association, 1992), p. 1. Indeed, Smith's antinomies define these 'contests' more fully. He writes that: '… *contemporaneity consists precisely in the constant experience of radical disjunctures of perception, mismatching ways of seeing and valuing the same world, in the actual coincidence of asynchronous temporalities, in the jostling contingency of various cultural and social multiplicities, all thrown together in ways that highlight the fast-growing inequalities within and between them*' (emphasis original). Smith, 'Contemporary art and contemporaneity', p. 704.

17 Smith, 'Contemporary art and contemporaneity', pp. 703–4. See also F. Jameson, *A singular modernity: An essay on the ontology of the present* (London and New York: Verso, 2002).

18 Consider also the problems that arise when Bourriaud calls for a 'strategic universalism' (p. 16) in art and curatorial practices, and thereby commits to a strain of nostalgic ethnocentrism. There is an essentialist closing quote in his *Altermodern* essay about the intractable differences between 'men' and '[Amazonian] Indians', whose 'knowledge is so perfect', while they avoid 'our' 'new jungle' (urban life). It is hard to see what is 'strategic' about the final line: 'Their world is not different from ours, they simply live in it, while we are still in exile'. *Altermodern*, p. 16.

19 Smith, 'The provincialism problem', p. 56.

20 Smith, 'Contemporary art and contemporaneity', p. 707.

Index

Note: 'n' after a page number indicates the number of a note on that page. Page numbers in **bold** refer to illustrations

EU authorised representative for GPSR:
Easy Access System Europe, Mustamäe tee 50,
10621 Tallinn, Estonia
gpsr.requests@easproject.com